ATLAS of LITERACY AND DISABILITY

CANADIAN ABILITIES FOUNDATION

by Marcia Rioux
Ezra Zubrow
Mary Stutt Bunch
Wendy Miller

Copyright © Abilities Foundation 2003. All rights reserved. No part of this book may be reproduced or transmitted in any form or by any means, electronic or mechanical, including photocopying, or by any information storage or retrieval system, without permission in writing from the publisher.

The analysis, views and opinions expressed in this book are those of the authors and do not necessarily reflect the position or policies of the National Literacy Secretariat of Human Resources Development Canada or the Canadian Abilities Foundation.

This book was made possible with support from the National Literacy Secretariat of Human Resources Development Canada, the School of Health Policy and Management York University, the National Center for Geographic Information Analysis and the Applied Social Systems Laboratory at the University at Buffalo and the Canadian Abilities Foundation.

Canadian Cataloging in Publication Data
Rioux, Marcia. H., Ezra B.W. Zubrow, Mary Stutt Bunch, Wendy Miller
    Atlas of Literacy and Disability
Includes bibliographical references
    1. Disability -- Canada -- rights

    2. Literacy -- Canada – critical -- functional -- basic

    3. Atlas – geography – maps   4. Policy   5.Title

ISBN 0-9681120-8-0

Published by
    Canadian Abilities Foundation
    340 College Street, Suite 650
    Toronto, Ontario   M5T 3A9   Canada
    Phone: (416) 923-1885
    Fax: (416) 923-9829
    e-mail: able@abilities.ca
    website: www.abilities.ca

Table of Contents

Foreword

I *Introduction and Tips for Reading Maps*

II *The Geography of Literacy and Disability in Perspective*
    Trends in Defining Literacy
    Trends in Measuring Literacy
    Trends in Defining Disability
    Trends in Measuring Disability
    New Directions

III *The Geography of Literacy*
    Provincial Literacy Scans (IALS)
    Toward Critical Literacy: Realizing Literate Citizenship
    Geography of Literacy Organizations

IV *The Geography of Disability*
    Provincial Disability Scans
    Assessing Environments, Supports and Inclusion
    Geography of Disability Organizations

V *Literacy and Disability at the Crossroads*
    Basic Literacy and Disability
    Functional Literacy and Disability
    Critical Disability: Literate Citizenship for People with Disabilities

VI *Conclusions*

Appendix A   Methodology

Foreword

Combining the expertise of researchers from the fields of disability policy analysis and Geographic Information Science (GIS), this interdisciplinary project created an atlas of maps that show, at a glance, the relationship between literacy and disability. This spatial look at the issues provides a tool for policy and service development. It reveals information about what promotes or hinders literacy, opportunities for communication and participation in society. The objective was to investigate the spatial characteristics of literacy and disability in Canada and the spatial characteristics of their relationship. The study:

- used GIS methodology and spatial data to uncover and analyse the relationship between literacy and disability
- provides a set of spatial data to be used in policy development
- applies a rights and inclusion perspective to literacy and disability data
- makes recommendations regarding policy in the area of disability and literacy, and
- shows how GIS can be used to inform social policy.

Mapping disability and literacy variables, both on their own and in combination, allows us to see issues in an inventive way. Maps are defined in cartographical theory as "graphic representations that facilitate a spatial understanding of things, concepts, conditions, processes, or events in the human world"[1] Thus mapping, as well as the varying perspectives on disability and literacy used in the study, facilitate a fresh look at the issues involved. With spatial representations, as opposed to linear, numerical or narrative depictions, the viewer's attention is drawn to visual features of the data, and relationships between those features that may have been previously concealed. The visual perspective allows some different ideas to be pursued in the interpretation of the data.

This atlas is intended to be an accessible and informative tool for use by policy-makers, program developers and people in the literacy and disability movements. It is intended to make relationships between literacy and disability transparent. Far from being simply an atlas of information about disability and literacy, it jumps into the arena of analyzing the data to see how it can accommodate understanding disability from a rights perspective - and literacy as a critical phenomenon. The study provides information that makes it possible to track the needs and rights of Canadians with disabilities in policy development, planning, and service delivery.

This atlas was the joint effort of several organizations and a number of individuals. It was financed by a grant from the National Literacy Secretariat of Human Resources Development Canada to the Canadian Abilities Foundation. The authors wish to thank them, as well as the School of Health Policy and Management, York University, the National Center for Geographic Information Analysis, and the Applied Social Systems Laboratory of the University at Buffalo. The researchers are also grateful for access to and use of the Statistics Canada Research Data Centre at the University of Toronto and in Ottawa.

No project is the sole achievement of it authors and this one is no exception. There were many individuals who supported this work both in the conceptualization of the ideas and the methodology. At the early stages, people in the field of GIS gave input into the possibility of using GIS to look at social phenomena of this nature. They gave further feedback on the first foray into the terrain. Individuals in the field of literacy were proactive in encouraging that we "go for it". And people in the disability movement recognized the potential of having data in forms that would expose information often so obscured by tables and graphs. During the project, there were individuals who gave generously of their knowledge in statistical surveys and of their time to support the statistical data manipulation, working the data around innovative formulations of ideas. A number of students worked on various aspects of the project, work which contributed in important ways to the overall task. We appreciate all of these efforts. While the authors are responsible for the outcome, none of this could have been accomplished without the benefit of widespread support.

There is always a challenge and a danger in trying to develop novel ways of looking at data, particularly quantitative data, and of using new paradigms. It leaves one vulnerable to criticism that may be fair but could also be silencing. We will be satisfied if we have moved the agenda along a little towards greater understanding of the relationship of literacy and disability and if we have even the slightest impact on the introduction of disability rights and critical literacy into the collection of survey data. We dedicate this work to those people who have faced the double jeopardy of being marginalized by their disability and by their experience of literacy.

---

1 Harley, J.B and Woodward, D., 1987. "Preface." In Harley, J.B and Woodward, David (Eds). The History of Cartography, Volume I. Chicago and London: University of Chicago Press, p. xvi

"An atlas never just shows you where you are, where you want to go to and how to get there. It also fires the imagination. Maps which chart rivers, mountains, towns, countries, faraway regions, oceans and continents can arouse intense feelings..."

The Atlas of Experience,
by Louise Van Swaaij & Jean Klare fwd.
2000 Bloomsbury. London

ATLAS *of* LITERACY AND DISABILITY[2]

I. Tips for Reading Map

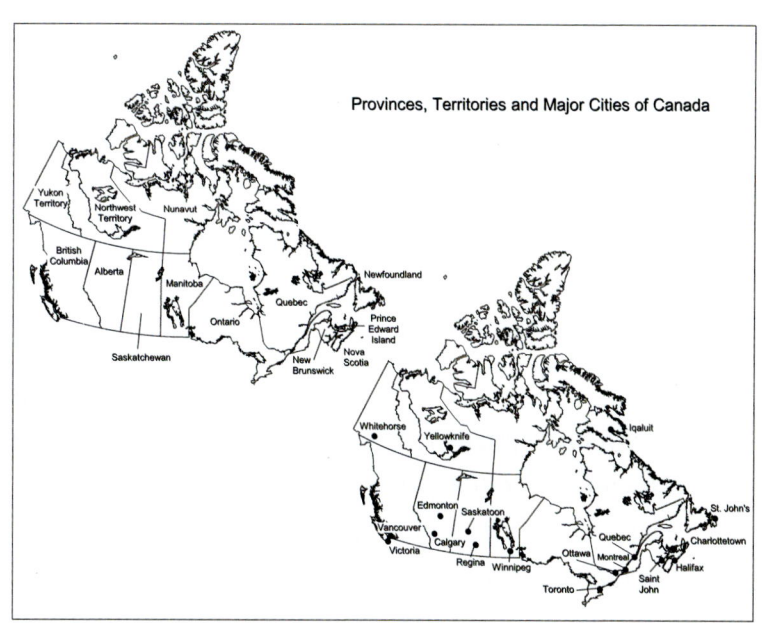

A map is a spatial representation of the earth's surface. Scalar pictures, they reduce the size of their object according to some proportional rules. Maps often give a bird's-eye view, usually placing the objects of interest in the centre of the image.
Using colours, symbols and labels to represent features found on the ground, a cartographer frequently uses a single symbol for multiple representations. Thus, a line may be a river, a road or a provincial border. A dot may be the location of a town or a "literacy organization," depending on the context.

Because the earth is three-dimensional and cartographic representations are two-dimensional, there is always geometric distortion. Map makers have developed a standard set of projections to do this transformation of the area, shape, distance and direction. Unfortunately, there is no perfect solution, and one always needs to distort one of the parameters. If one wishes to maintain area, shape and distance, direction is distorted; or, if one tries to keep area, distance and direction, then shape is distorted. Most readers will be familiar with Mercator's projections and will see that Canada is a different shape in this atlas than Mercator's. This is because the atlas follows the Canadian national standard and uses the Lambert Conformal Conic map projection.

The maps in this atlas were made using GIS. The abbreviation "GIS" stands for both Geographic Information Science, the subject, and Geographic Information Systems, the computerized map-making technology. In this atlas, both were used. You will find that all the maps in this atlas follow the same general format based on their GIS templates. Every map includes a base map of Canada showing the provinces, and a descriptive box on the side of the page nearest the bookbinding. In the descriptive box, you will find the title of the map and where the data comes from. These boxes are colour coded based on the data source, as the following diagram shows:

- *Health and Activity Limitation Survey* → *yellow box*
- *International Adult Literacy Survey (IALS)* → *blue box*
- *Participation and Activity Limitation Survey (PALS)* → *peach box*
- *National Population Health Survey (NPHS)* → *green box*

Inside the descriptive box is an explanation of the map and national figures for the map topic. See Figure 1.1 for a more complete description of the maps within this atlas.

I. INTRODUCTION   3

Figure 1.1.
Labeled GIS map for ease of understanding

GIS creates maps by defining layers. Each layer is one type of data. A good way to think of this is to visualize a layer cake.

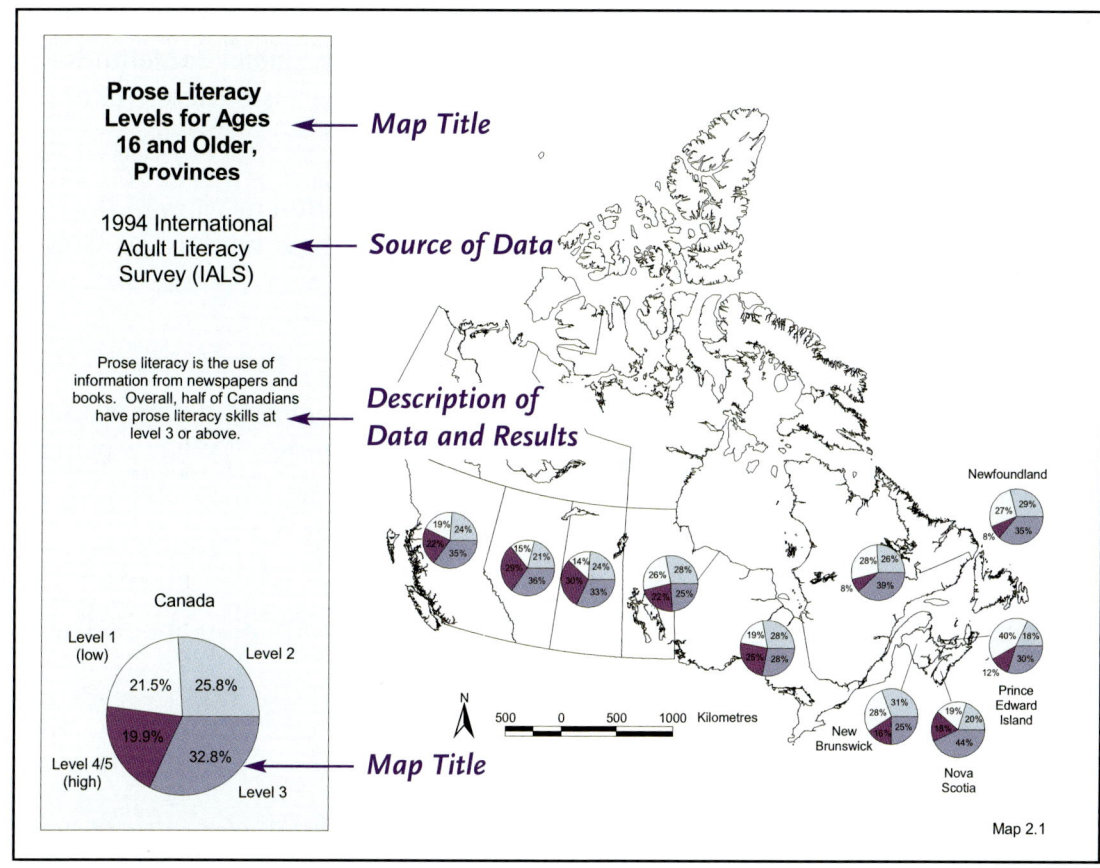

Figure 2.1.
Thematic layers in the atlas

Each layer represents a theme. Thus, the top layer might be the educational attainment and the lowest level–the base geography of Canada.

The maps are multi-thematic. Each layer represents a theme. Thus, the top layer might be the educational attainment and the lowest level the base geography of Canada. Usually, a theme will be a single variable. Sometimes the variables have been recalculated and the new transformed variable is presented. In some cases there will be three themes on a single map.

Information drawn from the surveys about literacy and disability is shown in a variety of different ways in the atlas. Data is displayed in this atlas using colour coding, bar graphs or pie charts. The way these work is described below.

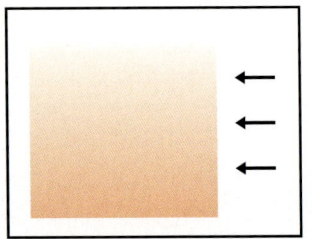

COLOUR CODING

In maps using colour coding to scale information, light to dark shades of colour are used to show differences in what is being measured. As a general rule, light colours mean less, and dark colours mean more of what is being measured. For example. the darker the area, the higher the disability rate.

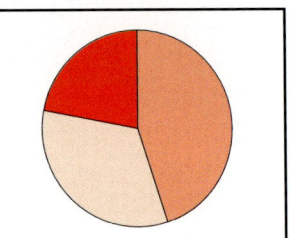

BAR GRAPHS

In these graphs, a series of bars are located in the province or territory they are showing information about. The taller bars mean more of what is being measured, and the shorter bars mean less.

PIE CHARTS

Similarly, the circles are sited in the province or territory for which they provide information. Bigger slices of the pie represent more of what is being measured, and smaller slices represent less.

The colour schemes for most of the maps in this project were created using ColorBrewer(TM), a web tool for selecting map colours. This tool is accessible through www.colorbrewer.org and is discussed in Brewer (2001). We selected this tool because the colour schemes were tested for numerous display techniques and readability, and are legible to people who are colour-blind. All of the maps, with the exception of Maps 6.1, 6.2 and 6.3, are readable for those with red-green colour-blindness.[5]

---

2   This atlas was the joint effort of several organizations. It was financed by a grant from the National Literacy Secretariat of Human Resources Development Canada, to the Canadian Abilities Foundation. The authors also wish to thank the School of Health Policy and Management, York University, the National Center for Geographic Information Analysis and the Applied Social Systems Laboratory of the University at Buffalo. ArcView 3.2 is a registered trademark of the ESRI Corporation.
3   www.landolakes.com/images/ recipes/4484b_r.jpg
4   www.informatics.org/ france/cake.jpg
5   Brewer, C. 2001. "Reflections on Mapping Census 2000." Cartography and Geographic Information Science, 28: 4, 213-235.

II. *The Geography of Literacy and Disability in Perspective*

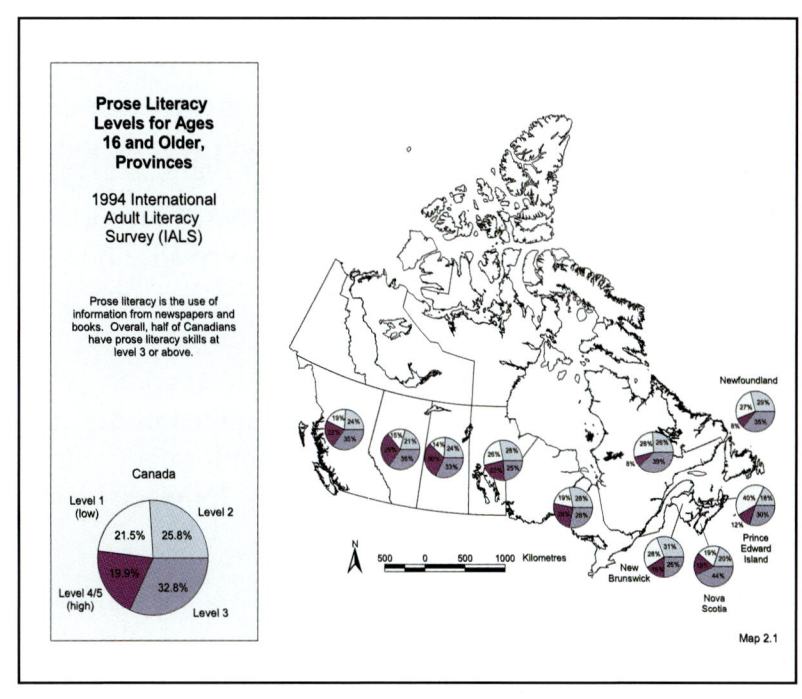

This atlas shows, at a glance, the relationship between literacy and disability. It reveals some factors that promote or hinder literacy, opportunities for communication and participation in society. It is a product of a study on literacy and disability that used Geographical Information Science (GIS) to create maps and look at statistics in new and creative ways. The maps are intended for use by policy makers, program developers and literacy and disability organizations. They can help these groups track where the needs and rights of Canadians with disabilities are being taken into account in policy development, planning, and services in the area of literacy.

Seeing literacy and disability in new ways is a theme in this atlas. Mapping allows us to understand issues in a new way because we can see the issues come alive on the page. The maps in the atlas show different definitions of disability that are used in statistical studies, or that could be used in literacy and disability surveys. The methods used to produce this atlas allow us to see literacy and disability together. It is difficult for researchers to use statistics to find the relationship between literacy and disability, because the statistics on literacy and disability are found in separate surveys in Canada. The research team used a creative and experimental approach to the concepts of literacy and disability, which are based on social inclusion and human rights. An innovative approach was also used in creating maps to help people visualize how literacy and disability play out across the country.

MAPS

The outline maps of Canada that are presented in the atlas are modified from ESRI's digitized dataset. They have been transformed to a Lambert formal Conformal Conic map projection. Moreover, the detailed subprovincial map units at the Census subdivision level were by made by modifying digitized Enumeration Level maps.

THE PROJECT

This atlas was created by an integrated team approach that focused on two areas of specialty. One was disability and literacy the other was geography and GIS.

After the project was designed, the best available data on literacy and disability from a variety of private, NGO and government studies were obtained. This information was supplemented by interviewing various experts. More detailed data was acquired from the Research Data Centre of Statistics Canada and was analyzed in Toronto and Ottawa. The files were then transferred to the Applied Social Systems Laboratory and the National Center for Geographic Information Analysis in Buffalo, New York, where they were transformed, using GIS, into maps and charts that were then incorporated into a variety of Canadian lectures, publications, articles and books, as well as this atlas.

II. THE GEOGRAPHY OF LITERACY AND DISABILITY IN PERSPECTIVE | 7

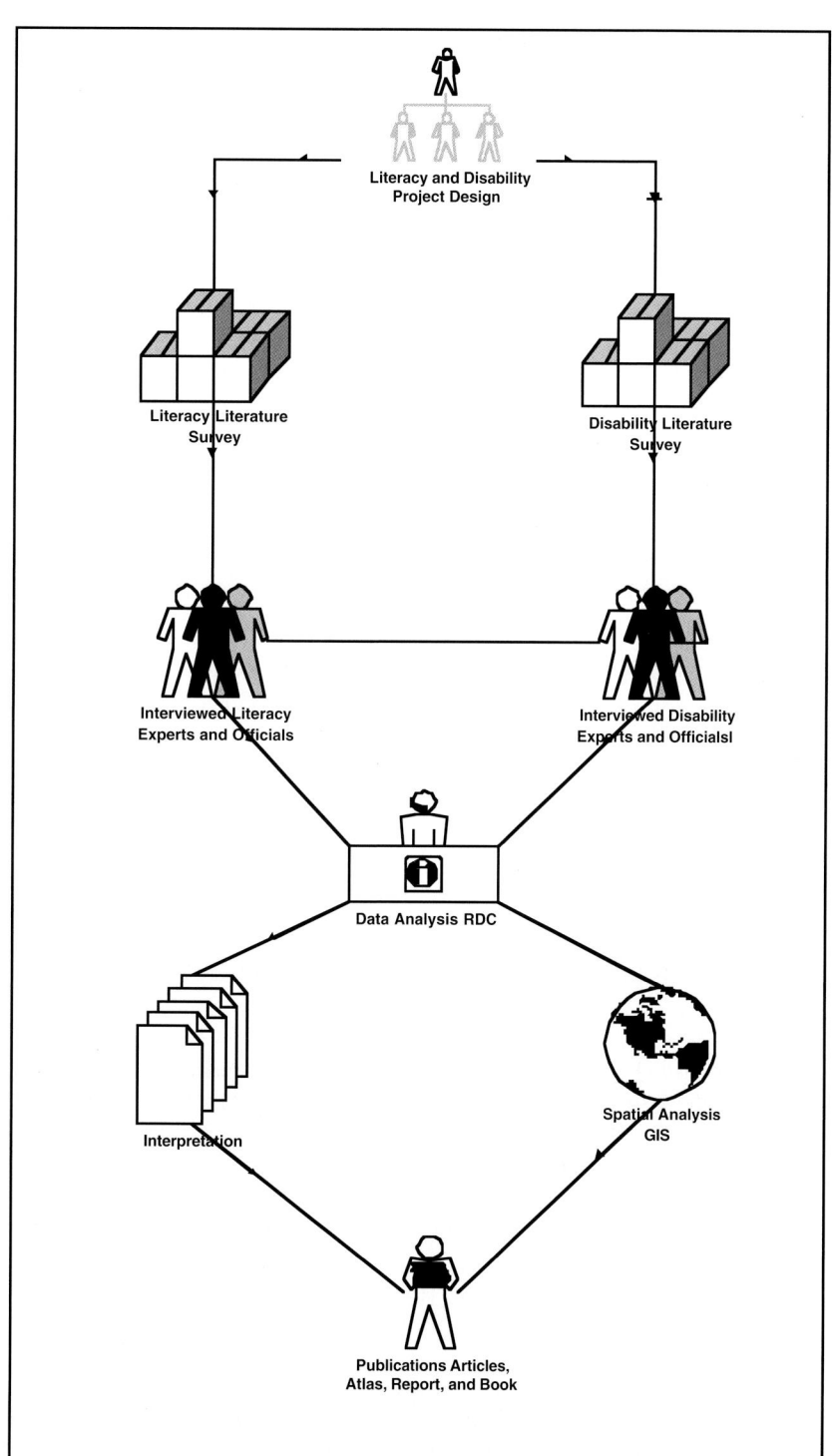

Figure A.1
The project design

TRENDS IN DEFINING LITERACY

> *Basic literacy* – rudimentary reading, writing and numeracy skills
>
> *Functional literacy* – ability to use reading, writing and numeracy skills to participate in the social and economic life of the community
>
> *Critical literacy* – the ways that marginalized individuals and groups communicate their experience and interests in public discourse.

There are many different ways to define and understand literacy. The maps in this atlas show a variety of meanings of literacy that have been used in western societies in recent decades. The literacy models used in this study include basic, functional and critical literacy.

Basic Literacy refers to the acquisition of a set of reading and writing skills. In 1948, the United Nations defined literacy as the ability to read and write a short statement.[6] People were either literate or illiterate. Basic literacy is thus a binary concept. Basic literacy does not show a range in level of skill, or changes in skill levels.[7] This approach also fails to account for the impact of differing social demands for types and levels of literacy skills. In today's knowledge-based society, this definition is considered too simple.

Functional Literacy reflects new demands for literacy in technologically advanced societies. Functional literacy is the ability to do the everyday activities that require the use of reading and math skills, and that are necessary for people to function and for communities to develop.[8] This way of understanding literacy is more flexible than basic literacy. It shows a continuum, or range, of literacy skill, and takes into account the different kinds of situations and environments in which people find themselves every day.

Critical Literacy refers to the ways that marginalized individuals and groups communicate their experience and interests in public discourse. This approach looks at whether or not society recognizes the differing ways people have of communicating.[9] It presumes there is a social responsibility to provide opportunities for everyone to

---

6 McKenzie, Helen. 1989. Illiteracy in Canada. Research Branch, Library of Parliament. Ottawa: Minister of Supply and Services Canada.

7 Godin, Joanne (Ed). 1996. Working in Concert: Federal, Provincial and Territorial Actions in Support of Literacy in Canada. Ottawa: National literacy Secretariat; Roeher Institute, 1999. Literacy, Disability and Communication. Toronto: The Roeher Institute; Satin, Alvin 1991. "An International Review of the Concepts, Definitions and Measurement Approaches Underlying Literacy Statistics." In Adult Literacy in Canada: Results of National Study. Statistics Canada, Labour and Household Surveys Division. Ottawa: Minister of Industry, Science and Technology.

8 Satin, Alvin 1991. "An International Review of the Concepts, Definitions and Measurement Approaches Underlying Literacy Statistics." In Adult Literacy in Canada: Results of National Study. Statistics Canada, Labour and Household Surveys Division. Ottawa: Minister of Industry, Science and Technology. p. 58

9 Freire, Paulo. 1993. Pedagogy of the Oppressed. New York: Continuum Publishing Co.; Brosksy, Linda. 1991. "Tropics of Literacy." Mitchell, C. and Weiler K. (Eds.) Rewriting Literacy: Culture and the Discourse of the Other. Toronto: OISE Press; Roeher Institute, 1999. Literacy, Disability and Communication. Toronto: The Roeher Institute; Mitchell, Candace. 1991. "Preface." Mitchell, C. and Weiler K. (Eds.) Rewriting Literacy: Culture and the Discourse of the Other. Toronto: OISE Press; Pratt, Syney., Nomez, Naldi and Patricio Urzua, 1977. Literacy: Charitable Enterprise or Political Right.. Prepared by the Literacy Working group, The St. Christopher House, Toronto. http://www.nald.ca/fulltext/lce/lce.htm

develop literacy skills that are meaningful, and to ensure that environments such as the health care and legal systems are sufficiently flexible to accommodate people's various styles of communication and literacy.

TRENDS IN MEASURING LITERACY

In 1978 UNESCO recommended that educational attainment be used as a crude measure or proxy (fill-in or substitute) for basic literacy.[10] Completion of grade nine was set as the cut-off for the minimum level of education needed to acquire the basic reading and writing skills considered necessary to function in industrialized societies at that time. Using this crude measure, less than grade nine defined illiteracy, while grade nine or more defined literacy. It is a simple, tangible measure of literacy. Level of education is asked in the **1996 Census** (Map 2.4), as well as in all the other surveys used in the study. An advantage of a measure like this is that it is concrete and common to many surveys, which is not the case with measures for functional and critical literacy proxies.

Functional literacy surveys that were developed through the 1980s in Canada and the United States measured a continuum of literacy in various skill areas. The most recent is the **International Adult Literacy Survey**, conducted in 1994.[11] This survey measures the skills people have, compared to the skills that they need, in daily life. To measure this, the IALS tested people's skills in using materials from real life in three kinds of literacy. These are prose literacy (Map 2.1), document literacy (Map 2.2) and quantitative literacy (Map 2.3). Scores were divided into five levels, with level 1 as the lowest and level 5 as the highest. Level 3 is considered the "suitable minimum skill level for coping with the demands for modern life and work."[12]

TRENDS IN DEFINING DISABILITY

This study draws on a number of ways of understanding disability that have framed its interpretation in Canada and other western countries over the past century.

From the **Biomedical** perspective, disability is characterized as a disease, disorder or "abnormal" physical or mental characteristic. Disability-related problems are seen as a consequence of an individual pathology, and solutions are directed at "curing" or "treating" the individual. In other words, solutions aim to decrease the prevalence of the

---

Biomedical – disability is a consequence of a biological abnormality or medical condition in the individual

Functional/Environmental – disability is a restriction in ability or functioning in one's environment resulting from impairment in the performance of an activity in a range considered normal

Social/Environmental – disability is the result of barriers that prevent people with disabilities from participating in social and economic institutions

Disability Rights – disability is a product of social, economic and political conditions and the discrimination and inequality attached to them

Prose literacy – use of information from texts such as newspapers, poems and fiction

Document literacy – use of information in formats such as job application forms, schedules, maps, tables and charts

Quantitative literacy – use of arithmetic operations in the context of printed materials such as balancing an account, figuring out a tip or completing an order

---

10 ibid
11 Data collection for a new survey, the International Adult Literacy and Lifeskills Survey, began in January 2003.
12 Organization of Education, Cooperation and Development (OECD). 2000. Literacy in the Information Age: Final Report of the International Adult Literacy Survey. p. xiii.

disability by addressing it within the individual. This formulation of disability has been critiqued recently for perpetuating stereotypes about people with disabilities and failing to account for the social context of disability.[13]

Functional/Environmental definitions of disability incorporate an understanding of disabilities as individual pathologies or abnormalities, but also focus on how people function in various environments. Rehabilitation is a common way of addressing disability. This includes such services as physical rehabilitation and skills for independent living. The purpose of disability rehabilitation services are to provide people with the skills to live lives comparable to other people that are as "normal" as possible, regardless of their disability.[14]

A **Social/Environmental** definition of disability emerged out of the disability community. Disability is seen as a form of social oppression, comparable to sexism and racism.[15] The focus is on the barriers that people encounter in their environments, and whether or not these are being addressed. Social responses focus on removing barriers and increasing the participation of people with disabilities at home and in communities, schools and workplaces.

The Disability Rights model of disability presumes that all people have the same rights, regardless of disability.[16] Disability is seen as a product of discrimination and inequality in social, economic and political life. The focus is on broad systemic factors that enable or restrict people from participating as equals in societies. Disability is a consequence of the overriding social causes of inequity in society.[17] Ensuring that people are provided with the supports they need to fully participate in and contribute to society is considered a societal responsibility.

TRENDS IN MEASURING DISABILITY

The first major statistical survey of disability in Canada was the **Health and Activity Limitation Survey (HALS)**, which measured functional disability. It was conducted in 1986 and 1991. It was based on the World Health

---

13 Rioux, M.H. 1997. "Disability: The Place of Judgement in a World of Fact." Journal of Intellectual Disability Research, Vol. 41, No. 2, April, Cohen, S. Visions of Social Control: Crime, Punishment and Classification. Cambridge: Polity Press, 1985; Sutherland, N. Children in English-Canadian Society. Toronto: University of Toronto Press, 1976.

14 Meyer, L.H and C. A. Peck et al., Critical Issues in the Lives of People with Severe Disabilities. Baltimore, Md.: Paul H. Brookes, 1990; Wolfensberger, W. Normalization: The Principle of Normalization in Human Services. Toronto: National Institute on Mental Retardation, 1972.

15 Colin Barnes, Geoff Mercer, Tom Shakespeare. Exploring Disability: A Sociological Analysis, Cambridge: Polity Press, 1999; Len Barton and Michael Oliver, Disability Studies, Past Present and Future, Leeds: The Disability Press, 1997; Michael Oliver, The Politics of Disablement, Basingstroke: McMillan, 1990.

16 UN High Commission on Disability, Resolution 2000/51; UN Special Rapporteur on Disability, Let the World Know: Report of a Seminar on Human Rights and Disability, November 5-9, 2000; M. H. Rioux, "Disability: The Place of Judgement in a World of Fact." Journal of Intellectual Disability Research, Vol. 41, No. 2, April, 1997

17 Beresford, P. and J. Campbell, "Disabled People, Service Users, User Involvement and Representation," Disability and Society, vol. 9, pp. 315-325, 1994; Fougeyrollas, P. Canadian Society for ICIDH, "The Handicap Creation Process," ICIDH International Network, vol. 4, 1991; Oliver, M. The Politics of Disablement. London: McMillan, 1990.

Organization's definition of disability as a four-stage process involving impairments, their causes and their disabling consequences in the context of daily life.[18] A person was identified as having an activity limitation through screening questions in the census. HALS then measured the nature and extent of limitations in activity resulting from an identified physical condition or health problem, or from an emotional, psychological, nervous or psychiatric condition. Limitations at home, at school, in the workplace and in the community were included (Map 2.5).

The Participation and Activity Limitation Survey (PALS) was conducted in 2001.[19] PALS used an approach similar to HALS, with some differences that affected who was included in the sample. These differences are likely the reason PALS has a lower disability rate than HALS. Learning from the earlier HALS survey, PALS added important questions about pain and expanded the questions dealing with learning, psychological, emotional and psychiatric conditions Map 2.6).

The 1996 National Population Health Survey (NPHS) measured functional disability in a different way from HALS and PALS. It asked about limitations in activities at home, at school, at work and in other activities such as leisure activities, but in less detail than the other two surveys. It also asked if the individual had any long-term disabilities or handicaps. As a result of these differences, NPHS has different findings about disability than HALS or PALS (Map 2.7).

The International Adult Literacy Survey (IALS) used a very broad definition of disability. It included anyone who ever had a disability, whether or not it was still present, at any degree of severity, and without regard to whether the respondent felt restricted in activities of daily living. Disability data from this measure was much higher than in the other surveys, and is, therefore, considered exploratory and probably less reliable than that in other surveys (Map 2.8).

NEW DIRECTIONS

This study emphasizes perspectives of literacy and disability grounded in inclusion, rights and equality. Critical literacy and disability rights portray both literacy and disability as social issues with systemic causes. Surveys to date have not been designed to measure these concepts. To overcome this gap in this study, exploratory proxies for functional and critical literacy were created from the IALS and HALS surveys, and a Barriers and Accommodations Index was derived from HALS.

Functional literacy proxies from IALS and HALS were based on a combination of indicators that suggest skills that directly affect individual functioning in daily life. The functional literacy proxy derived from IALS included four

---

18 World Health Organization, 1980. International Classification of Impairments, Disabilities and Handicaps. Geneva: World Health Organization
19 Data from this survey began to be released near the end of the research for this atlas, at the end of 2002.

kinds of questions. In the first, respondents were asked to rate the adequacy of their reading, writing and math skills in terms of their daily life. The second inquired about the frequency with which people used literacy skills for such tasks as writing letters in daily life. Respondents were also asked if they needed assistance in reading and writing, and if they were satisfied with their literacy skills.

In a similar manner, eight questions were selected from HALS and combined to create a composite measure. These included queries about individual perception of the adequacy of their reading and writing skills, the frequency with which they used literacy or communication skills for such activities as reading newspapers, talking on the phone or shopping, and difficulty with everyday functions.

Critical literacy proxies were based on questions about how communication or literacy skills related to a person's control over his or her life, and the level of participation in public life. The idea was to determine whether one experienced inequality or marginalization in relation to the way he or she communicated. Evaluating Canada's success at creating such barrier-free environments for "literate citizenship" has not previously been incorporated into literacy surveys.

HALS Functional Literacy Proxy

Do you consider your reading/writing skills to be adequate in everyday life?

Frequency of reading.

Do you have difficulty telling right from left?

Are you often told you are not doing the right thing at the right time?

Do you have difficulty doing activities with multiple steps?

Do you often have difficulty solving day-to-day problems?

Frequency of talking on telephone.

Frequency of shopping.

HALS Critical Literacy Proxy

Does someone else organize the drugs or medication that you have to take?

Do you have any difficulty explaining your ideas when speaking?

Do you often need help to talk to people you don't know very well?

Do you often need help to understand people you don't know very well?

How often do you talk on the telephone? (Never/all other responses)

How often do you shop? (Never/all other responses)

IALS Critical literacy Proxy

How often do you do the following activities: use a public library; attend movie/play/concert; attend or take part in a sporting event; participate in volunteer or community organizations; listen to radio, records, tapes, cassettes, or compact discs?

Which of the following materials do you currently have in your home: daily newspapers; weekly newspapers/magazines; more than 25 books; a (multi-volume) encyclopedia; a dictionary?

How often do you read or use information as part of your daily life: manuals or reference books, including catalogues; bills, invoices, spreadsheets or budget tables; directions or instructions for medicines, recipes or other products?

How much information about current events, public affairs, and the government do you get from: newspapers; magazines; radio; television; family members, friends or co-workers?

IALS Functional Literacy Proxy

How would you rate your reading/writing/math skills in English needed in daily life?

Rate reading/writing/math skills in English at work.

Extent of reading/writing/math skills in English limit job opportunities.

How often do you do the following activities: write letters, read books?

How often do you read or use information as part of your daily life (letters or memos; reports, articles, magazines or journals; diagrams or schematics; material written in a language other than English)?

How often do you need help from others with: reading newspaper articles; reading information from government agencies, business or other institutions; filling out forms such as applications or bank deposit slips; reading instructions such as on a medicine bottle; reading instructions on "packaged" goods in stores or supermarkets; doing basic arithmetic – that is, adding, subtracting, multiplying, and dividing; writing notes and letters?

Which parts of the newspaper do you read?

How satisfied are you with reading and writing skills in English?

The critical literacy proxy from IALS was derived from four questions that reflect social participation, access to information and use of skills and information. It included questions about participating in community events and using community resources, having and using resources with information about public events, and using literacy skills in everyday life.

A composite critical literacy variable was devised from HALS out of six questions. Included were questions about the degree to which people had control over their use of medication and about their independence or reliance on others for day-to-day communication. Additional questions were intended to determine if a person was isolated or dependent on others.

The Barriers and Accommodations Index was designed as an alternative to the Severity Index used in HALS. The BAI shifts the focus of disablement from the individual to environments and systems of support. There are three parts to the Barriers and Accommodations Index. The first shows the relationship between barriers encountered and accommodations received. The second shows the number of barriers encountered, and the third shows numbers of accommodations received.

The 2001 Relative Indices show finer geographic and temporal scale than the other maps included in this atlas. These are relative indices of barriers and accommodations making predictions using HALS, IALS, PALS, NPHS and the Census. These were tested (see the detailed methodology) and found to be reliable predictions within about 2%. Once validated, they were projected onto data at very small spatial scale to show how strong the barriers and accommodations would be for people with disabilities in 2001 at the local level. In addition to these two relative indices, a combined index predicts how well the barriers are accommodated.

These proxy literacy measures, the BAI and the relative indices are experimental. Despite some limitations, these measures do reveal useful information. They reveal possible trends in critical literacy and disability rights. They point to some directions for survey designers interested in measuring the concept of critical literacy and disability rights.

II. THE GEOGRAPHY OF LITERACY AND DISABILITY IN PERSPECTIVE | 15

Prose Literacy Levels for Ages 16 and Older, Provinces

1994 International Adult Literacy Survey (IALS)

Prose literacy is the use of information from newspapers and books. Overall, half of Canadians have prose literacy skills at level 3 or above.

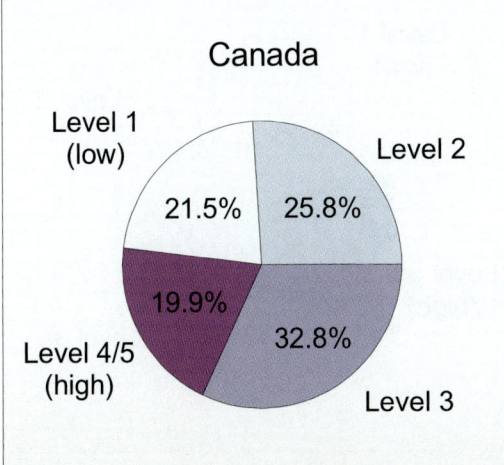

Canada

Level 1 (low) 21.5%
Level 2 25.8%
Level 3 32.8%
Level 4/5 (high) 19.9%

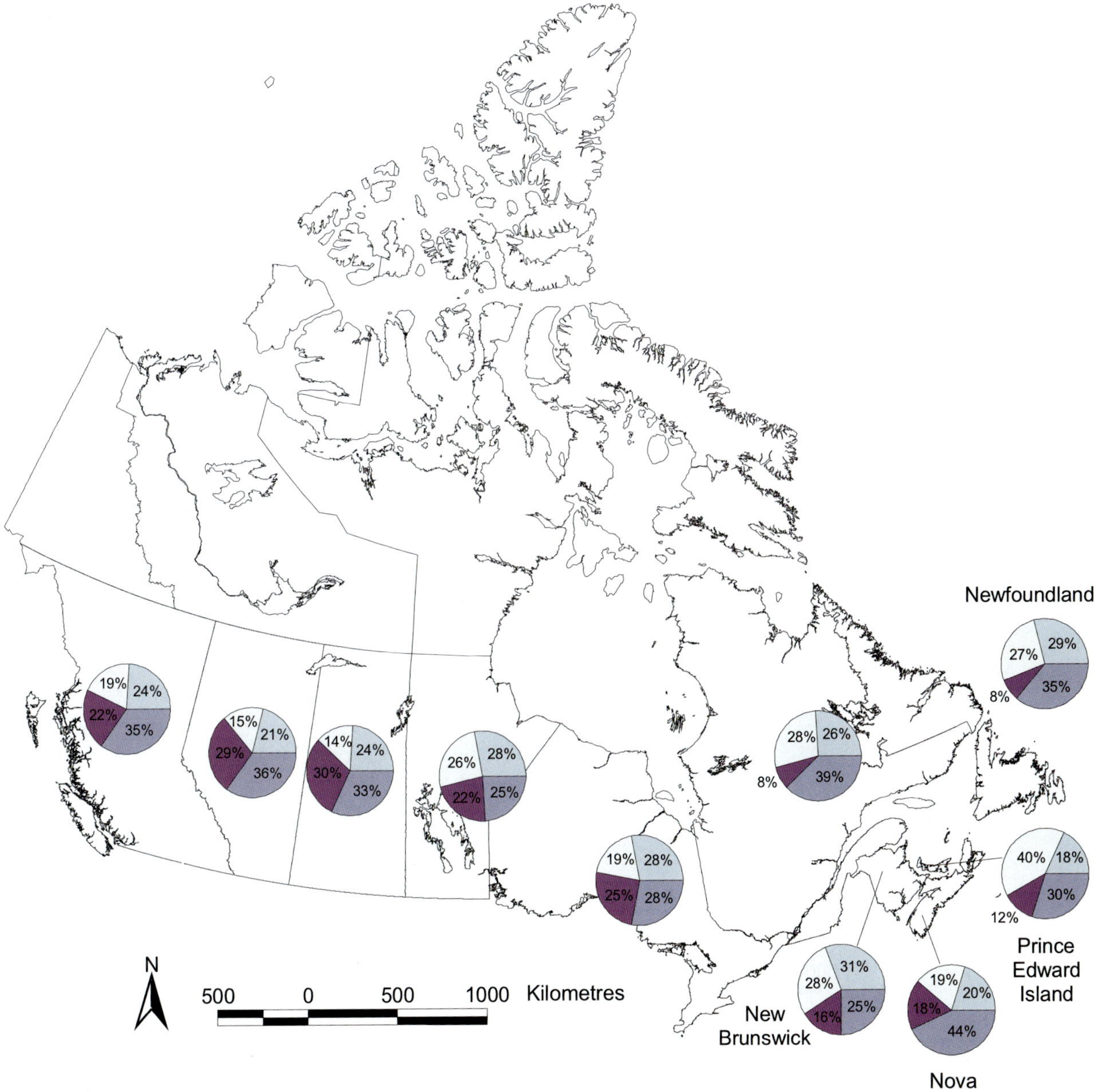

Map 2.1

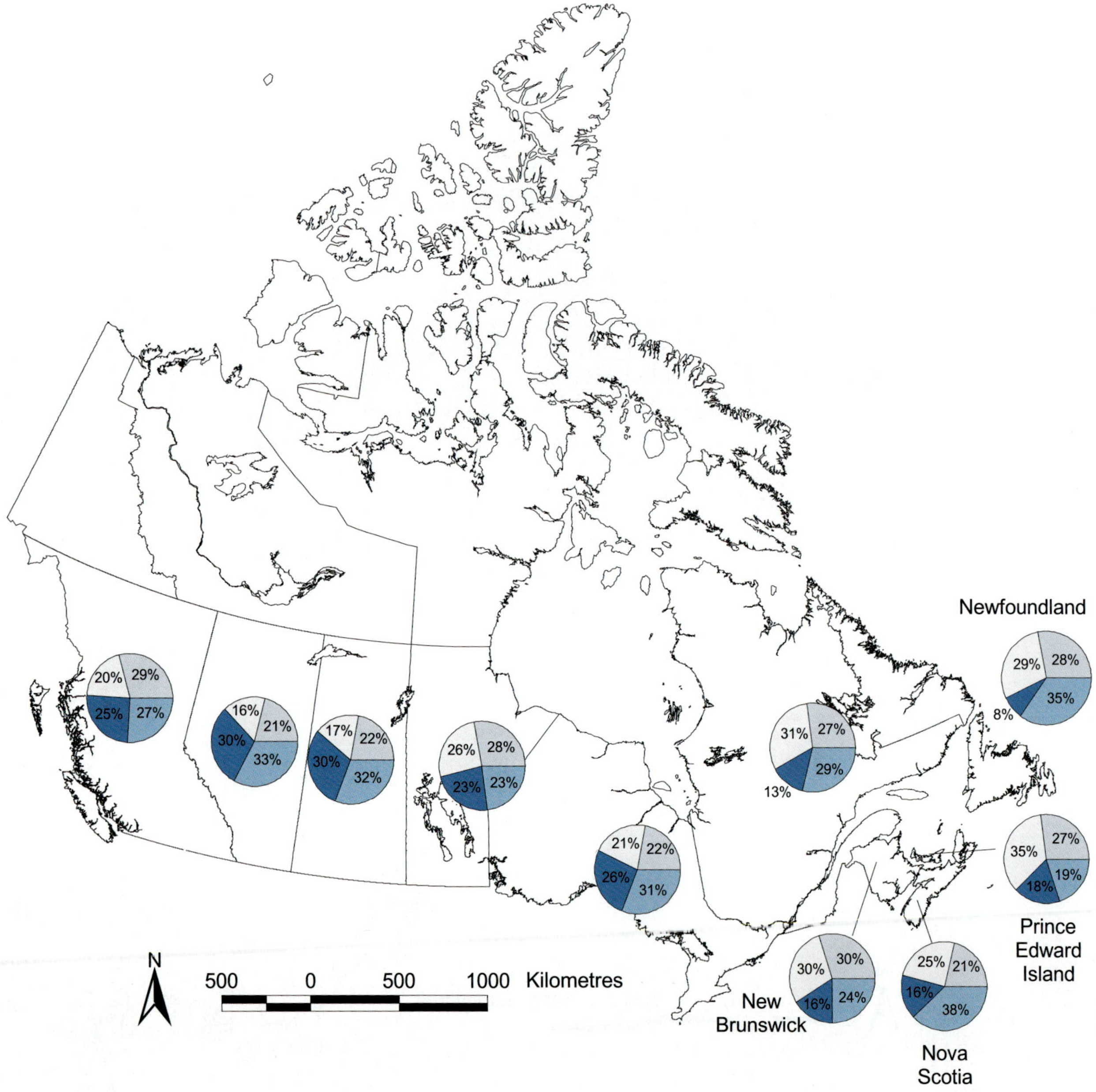

16 ATLAS OF LITERACY AND DISABILITY

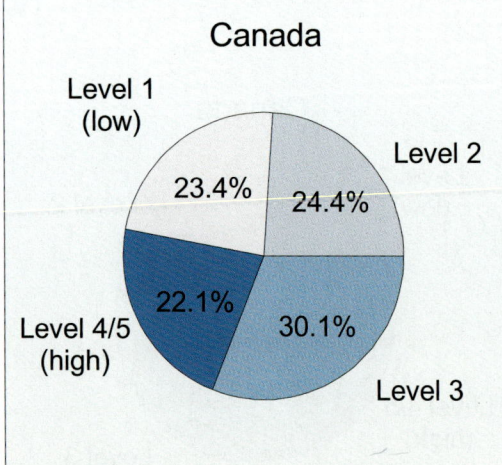

Document Literacy Levels for Ages 16 and Older, Provinces

1994 International Adult Literacy Survey (IALS)

In 1994 when IALS was carried out, there were differences noted in document literacy between the provinces west and east of Ontario. Provinces in the east (except Nova Scotia) reported slightly lower proportions and provinces in the west (except for Manitoba) reported similar or higher proportions.

Map 2.2

II. THE GEOGRAPHY OF LITERACY AND DISABILITY IN PERSPECTIVE | 17

Quantitative Literacy Levels for Ages 16 and Older, Provinces

1994 International Adult Literacy Survey (IALS)

Just under half of the adult population in Canada has some difficulty in their everyday use of numbers and math skills. 21.8% scored at level 1 and 26.1% scored at level 2 in quantitative skills. In some provinces, well over half the population reported these lower levels.

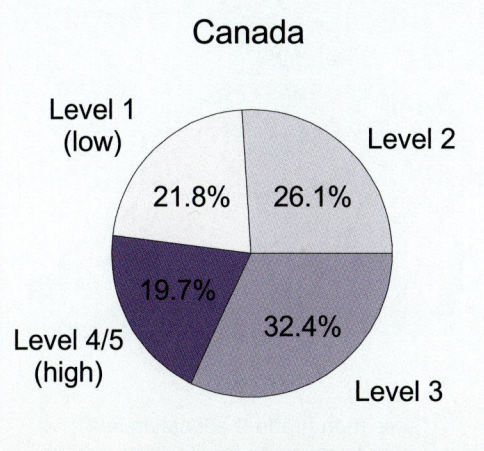

Canada

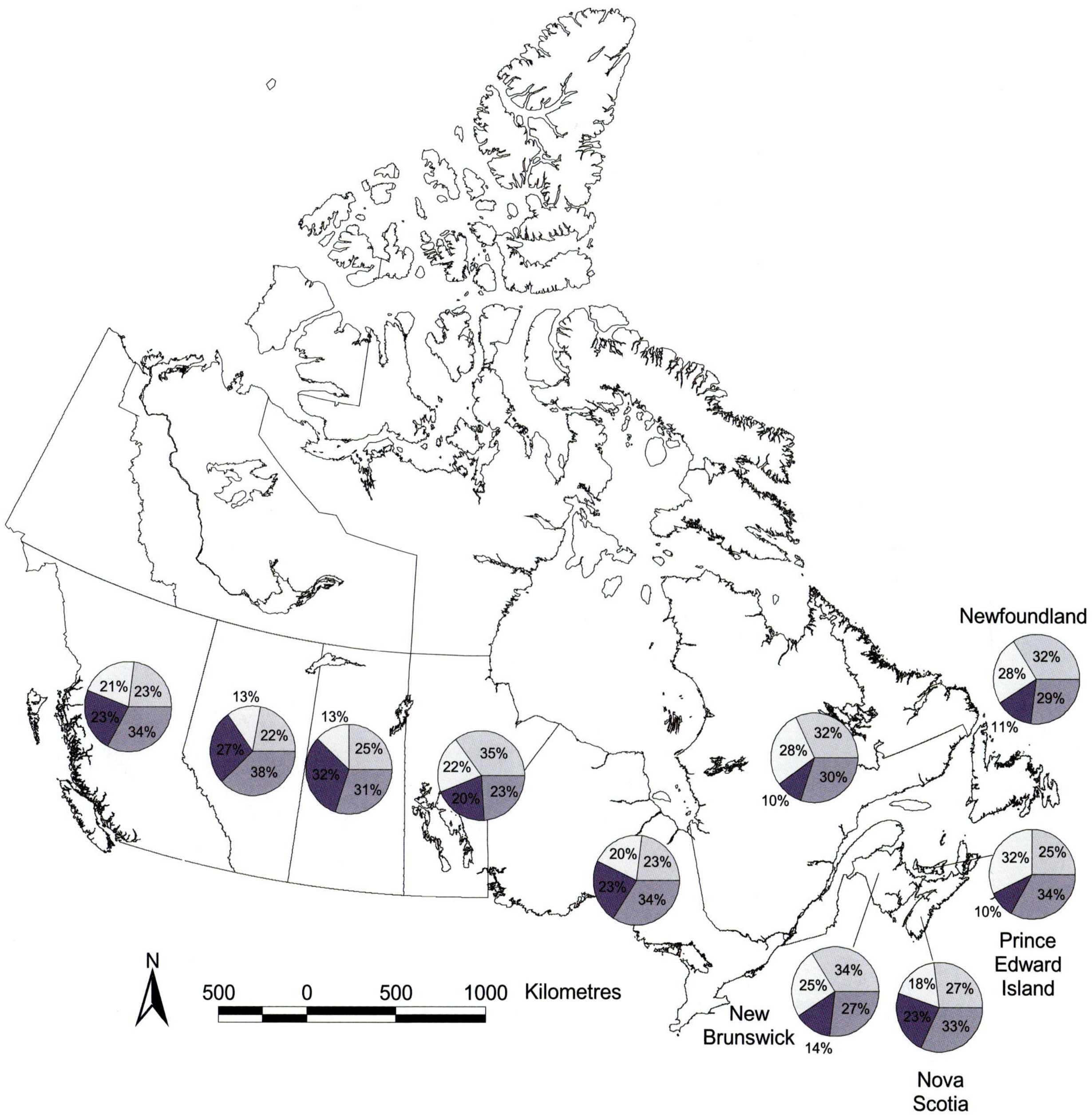

- Level 1 (low): 21.8%
- Level 2: 26.1%
- Level 3: 32.4%
- Level 4/5 (high): 19.7%

Map 2.3

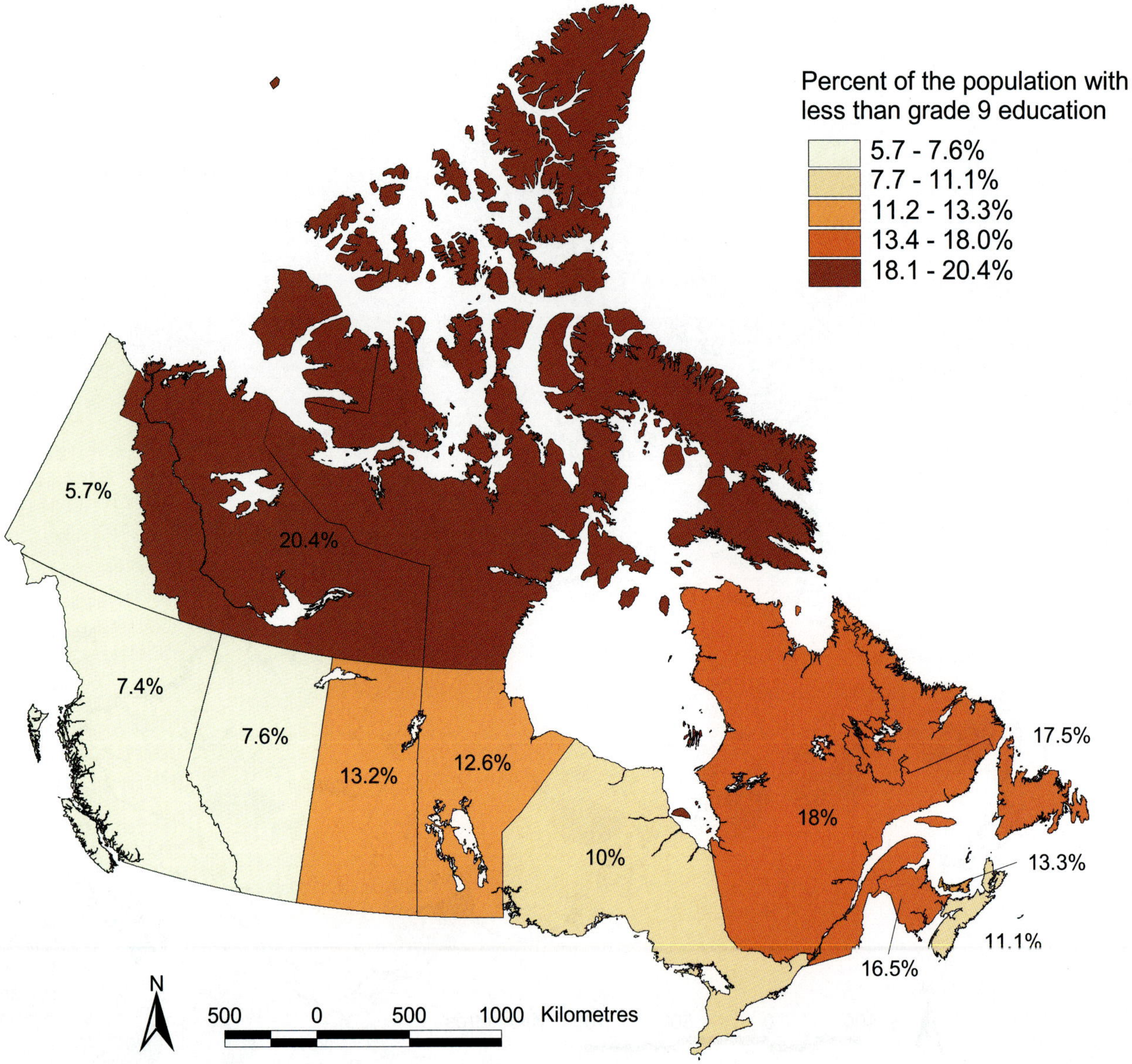

ATLAS OF LITERACY AND DISABILITY

Percent of the Population Ages 15 and Older with Less than Grade 9 Education*, Provinces and Territories

1996 Census of Population

On average, 12.1% of Canadian adults have less than grade 9 education, a measure of low basic literacy skills. Those who live in the Northwest Territories (20.4%), Quebec (18%), New Brunswick (16.5%) and Newfoundland (17.5%) are less likely to go to school past grade 8 than other Canadians.

Canada -- 12.1%

*Less than grade 9 education is a crude measure for illiteracy.

Percent of the population with less than grade 9 education
- 5.7 - 7.6%
- 7.7 - 11.1%
- 11.2 - 13.3%
- 13.4 - 18.0%
- 18.1 - 20.4%

Map 2.4

II. THE GEOGRAPHY OF LITERACY AND DISABILITY IN PERSPECTIVE | 19

Disability Rates for Ages 15 and Older Residing in Households, Provinces and Territories

1991 Health and Activity Limitation Survey (HALS)

While the overall percentage of adults with disabilities is 16.8%, the range varies among the provinces and territories. Nova Scotia, New Brunswick, Manitoba, and Saskatchewan have the highest percentage of adults with disabilities. Newfoundland, Quebec, the Yukon and Northwest Territories all have disability rates lower than the national average.

Canada -- 16.8%

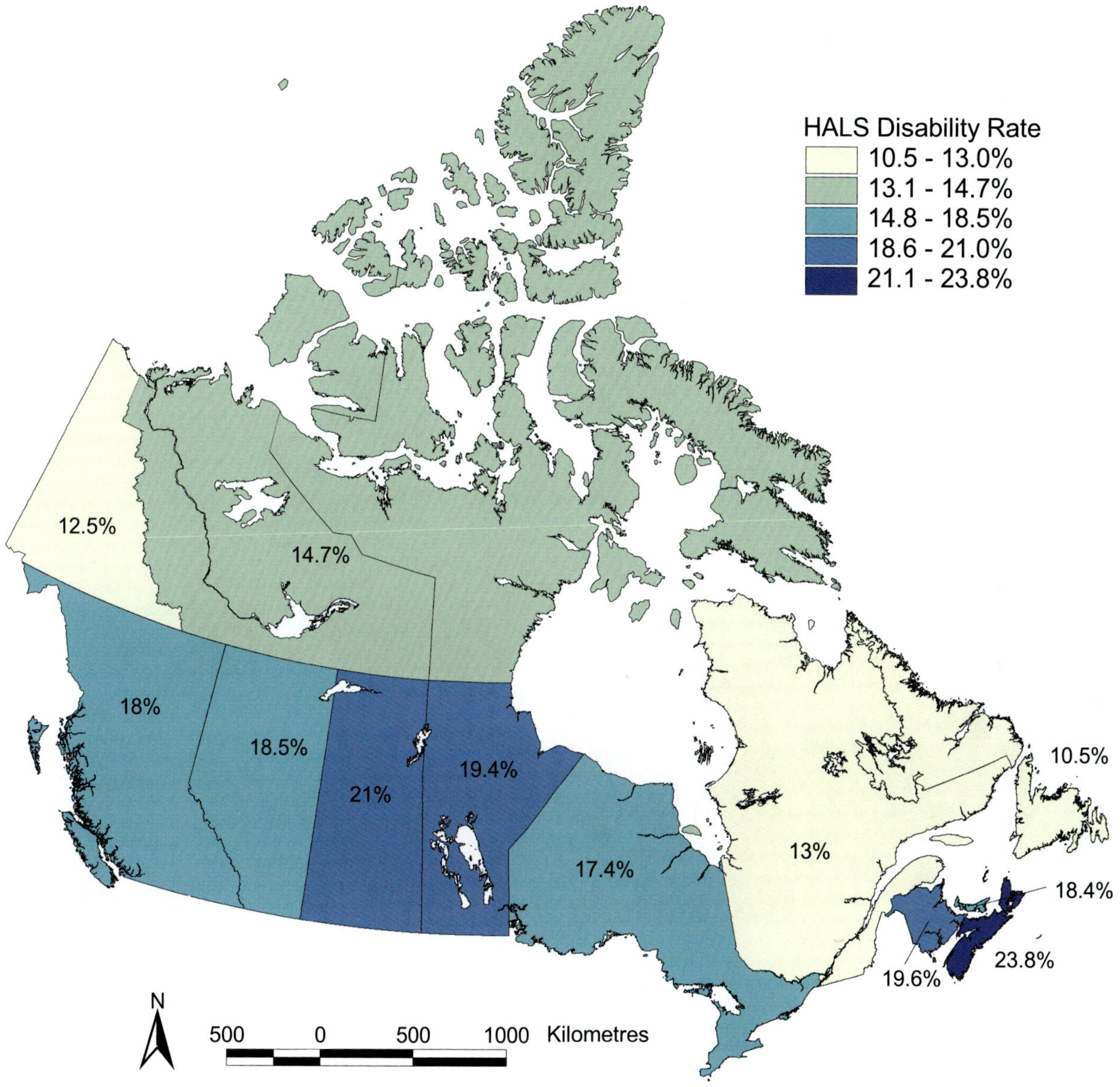

HALS Disability Rate
- 10.5 - 13.0%
- 13.1 - 14.7%
- 14.8 - 18.5%
- 18.6 - 21.0%
- 21.1 - 23.8%

12.5% — 14.7% — 18% — 18.5% — 21% — 19.4% — 17.4% — 13% — 10.5% — 18.4% — 19.6% — 23.8%

Map 2.5

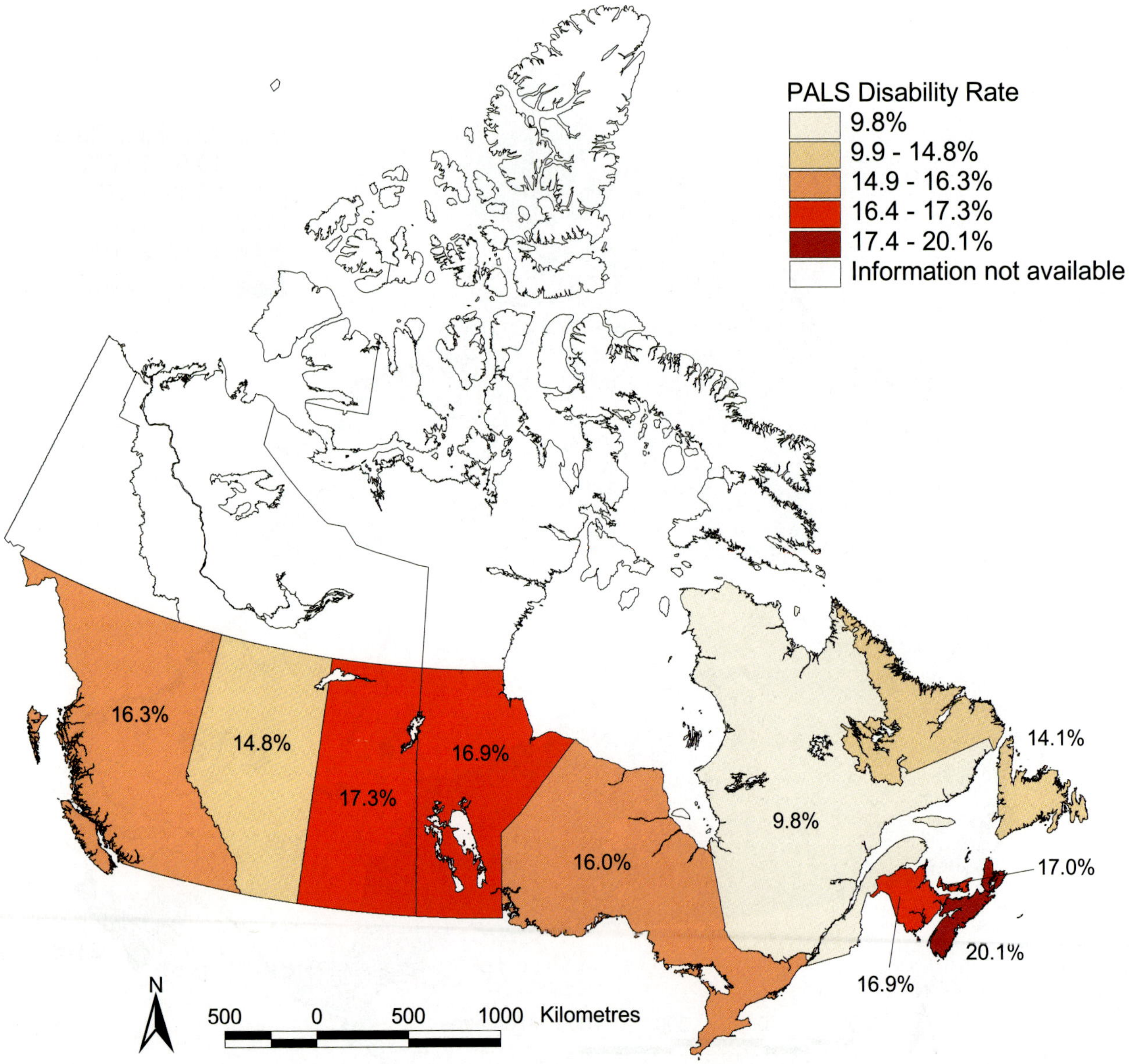

20 ATLAS OF LITERACY AND DISABILITY

Disability Rates for Ages 15 and Older, Provinces

2001 Participation and Activity Limitation Survey (PALS)

PALS shows an overall disability rate of 14.6% compared to HALS 16.8% (see previous map). The PALS provincial disability rates are consistently lower than those seen in HALS (except for Newfoundland). Quebec has the lowest rate at 9.8%. These differences likely reflect findings from different years and from modifications in survey design.

Canada -- 14.6%

Map 2.6

II. THE GEOGRAPHY OF LITERACY AND DISABILITY IN PERSPECTIVE | 21

Disability Rates* for Ages 15 and Older, Provinces

1996 National Population Health Survey (NPHS)

The rates and patterns of disability in the NPHS are quite different than the PALS and HALS findings. NPHS used a different method than the others to measure disability. Disability rates in NPHS ranged from about 13% to 22%. The national average was 15.3%.

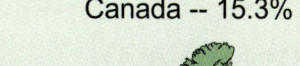

Canada -- 15.3%

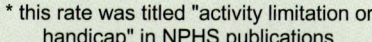

* this rate was titled "activity limitation or handicap" in NPHS publications

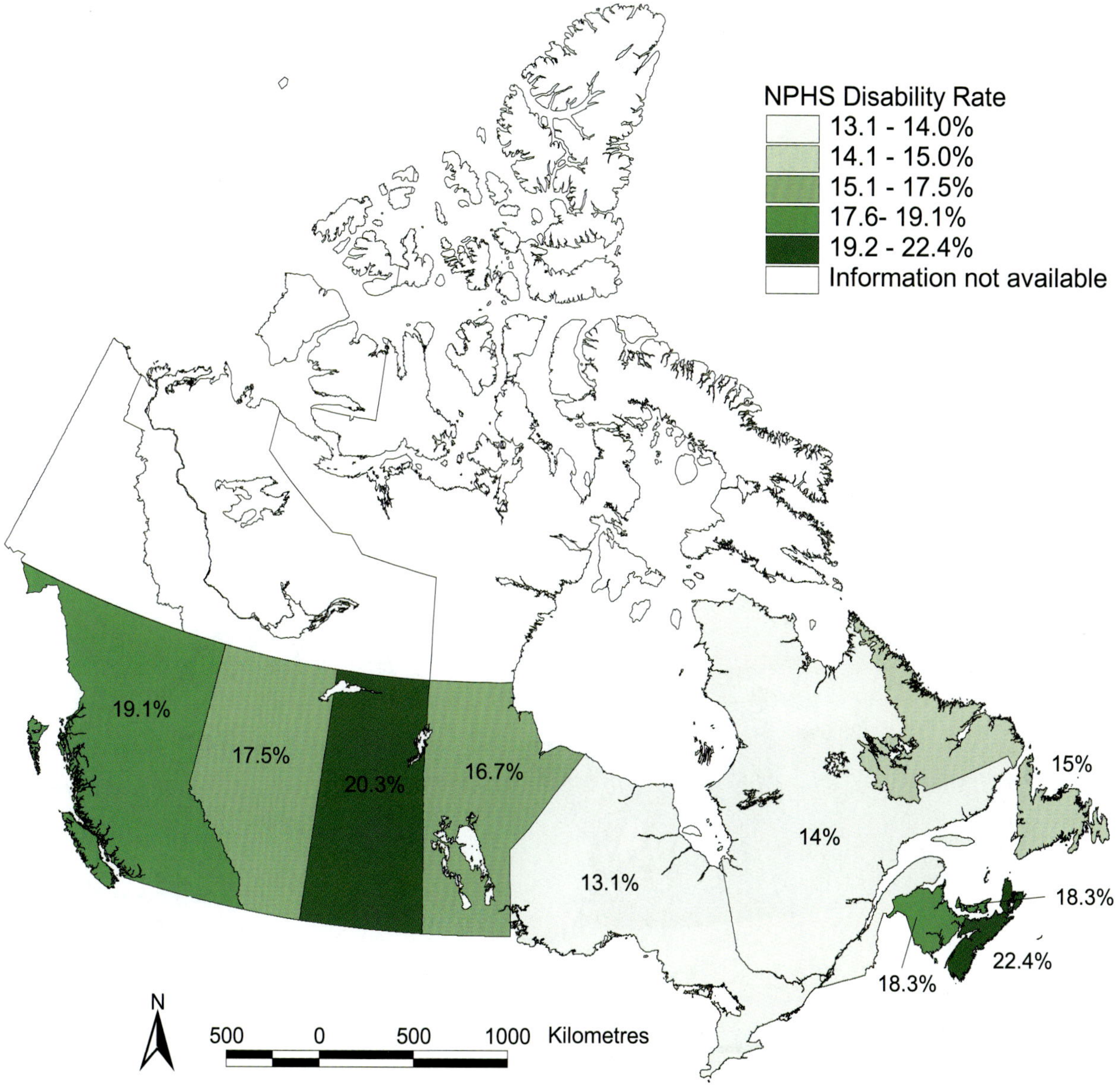

NPHS Disability Rate
- 13.1 - 14.0%
- 14.1 - 15.0%
- 15.1 - 17.5%
- 17.6 - 19.1%
- 19.2 - 22.4%
- Information not available

Map 2.7

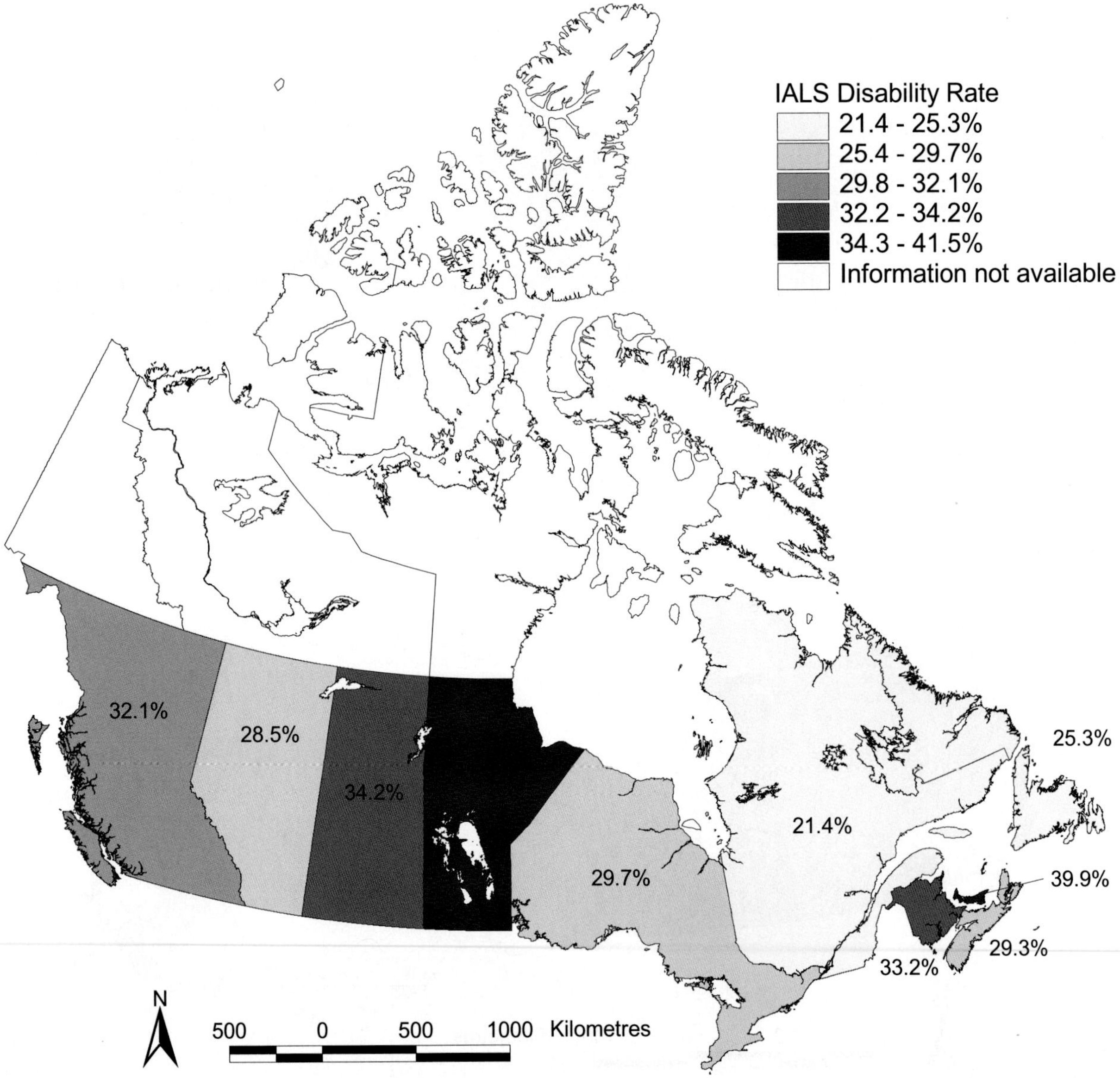

ATLAS OF LITERACY AND DISABILITY

Disability Rates for Ages 16 and Older, Provinces

1994 International Adult Literacy Survey (IALS)

IALS Disability Rate
- 21.4 - 25.3%
- 25.4 - 29.7%
- 29.8 - 32.1%
- 32.2 - 34.2%
- 34.3 - 41.5%
- Information not available

According to IALS, 28.4% of Canadian adults ages 16 and older are disabled - a rate considerably higher than those reported in HALS, PALS and NPHS. The distribution of disability among provinces is also different. Disability rates vary depending on the questions used to identify the population with disabilities. IALS used a broad and general definition.

Canada -- 28.4%

32.1% 28.5% 34.2% 25.3% 21.4% 29.7% 39.9% 33.2% 29.3%

Map 2.8

III. *The Geography of Literacy*

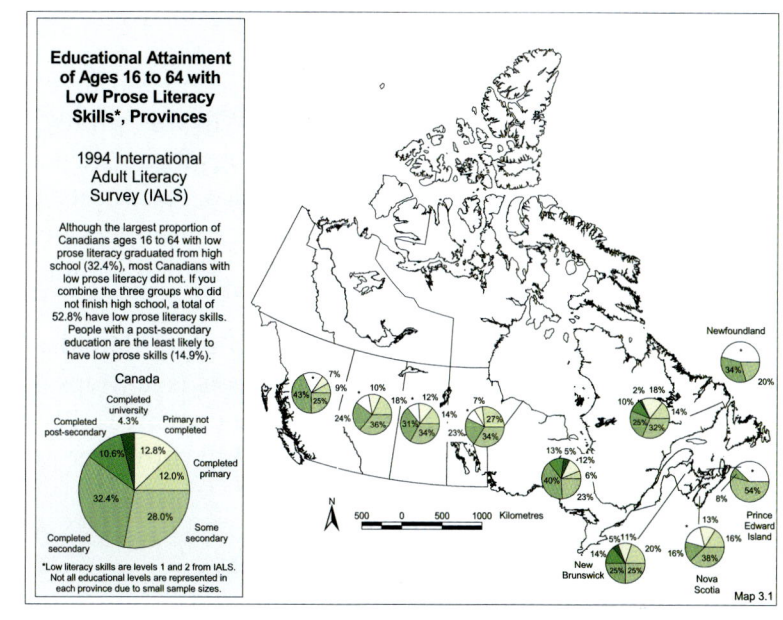

PROVINCIAL LITERACY SCANS (IALS)

	Prose	Document	Quantitative
Level 1	21.5	23.4	21.8
Level 2	25.8	24.4	26.1
Level 3	32.8	30.1	32.4
Levels 4 & 5	19.9	22.1	19.7
Total	100.0	100.0	100.0

The first series of maps in this chapter show socio-demographic information about the prose literacy rates of Canadians at the level of the provinces, from the IALS. The maps are restricted to prose literacy for a number of reasons. First, it would have been impossible to produce maps on all three types of literacy for the number of variables that needed to be included and so it was expedient to choose only one type to map. Second, while there are slightly different findings between the domains of literacy, the findings are similar. Third, we considered it important to do a scan by province.

This provincial scan is an investigational use of IALS literacy rates because the sample sizes were small in this survey. Most reports show literacy information at the regional level. We saw no need to repeat the findings from previous reports,[20] and wanted to show as much geographical detail as possible. As you look at these maps, remember that the findings shown are more reliable for Ontario, Quebec and New Brunswick than the other provinces because they had larger samples. However, even while provincial differences are exploratory, the general trends in differences between the east and the west are reliable.

The provincial scans show that almost half of all Canadian adults (47% to 48%) have prose, document and quantitative literacy skills in the lowest two levels (see Maps 2.1, 2.2 and 2.3). This is not considered an adequate level of skill.[21] There are differences among the provinces. People in the eastern provinces and Quebec tend to have lower levels of all three types of literacy skill compared to those in Ontario and the western provinces.

Literacy Levels and Demographic Characteristics

As the maps in chapter three show, certain factors are associated with level of prose literacy skill. Education attainment is one. Map 3.1 shows that the higher the level of a person's education, the higher their level of prose literacy. The same is true for document and quantitative literacy. There is also an association between literacy and age. IALS shows that seniors are nearly twice as likely to have prose literacy skills at the lower two levels than younger Canadian adults (Map 3.2). This is probably because seniors have lower levels of education than younger Canadians.[22] However, the gap in prose literacy level between age groups varied greatly from province to province.

Some demographic factors appear to have a stronger relationship with literacy than others. Gender differences are

---

20 These can be accessed through the National Literacy Secretariat or NALD websites at http://www.nald.ca/nls.htm
21 Organization of Education, Cooperation and Development (OECD). 2000. *Literacy in the Information Age: Final Report of the International Adult Literacy Survey*, p. xiii.
22 Statistics Canada and Human Resources Development Canada. 1996. *Reading the Future: A Portrait of Literacy in Canada*. Ottawa: Minister of Industry.

so small that they may not be significant (Map 3.3). There is a stronger correlation between literacy and immigrant status. Immigrants scored lower on all three measures of literacy in IALS, particularly prose and document literacy. This was especially true if, as Map 3.5 shows, a person immigrated within the last ten years. Immigrants probably score lower on IALS because they do not test well in English or French. This view is supported by the findings shown in Map 3.4. A much higher proportion of people with low literacy do not speak either official language (15.2%) than those with higher levels (1.5%). IALS did not test literacy skills in languages other than French and English.

Literacy in the Aboriginal population was measured using the grade nine cut-off measure, from Census data rather than IALS survey because few Native people were respondents in IALS.[23] Aboriginal persons are found to be considerably more likely not to have schooling beyond the grade nine level – 18.4%, compared to that of non-Aboriginal Canadians at 12.1% (see Map 3.6). These are conservative estimates because the definition of Aboriginal people includes those with official First Nations status, and those who reported having a First Nations ancestor or ancestors, a Métis ancestor and/or an Inuit ancestor. The disadvantage in educational attainment experienced by Aboriginal persons may be even higher than the statistics suggest.

Socio-Economic Factors and Literacy Skill Levels

Literacy skills are positively correlated with socio-economic factors such as labour force status and level of income. The higher the level of literacy, the more likely a person is to be in the labour force, as indicated in Map 3.7. People are considered to be in the labour force when they are either employed or actively seeking employment. Literacy skills are also related to income. Map 3.8 shows personal income. This is the income that is attached to a particular person, as opposed to household income. Those with higher levels of literacy tend to have higher incomes. Overall, more people with high levels of prose literacy have incomes of $35,000 or higher, and more people with low prose literacy skills have incomes between $15,000 and $24,999. Since this survey was carried out in 1994, it is probable that labour market and employment conditions have changed in some provinces.

TOWARD CRITICAL LITERACY: REALIZING LITERATE CITIZENSHIP

The second series of maps in this chapter examines types of literacy, departing from the usual modes of analyzing IALS, in an effort to draw out findings that compare basic, functional and critical perspectives of literacy. The basic crude measure of literacy tells us whether a person has completed grade nine. The functional literacy proxy designed for this study measures whether people consider themselves to have the skills needed to function in

---

23 Literacy data for the Aboriginal population was drawn from a Statistics Canada publication titled *Profile of Canada's Aboriginal Population* based on the 1996 Census. "Aboriginal person" was defined in this report according to a broad definition as including persons who report Aboriginal origin, as well as those who identify themselves as registered Indians. The survey included persons with Aboriginal status and Aboriginal ancestry living off-reserve. It excludes those living on reserves, as well as people in institutions and in the armed forces.

daily life. The critical literacy proxy is intended to reflect how literacy and communication skill affects people's participation and equality in society. Proxy variables for functional and critical literacy were designed that provide exploratory data, but have not been tested for validity and reliability.

Basic Literacy

Map 3.9 shows basic literacy according to the 1996 Census, highlighting differences between provinces and territories. It shows that, on average, 12% of Canadian adults would be considered illiterate at the basic level. It also shows that, in general, people in the Northwest Territories and eastern provinces have lower grade nine completion rates than the western provinces and Yukon. Map 3.10 shows basic literacy at the Census subdivision level. It shows that there are various differences within provinces in basic literacy.

Functional Literacy

Two functional literacy proxies that are different from the measures of prose, document and quantitative literacy were derived from IALS. The first of these is the overall literacy measure, which provides a sum of the prose, document and quantitative literacy scores, combined into one measure. Map 3.11 shows that nearly half of Canadians (46.3%) have an overall low score of literacy (levels 1 and 2), and just over half have levels of literacy that are adequate or better.

The proxy variable is referred to as the functional literacy measure. It was designed out of a selection of variables that were specifically chosen to more directly reflect functioning in daily life. It is represented in Maps 3.12 and 3.13. The first of these shows that the greatest proportion of Canadian adults has a moderate level of the literacy skills they need to function in daily life (41.1%). More people score at the highest level (34.4%) than at the lowest level (24.5%). The other maps reveal that educational attainment plays a role in functional literacy skills. More than half of Canadians ages 16 to 64 with low functional literacy did not finish high school (53.6%). Close to a third of Canadian adults with low functional literacy skills did complete high school.

Critical Literacy and Literate Citizenship

The proxy variable for critical literacy does not measure the skills of individuals, but whether or not they experience conditions related to literacy and communication that include or marginalize them in society. It is an exploratory measure of critical literacy at low (level 1), moderate (level 2) and high (level 3). Canadians score similarly in critical literacy to their scores in functional literacy. Map 3.14 shows that the largest proportion of Canadian adults experience critical literacy in the medium level (40%), a pattern that is consistent through much of the country. Yet a fairly high proportion (one-quarter) of Canadian adults experience low critical literacy. As is the case with functional literacy, critical literacy appears to be linked to high school completion. Map 3.15 shows that the largest proportion of Canadian adults who experience low critical literacy have not completed high school

(57%). An alarming 43% of people who did finish high school, college, or university experience marginalization in the form of low critical literacy.

A Comparison

Map 3.16 compares findings according to the three definitions of literacy in IALS. Canadians overall are more likely to have low functional and critical literacy (25% each) than low basic literacy skills (16.3%). This data suggests that having basic literacy does not ensure that a person is functionally or critically literate.

GEORGAPHY OF LITERACY ORGANIZATIONS

Literacy organizations shown in Map 3.17 were drawn from the NALD online database and categorized by the research team. Of the ten categories of literacy organizations, those that provide literacy and basic skills are by far the most common. The next most common types are those that provide literacy networking, awareness and advocacy. Ontario and Quebec have notably more literacy organizations than the other provinces.

III. THE GEOGRAPHY OF LITERACY   29

Educational Attainment of Ages 16 to 64 with Low Prose Literacy Skills*, Provinces

1994 International Adult Literacy Survey (IALS)

Although the largest proportion of Canadians ages 16 to 64 with low prose literacy graduated from high school (32.4%), most Canadians with low prose literacy did not. If you combine the three groups who did not finish high school, a total of 52.8% have low prose literacy skills. People with a post-secondary education are the least likely to have low prose skills (14.9%).

Canada

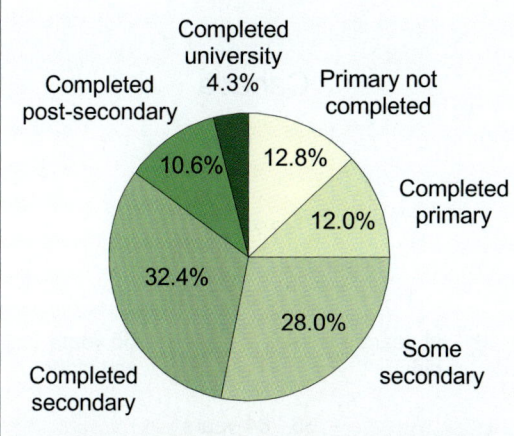

- Completed university 4.3%
- Completed post-secondary 10.6%
- Completed secondary 32.4%
- Some secondary 28.0%
- Completed primary 12.0%
- Primary not completed 12.8%

*Low literacy skills are levels 1 and 2 from IALS. Not all educational levels are represented in each province due to small sample sizes.

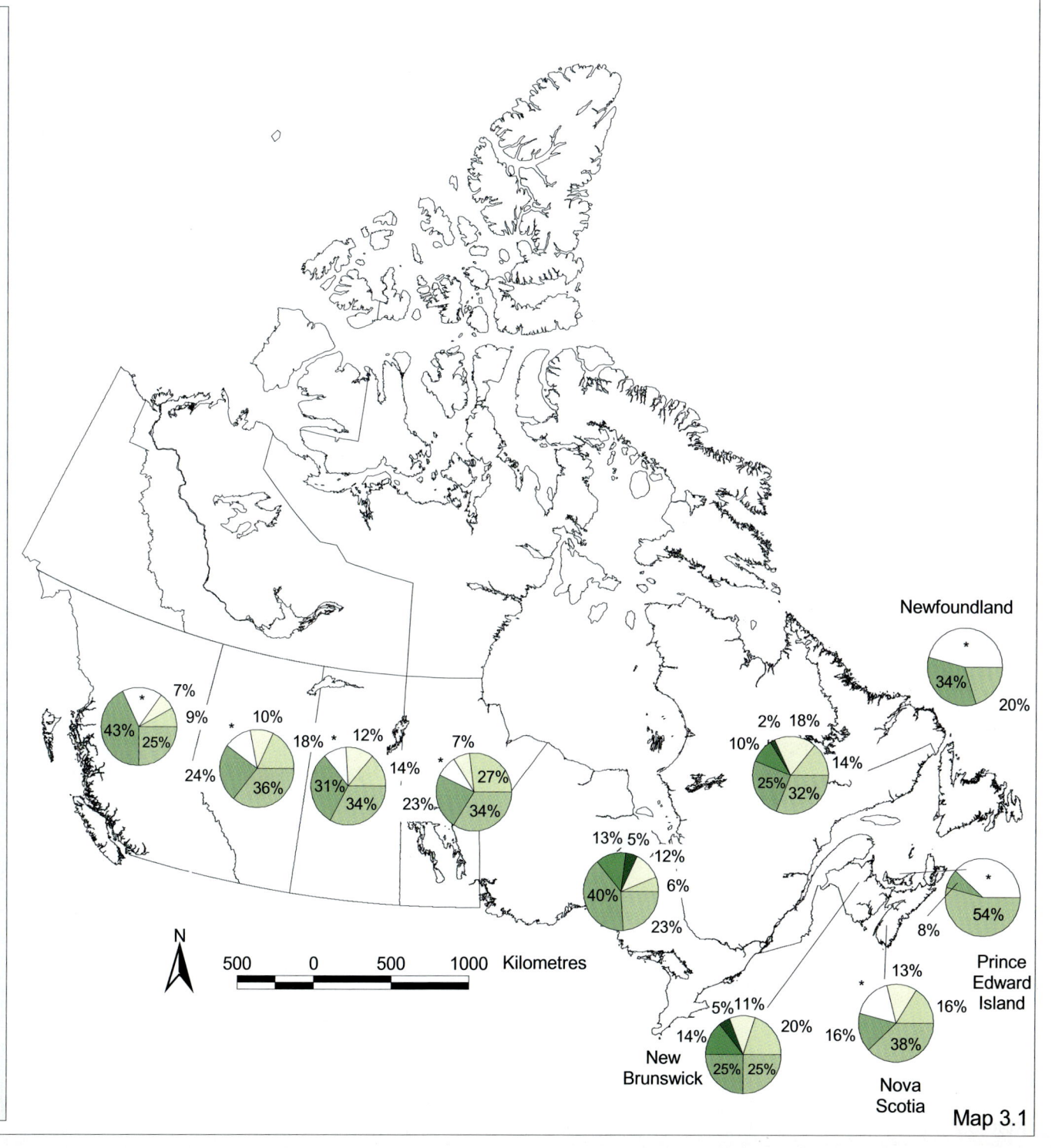

Map 3.1

ATLAS OF LITERACY AND DISABILITY

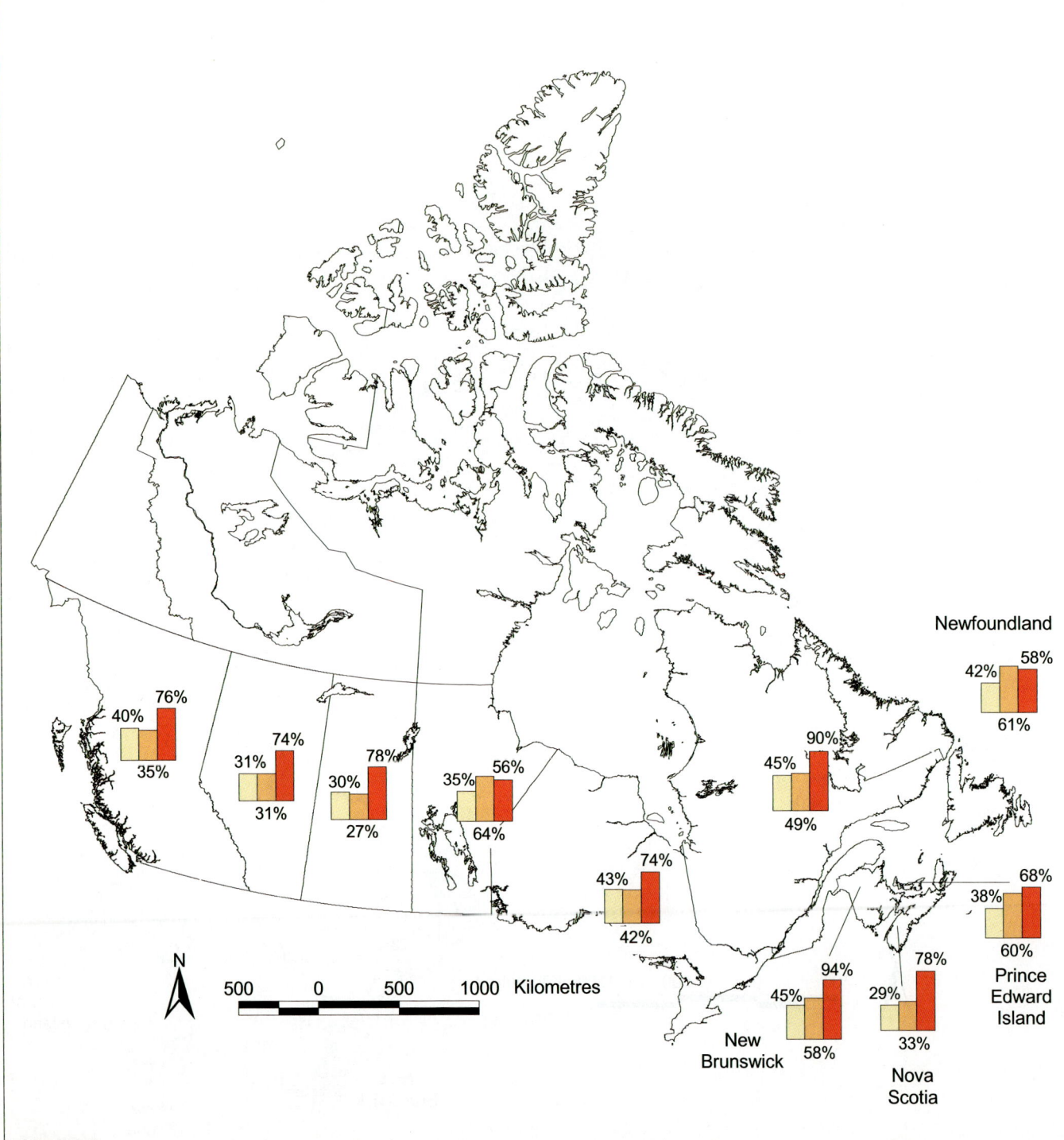

Age Distribution of Ages 16 and Older with Low Prose Literacy Skills*, Provinces

1994 International Adult Literacy Survey (IALS)

Seniors ages 65 and older are nearly twice as likely (79.1%) to have prose literacy skills at the two lowest levels than those between ages 35 and 64 years (42.7%) or between 16 and 34 years (40.8%). However the gap in skill level by age varied in different areas of the country.

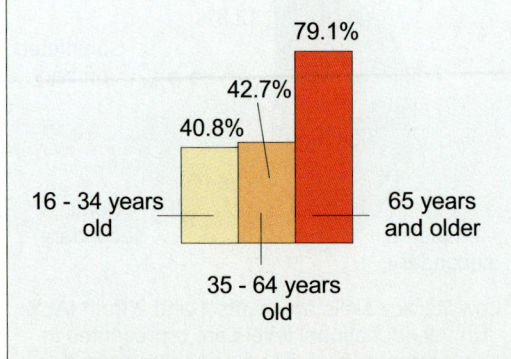

Canada

- 16 - 34 years old: 40.8%
- 35 - 64 years old: 42.7%
- 65 years and older: 79.1%

*Low literacy skills are levels 1 and 2 from IALS.

Provincial data (16-34% / 35-64% / 65+):

- Newfoundland: 42% / 61% / 58%
- Prince Edward Island: 38% / 60% / 68%
- Nova Scotia: 29% / 33% / 78%
- New Brunswick: 45% / 58% / 94%
- Quebec: 43% / 42% / 74%
- Ontario: 35% / 64% / 56%
- Manitoba: 45% / 49% / 90%
- Saskatchewan: 30% / 27% / 78%
- Alberta: 31% / 31% / 74%
- British Columbia: 40% / 35% / 76%

Map 3.2

III. THE GEOGRAPHY OF LITERACY | 31

Gender Distribution for Ages 16 and Older with Low Prose Literacy Skills*, Provinces

1994 International Adult Literacy Survey (IALS)

The difference between men and women in level of prose literacy is very slight. In Manitoba, Quebec, and Nova Scotia, equal numbers of men and women have limited literacy, while in British Columbia and Saskatchewan slightly more women than men struggle with reading texts, documents, and numbers in their daily lives.

Canada

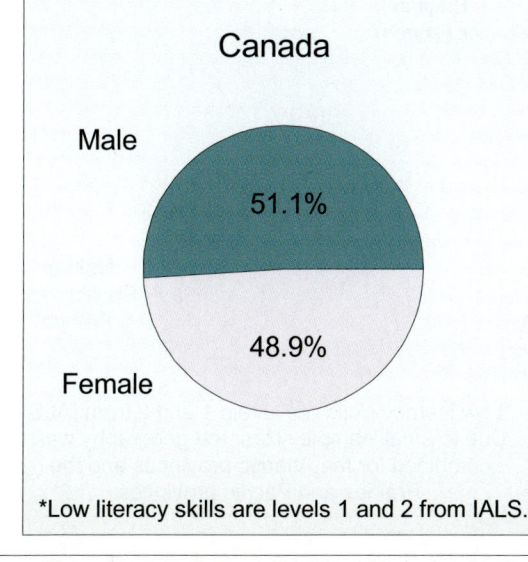

Male: 51.1%
Female: 48.9%

*Low literacy skills are levels 1 and 2 from IALS.

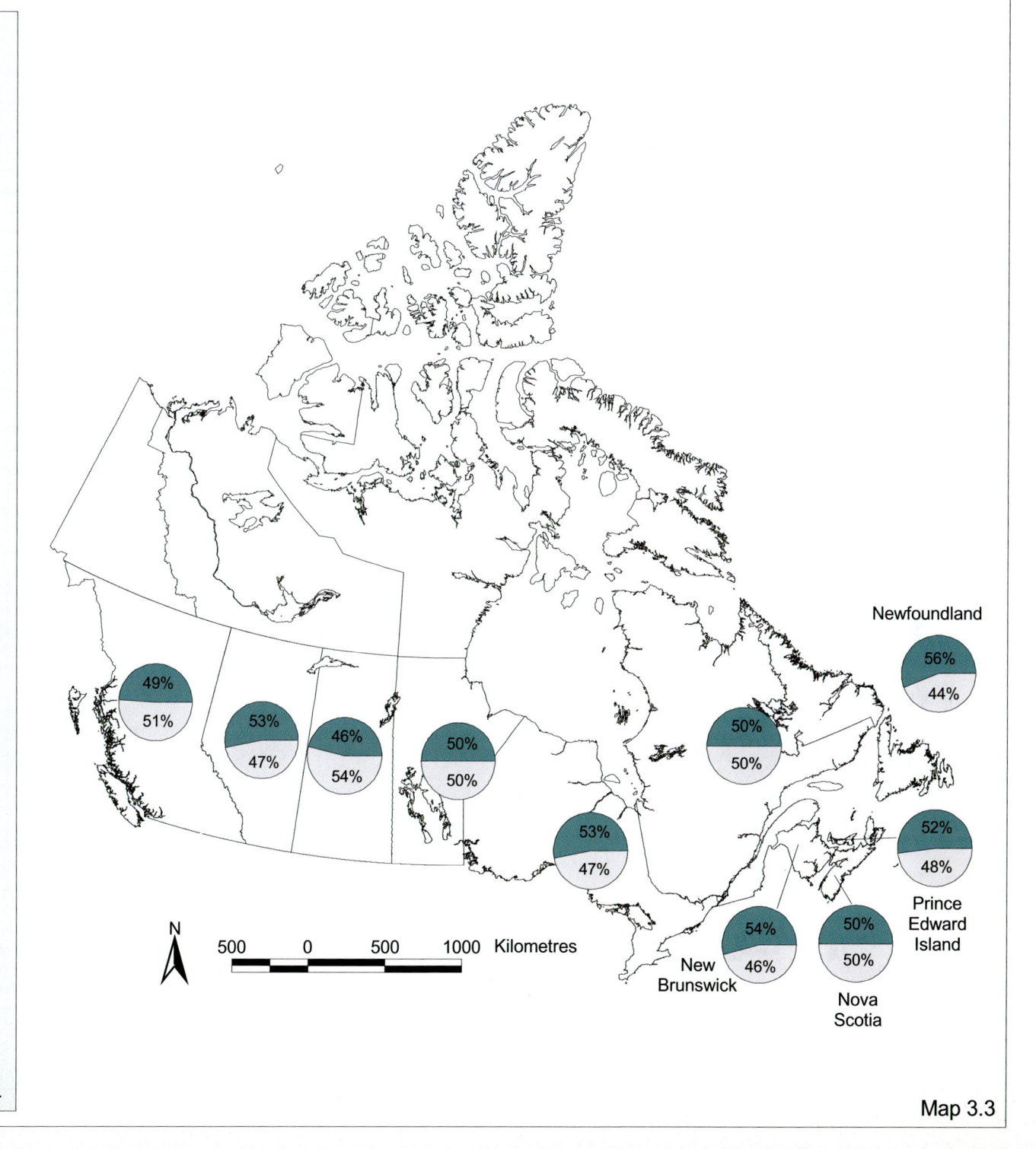

British Columbia: 49% / 51%
Alberta: 53% / 47%
Saskatchewan: 46% / 54%
Manitoba: 50% / 50%
Ontario: 53% / 47%
Quebec: 50% / 50%
New Brunswick: 54% / 46%
Nova Scotia: 50% / 50%
Prince Edward Island: 52% / 48%
Newfoundland: 56% / 44%

Map 3.3

ATLAS OF LITERACY AND DISABILITY

Use of Official Language by Ages 16 and Older with Low Prose Literacy Skills*, Provinces

1994 International Adult Literacy Survey (IALS)

The vast majority of Canadian adults with low prose literacy skills speak one of Canada's two official languages (85%). Both Ontario and Quebec show more individuals with low literacy skills whose language is neither English nor French. In Ontario it is 23%.

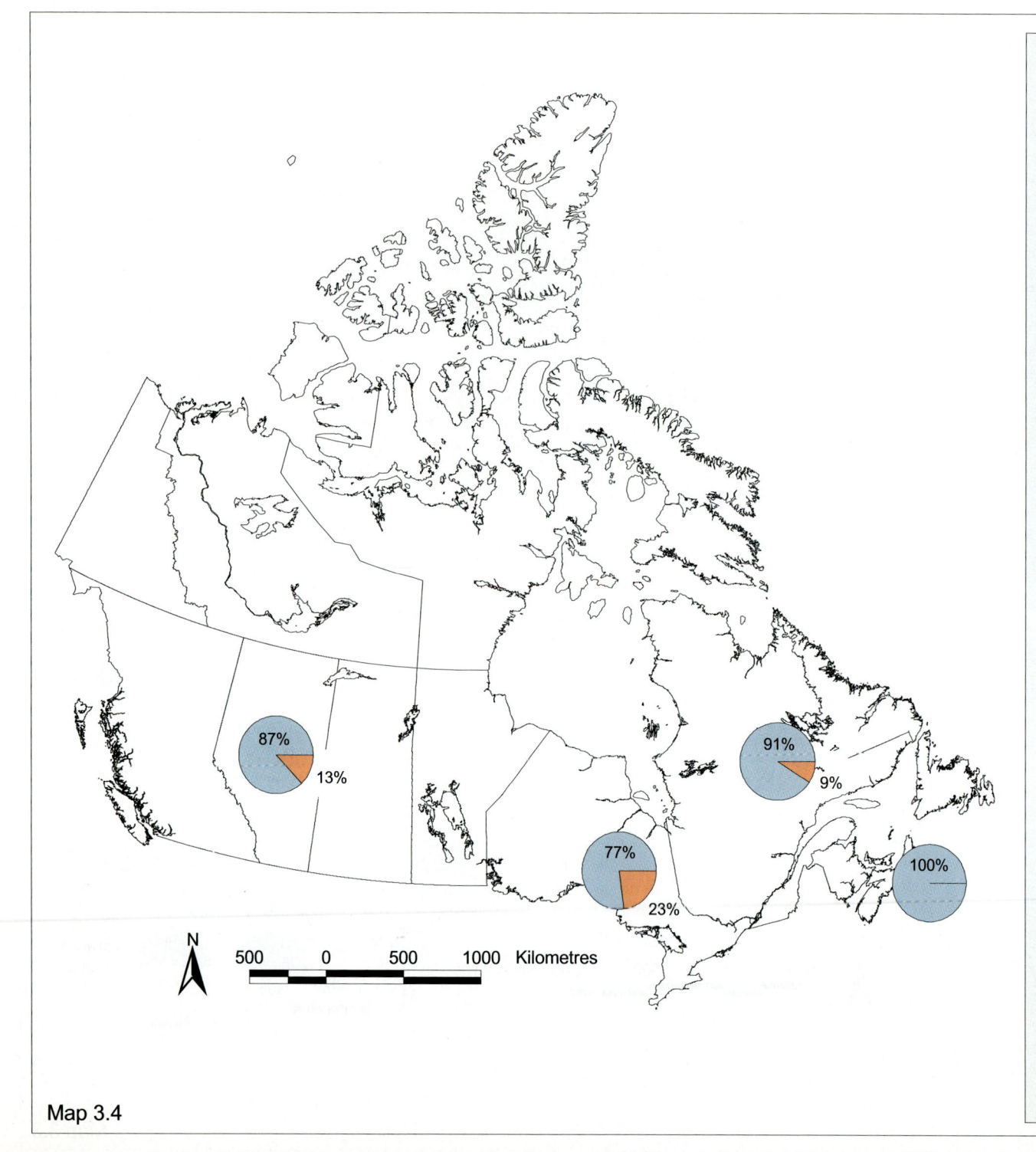

Canada

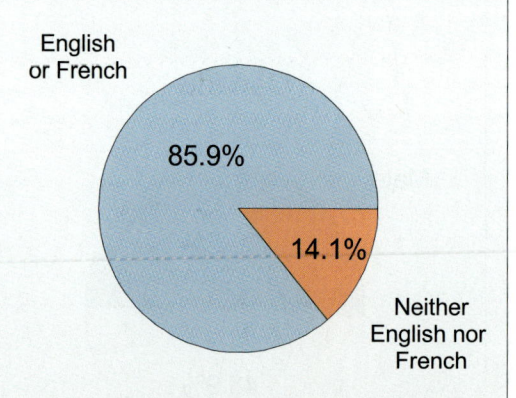

English or French: 85.9%
Neither English nor French: 14.1%

Provincial pie charts:
- Prairies/Pacific: 87% / 13%
- Ontario: 77% / 23%
- Quebec: 91% / 9%
- Atlantic: 100%

*Low literacy skills are levels 1 and 2 from IALS. Due to small sample sizes, the geography was combined for the Atlantic provinces and the Prairies and Pacific provinces.

Map 3.4

III. THE GEOGRAPHY OF LITERACY | 33

Immigration Status of Ages 16 and Older with Low Prose Literacy Skills*, Provinces

1994 International Adult Literacy Survey (IALS)

One in four adults with low prose literacy skills are immigrants to Canada. Of those, about 9% immigrated between 1984 and 1994, and their low skill levels may be related to difficulty with understanding English and French. Seventeen percent immigrated before 1984, and are more likely to be comfortable in Canada's official languages. The other 75% are Canadian born.

Canada

- Immigrated between 1984 and 1994: 8.9%
- Immigrated before 1984: 17.3%
- Canadian born: 73.8%

*Low literacy skills are levels 1 and 2 from IALS. Due to small sample sizes, specific immigration data was not available for all provinces.

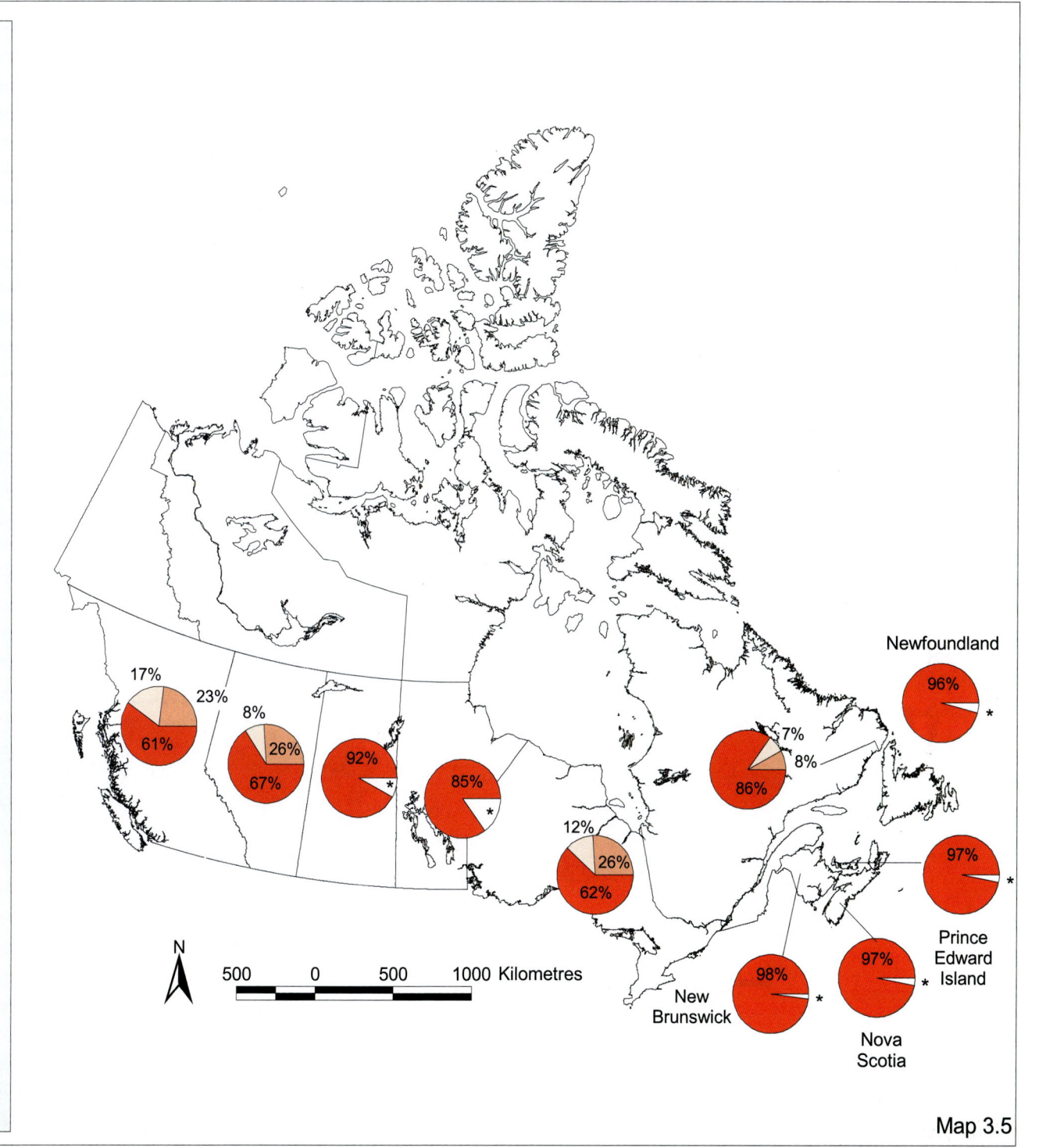

Provincial pie charts (Canadian born / Immigrated before 1984 / Immigrated 1984–1994):
- British Columbia: 61% / — / 17%, (23% before 1984 shown)
- Alberta: 67% / 26% / 8%
- Saskatchewan: 92% *
- Manitoba: 85% *
- Ontario: 62% / 26% / 12%
- Quebec: 86% / 8% / 7%
- New Brunswick: 98% *
- Nova Scotia: 97% *
- Prince Edward Island: 97% *
- Newfoundland: 96% *

Map 3.5

ATLAS OF LITERACY AND DISABILITY

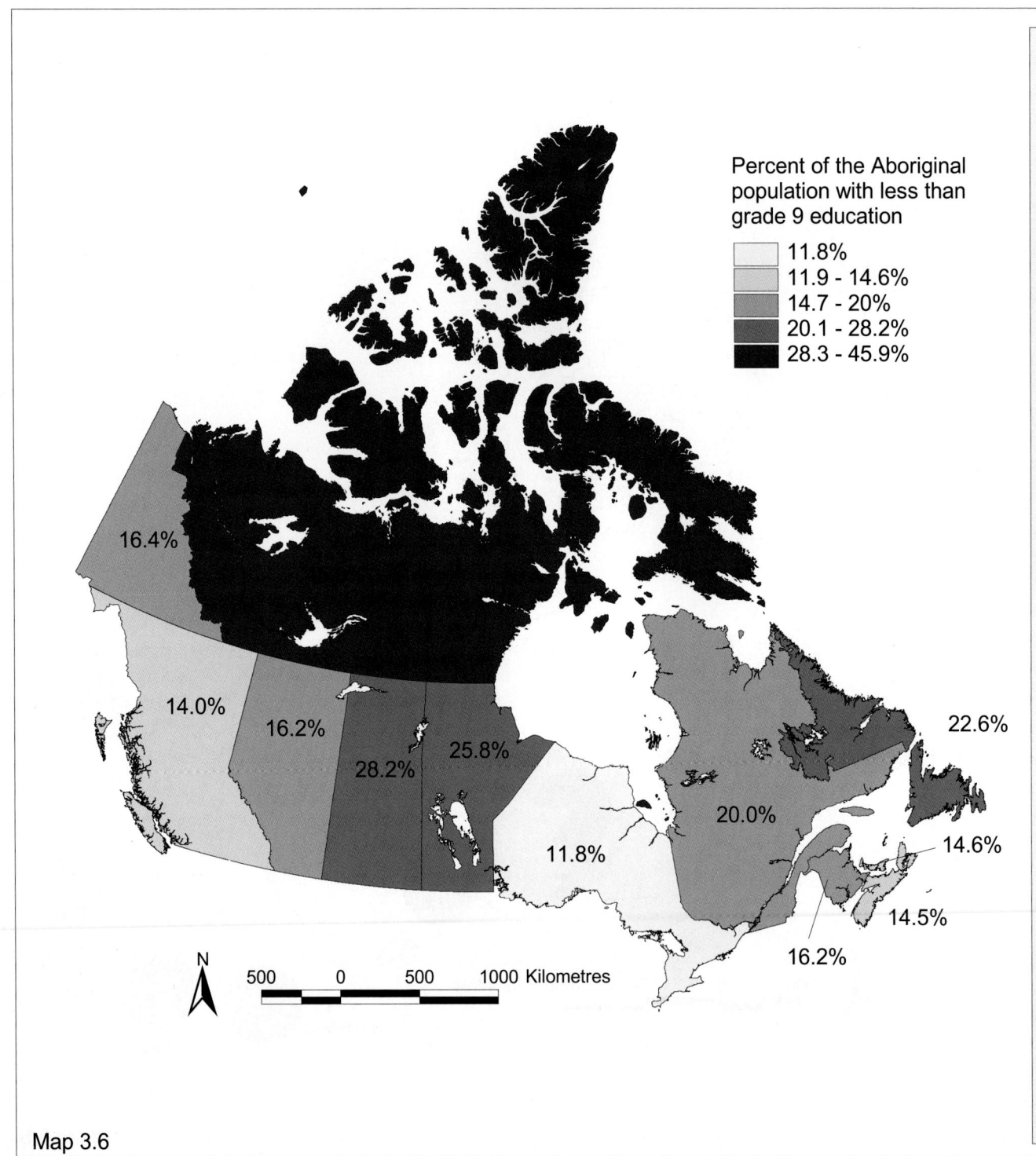

Percent of the Aboriginal population with less than grade 9 education
- 11.8%
- 11.9 - 14.6%
- 14.7 - 20%
- 20.1 - 28.2%
- 28.3 - 45.9%

16.4%
14.0%
16.2%
28.2%
25.8%
22.6%
20.0%
11.8%
14.6%
14.5%
16.2%

500 0 500 1000 Kilometres

Map 3.6

Percent of the Aboriginal Population* with Less than Grade 9 Education^, Provinces and Territories

1994 Statistics Canada "Profile of Canada's Aboriginal Population"

In Canada, about 18% of the Aboriginal population* had less than grade 9 education -- a measure of low basic literacy skills. Among this population in the Northwest Territories, this percentage rose to 45.9% and in Saskatchewan and Manitoba, the percentage was 28.2% and 25.8% respectively.

Canada -- 18.4%

*The Aboriginal population includes those who report being Registered Indians or having an Aboriginal ancestor.
^Less than grade 9 education is a crude measure for illiteracy.

III. THE GEOGRAPHY OF LITERACY | 35

Adults who are Active in the Labour Force by Prose Literacy Level*, Provinces

1994 International Adult Literacy Survey (IALS)

In the country, the higher the level of prose literacy, the more likely a persons is to be in the labour force. Only 40% of Canadian adults with the lowest prose literacy skills have worked in the past twelve months, while three quarters of those at the highest levels are working or have worked recently. There are some regional differences.

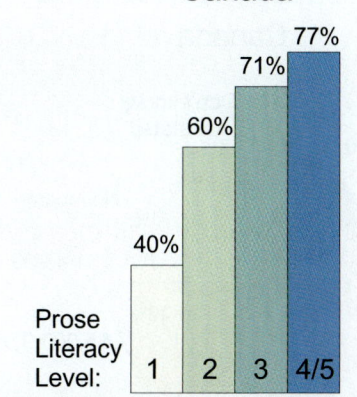

Canada

Prose Literacy Level:
- 1: 40%
- 2: 60%
- 3: 71%
- 4/5: 77%

*Includes people ages 15 to 64 who are employed and those who are looking for work. Levels taken from the survey, ranked 1-4/5 with 1 being the lowest level and 4/5 the highest.
^The sample size for level 4/5 for PEI was too small for the results to be released.

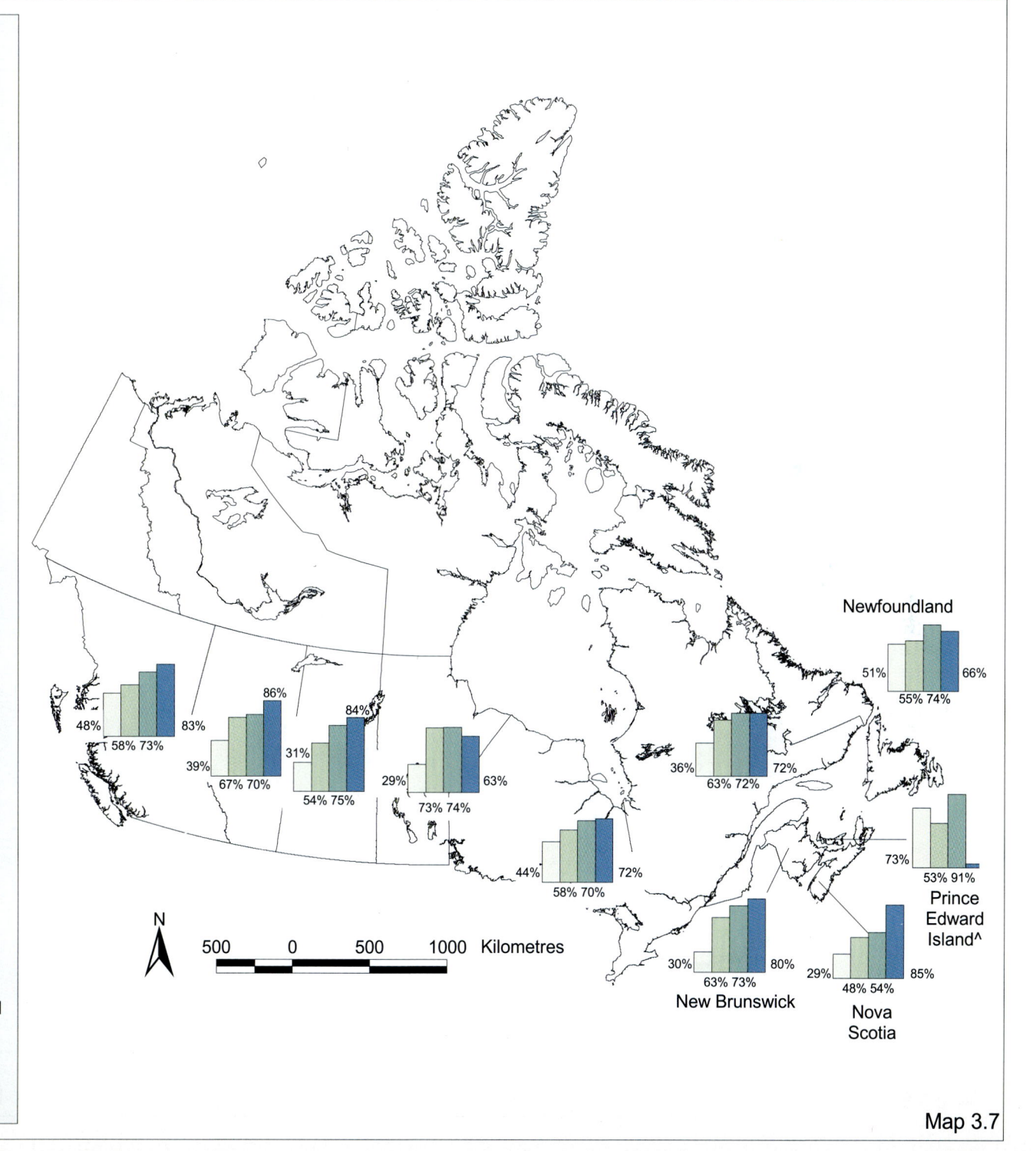

Provincial data (levels 1, 2, 3, 4/5):

- British Columbia: 48%, 58%, 73%, 83%
- Alberta: 39%, 67%, 70%, 86%
- Saskatchewan: 31%, 54%, 75%, 84%
- Manitoba: 29%, 73%, 74%, 63%
- Ontario: 36%, 63%, 72%, 72%
- Quebec: 44%, 58%, 70%, 72%
- New Brunswick: 30%, 63%, 73%, 80%
- Nova Scotia: 29%, 48%, 54%, 85%
- Prince Edward Island^: 53%, 73%, 91%
- Newfoundland: 51%, 55%, 74%, 66%

Map 3.7

ATLAS OF LITERACY AND DISABILITY

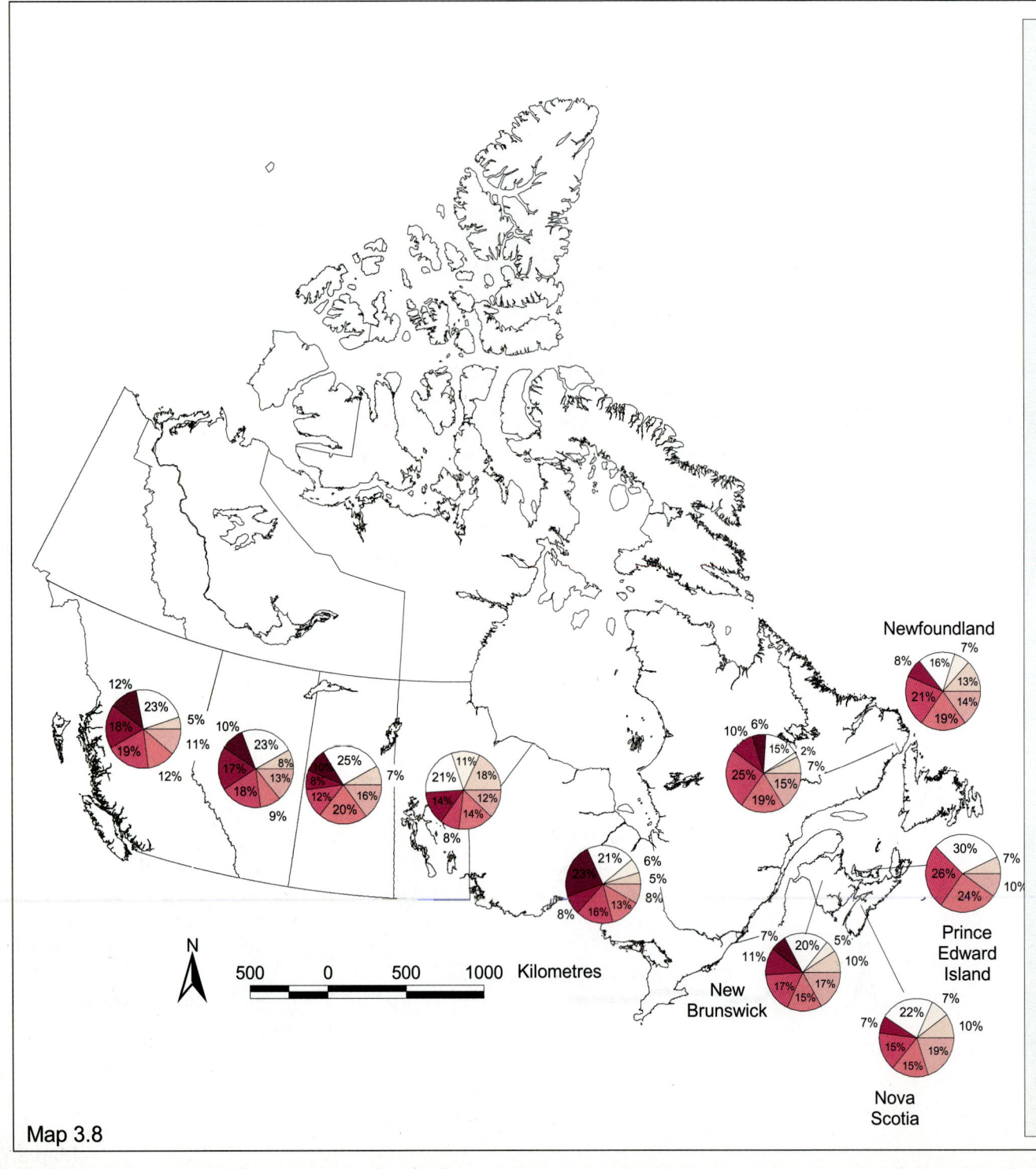

Personal Income Levels for Ages 16 and Older with Low Prose Literacy Skills*, Provinces

1994 International Adult Literacy Survey (IALS)

Adults with low prose literacy skills who live in the eastern provinces have lower incomes than those who live in the western provinces. For example, in Newfoundland, over half of this population (53%) makes less than $15,000 per year, compared to less than one third of the population in Alberta (30%).

Canada

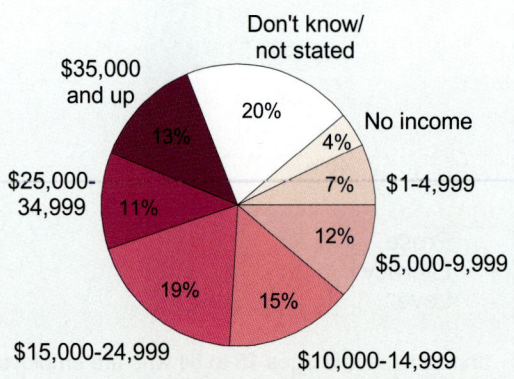

- $35,000 and up: 13%
- Don't know/not stated: 20%
- No income: 4%
- $1-4,999: 7%
- $5,000-9,999: 12%
- $10,000-14,999: 15%
- $15,000-24,999: 19%
- $25,000-34,999: 11%

*Low literacy skills are levels 1 and 2 from IALS. Not all income levels are represented in each province due to small sample sizes.

Map 3.8

III. THE GEOGRAPHY OF LITERACY | 37

Percent of the Population Ages 15 and Older with Less than Grade 9 Education*, Provinces and Territories

1996 Census of Population

On average, 12.1% of Canadian adults have less than grade 9 education, a measure of low basic literacy skills. Those who live in the Northwest Territories (20.4%), Quebec (18%), New Brunswick (16.5%) and Newfoundland (17.5%) are less likely to go to school past grade 8 than other Canadians.

Canada -- 12.1%

*Less than grade 9 education is a crude measure for illiteracy. This map was also printed as map 2.4

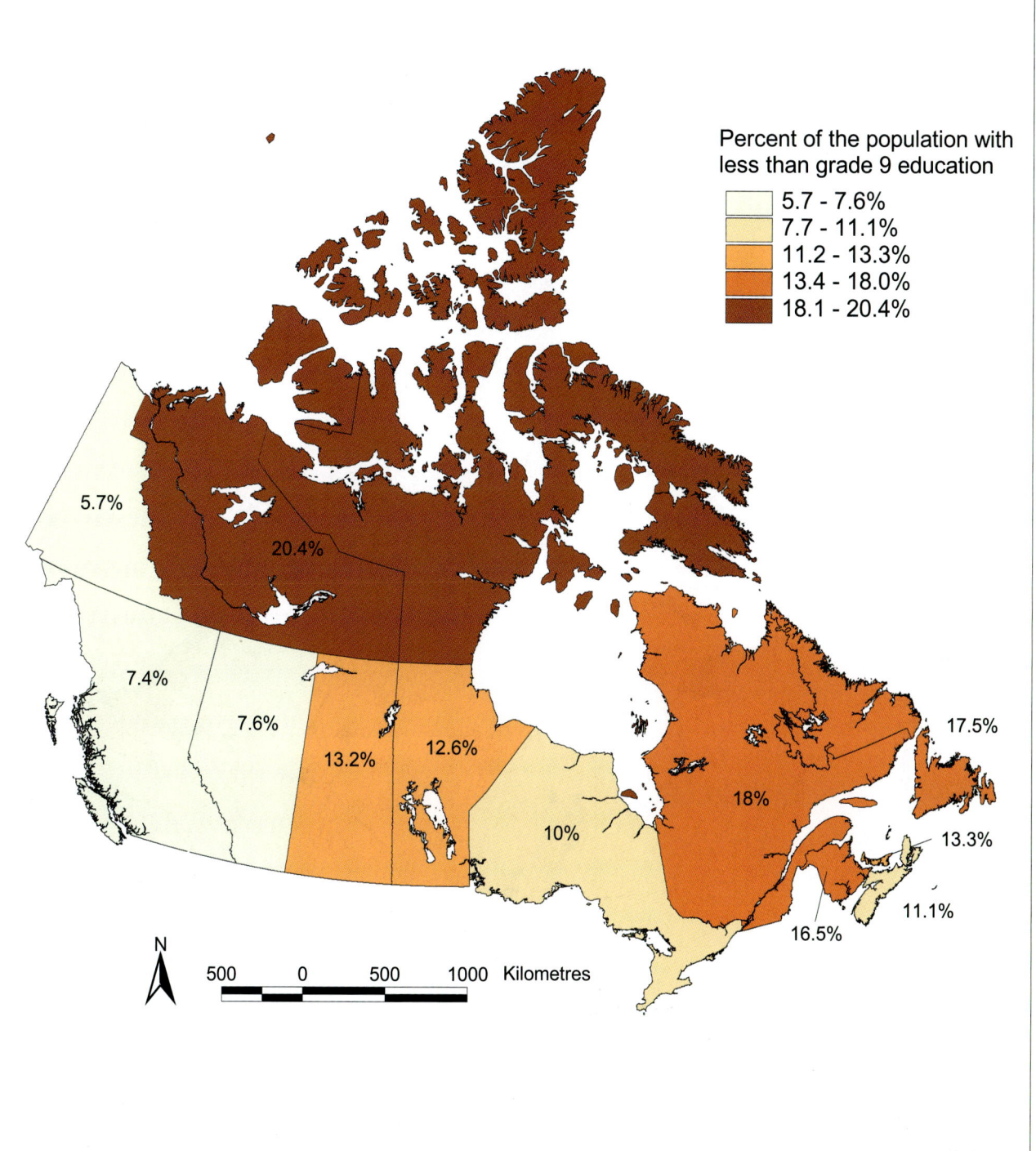

Percent of the population with less than grade 9 education
- 5.7 - 7.6%
- 7.7 - 11.1%
- 11.2 - 13.3%
- 13.4 - 18.0%
- 18.1 - 20.4%

Map 3.9

ATLAS OF LITERACY AND DISABILITY

Percent of the population with less than grade 9 education

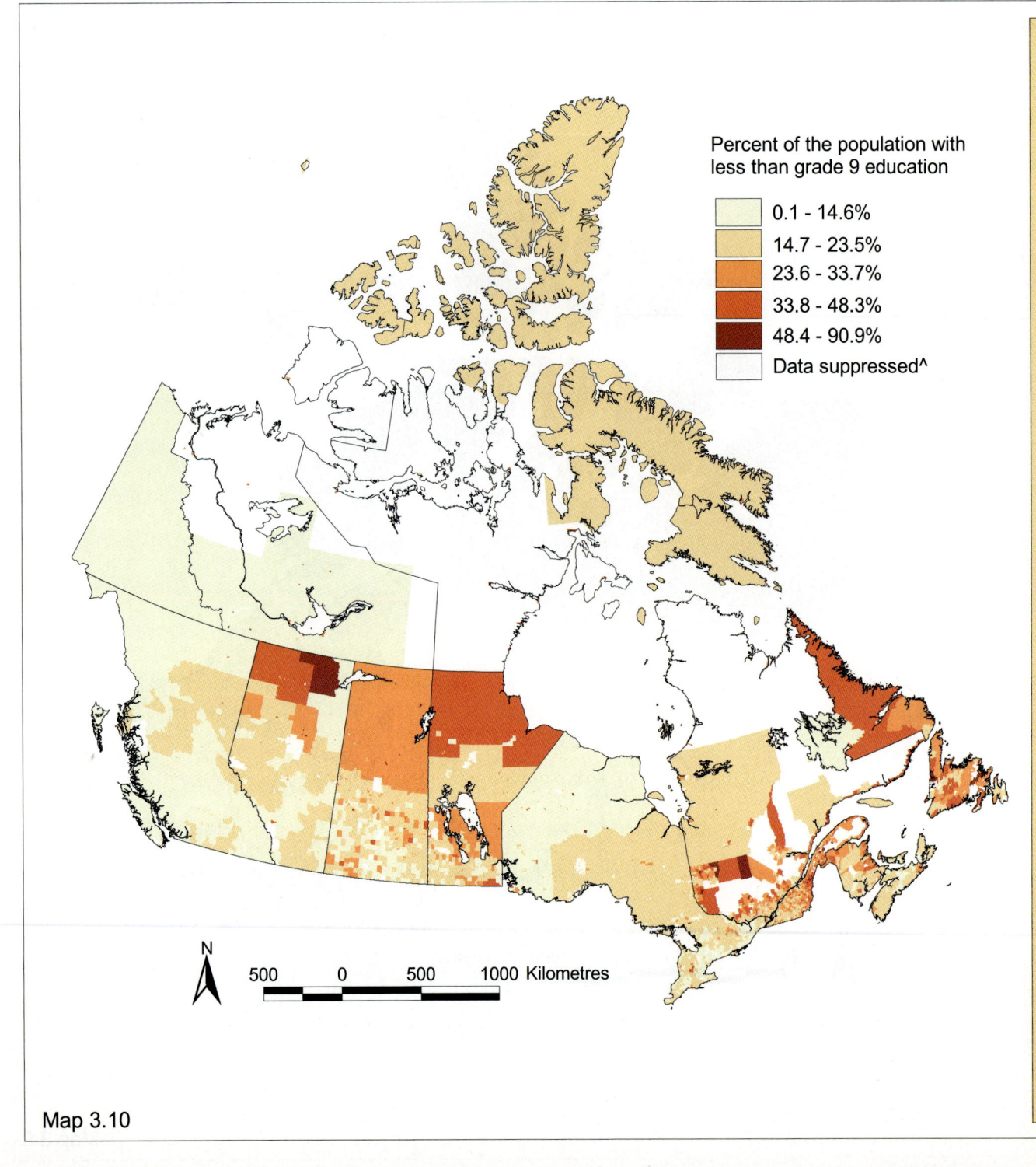

- 0.1 - 14.6%
- 14.7 - 23.5%
- 23.6 - 33.7%
- 33.8 - 48.3%
- 48.4 - 90.9%
- Data suppressed^

Percent of the Population with Less than Grade 9 Education*, Census Subdivisions

1996 Census of Population

The darkest colour shows areas where educational attainment is lowest. In these areas, between 48-91% of the population have not gone to high school. The light yellow colour identifies areas where less than 15% of the adult population have less than grade 9 education.

Canada -- 12.1%

* Less than grade 9 education is a crude measure of illiteracy.

^Data was suppressed when the CSD has a population less than 40 and for Indian Reserves, if the response rate was less than 25%.

Map 3.10

III. THE GEOGRAPHY OF LITERACY | 39

Overall Literacy Levels* for Ages 16 and Older, Provinces

1994 International Adult Literacy Survey (IALS)

One third of Canadians sixteen years old and older have an overall literacy score at level 3 (33.6%). Few people have literacy levels that are higher than that, but nearly half of Canadians have lower literacy levels (46.3%). In general, people have higher levels in the West.

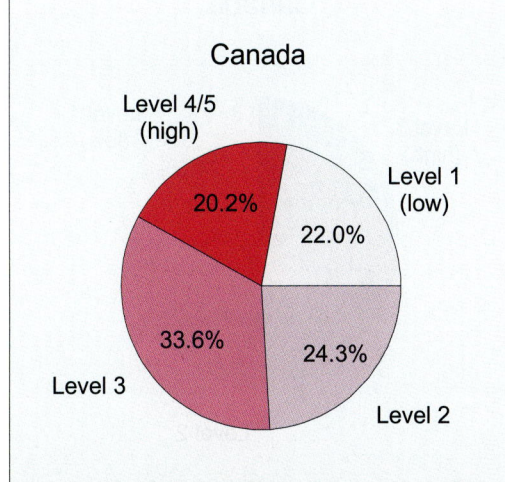

Canada

- Level 4/5 (high): 20.2%
- Level 1 (low): 22.0%
- Level 2: 24.3%
- Level 3: 33.6%

*Based on an alternative proxy derived from IALS.

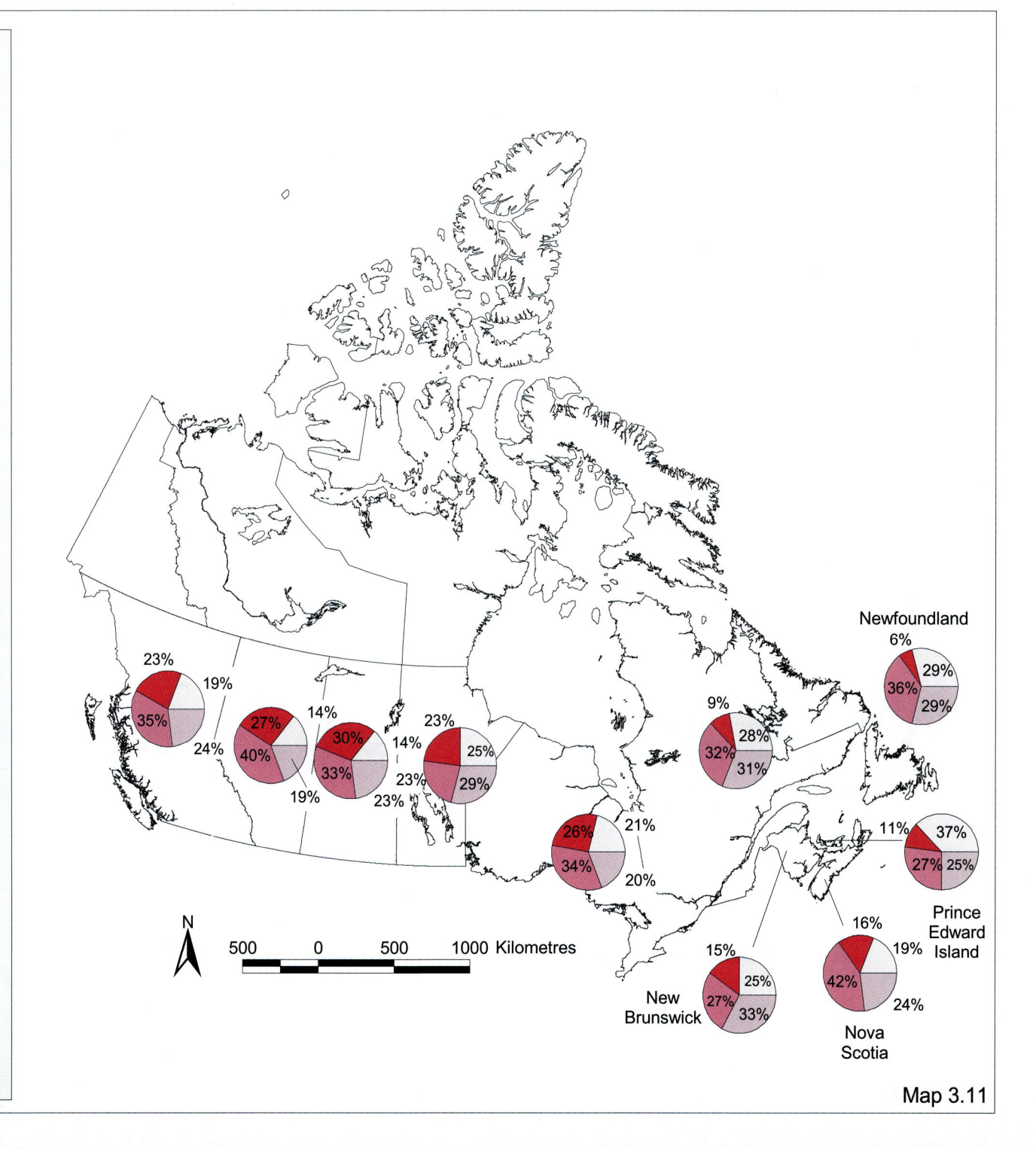

British Columbia: 23% / 19% / 35% / 24%
Alberta: 27% / 14% / 40% / 19%
Saskatchewan: 30% / 14% / 33% / 23%
Manitoba: 23% / 23% / 29%
Ontario: 26% / 21% / 34% / 20%
Quebec: 9% / 28% / 32% / 31%

Newfoundland: 6% / 29% / 36% / 29%
Prince Edward Island: 11% / 37% / 27% / 25%
Nova Scotia: 16% / 19% / 42% / 24%
New Brunswick: 15% / 25% / 27% / 33%

Map 3.11

ATLAS OF LITERACY AND DISABILITY

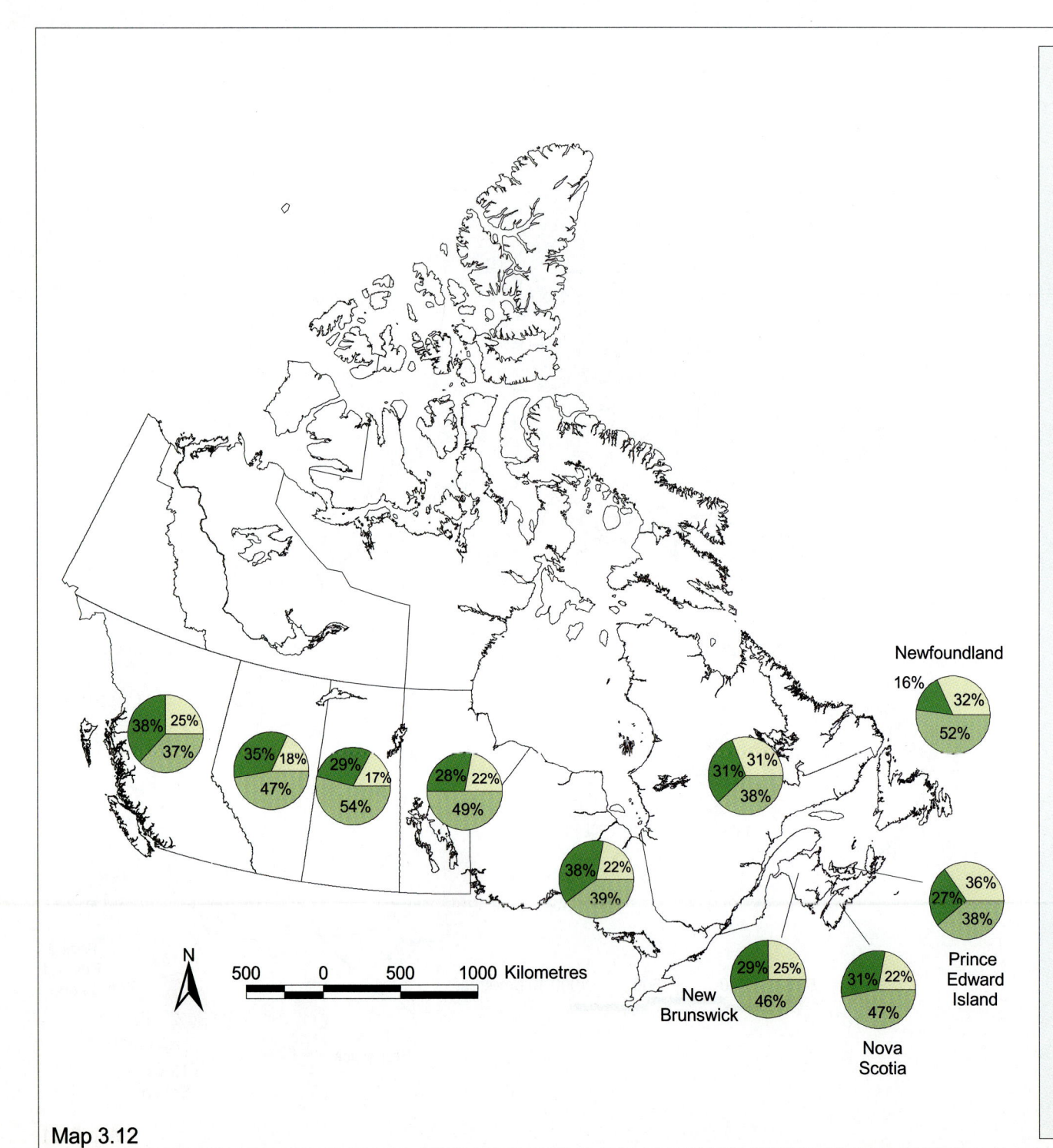

Functional Literacy* Levels for Ages 16 and Older, Provinces

1994 International Adult Literacy Survey (IALS)

Just over one third of adults ages 16 and older are classified as having a high level of functional literacy. However, almost one quarter of adults are classified as having a low level of functional literacy indicating they have some problems functioning in their daily activities.

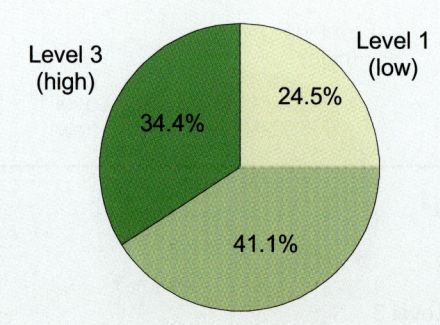

Province data (Level 3 high / Level 1 low / Level 2):

- British Columbia: 38% / 25% / 37%
- Alberta: 35% / 18% / 47%
- Saskatchewan: 29% / 17% / 54%
- Manitoba: 28% / 22% / 49%
- Ontario: 38% / 22% / 39%
- Quebec: 31% / 31% / 38%
- Newfoundland: 32% / 16% / 52%
- Prince Edward Island: 27% / 36% / 38%
- New Brunswick: 29% / 25% / 46%
- Nova Scotia: 31% / 22% / 47%

Canada:
- Level 3 (high): 34.4%
- Level 1 (low): 24.5%
- Level 2: 41.1%

*Based on an alternative proxy for functional literacy derived from IALS.

Map 3.12

III. THE GEOGRAPHY OF LITERACY | 41

Educational Attainment of Ages 16 to 64 with Low Functional Literacy Skills*, Provinces

1994 International Adult Literacy Survey (IALS)

More than half of Canadians ages 16 to 64 with low functional literacy have not finished high school (53.6%). This includes those who completed and did not complete primary school, and those with some high school. Close to one third did complete high school and just over one in ten finished college or university.

Canada

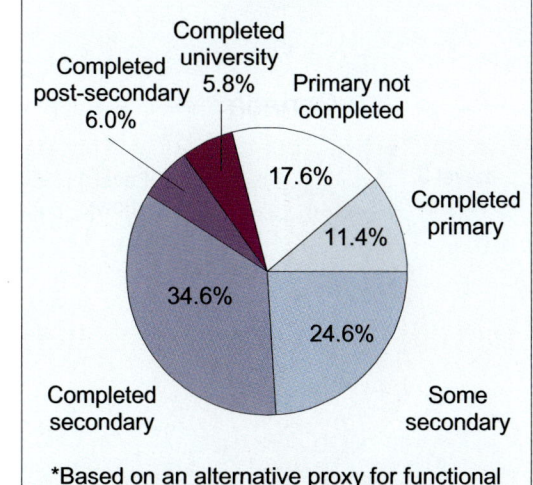

- Completed university 5.8%
- Completed post-secondary 6.0%
- Primary not completed 17.6%
- Completed primary 11.4%
- Some secondary 24.6%
- Completed secondary 34.6%

*Based on an alternative proxy for functional literacy derived from IALS. Low functional literacy skills are level 1. Not all educational levels are represented in each province due to small sample sizes.

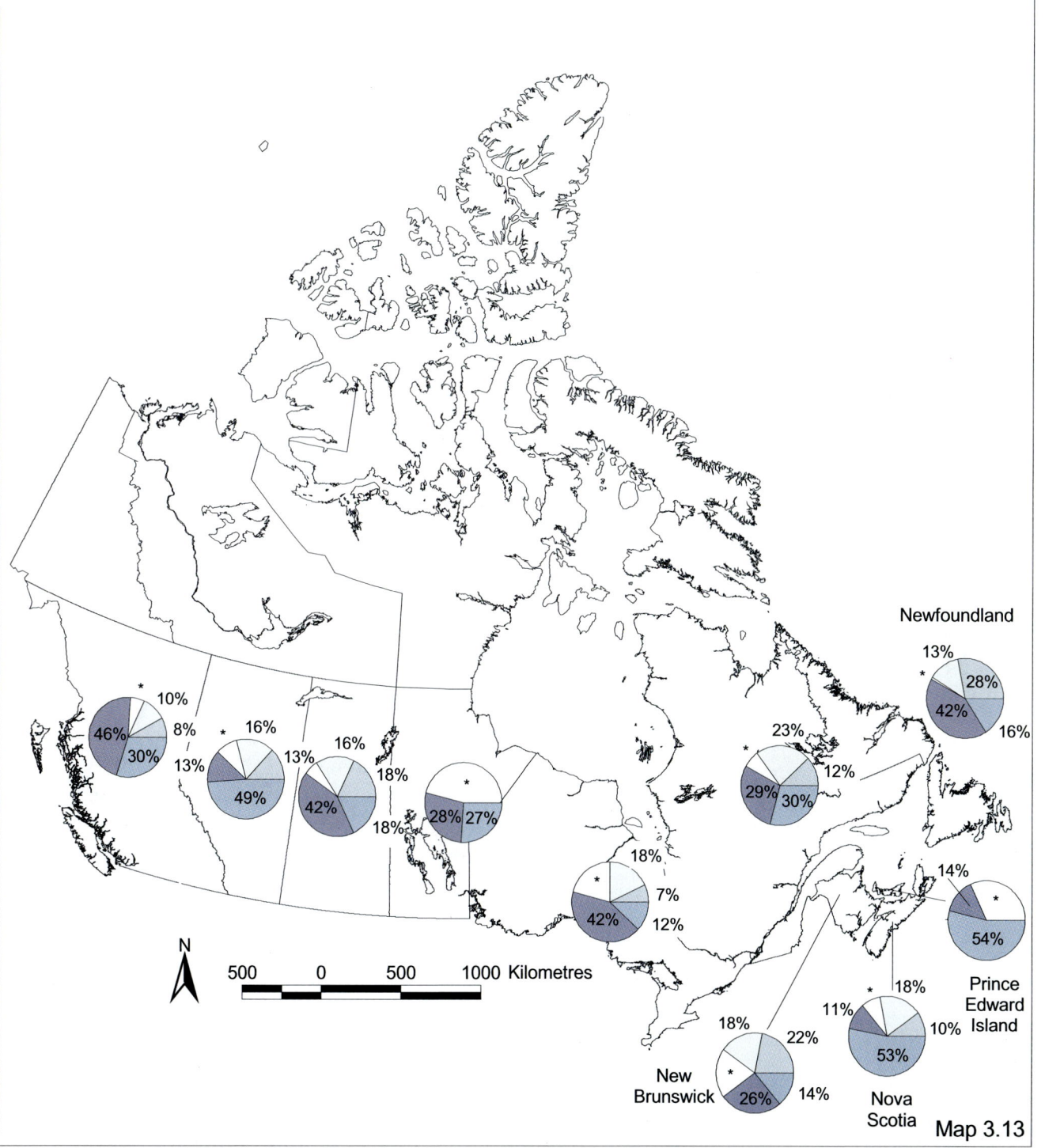

Newfoundland: 13%*, 28%, 42%, 16%

British Columbia: 46%, 30%, 10%*, 8%, 13%
Alberta: 16%, 13%, 49%
Saskatchewan: 16%, 18%, 42%
Manitoba: 28%, 27%, 18%, *
Ontario: 42%, 18%, 7%, 12%, *
Quebec: 23%, 29%, 30%, 12%, *
New Brunswick: 18%, 22%, 26%*, 14%
Nova Scotia: 11%, 18%, 53%, 10%, *
Prince Edward Island: 14%, 54%, *

Map 3.13

ATLAS OF LITERACY AND DISABILITY

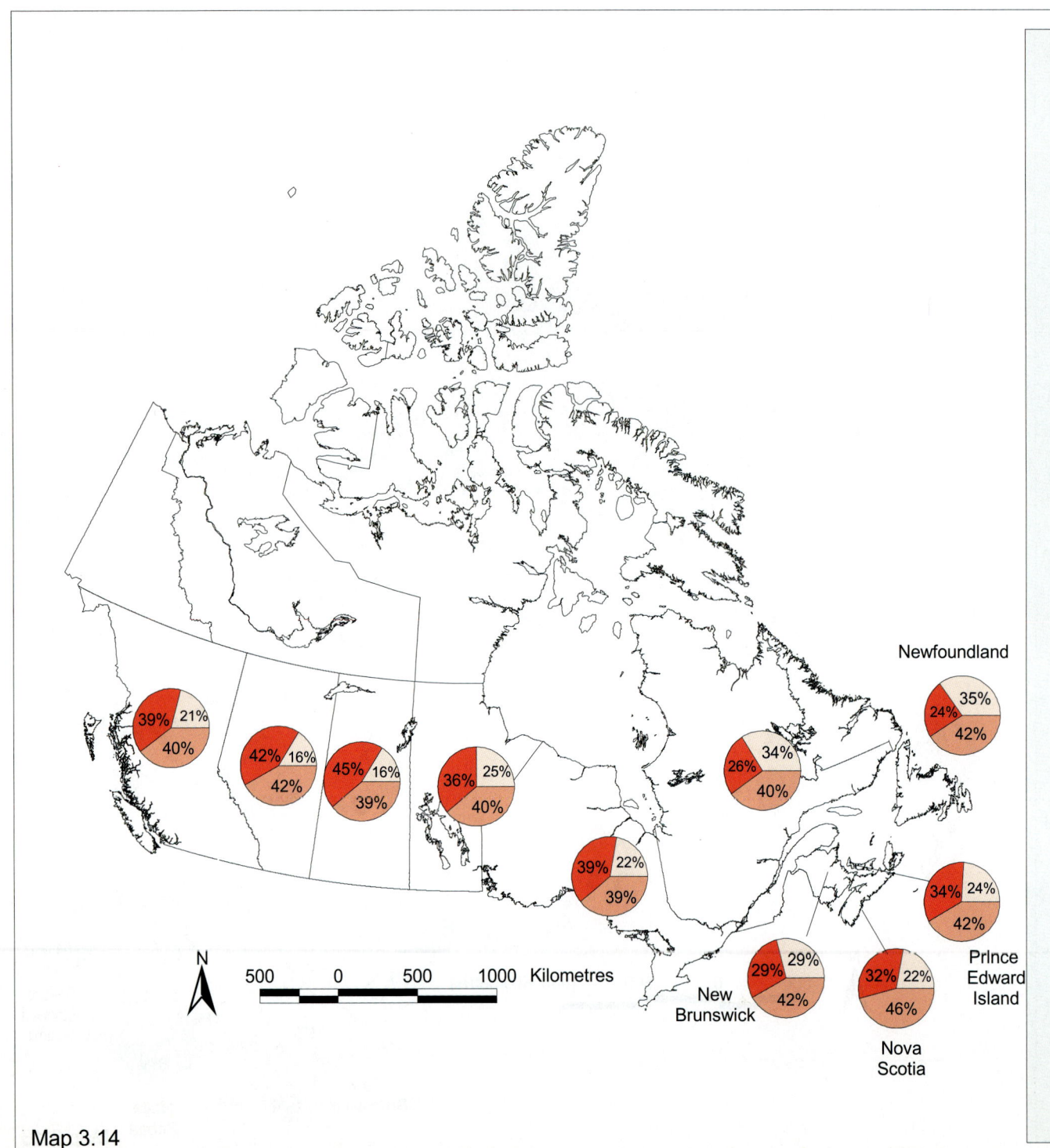

Critical Literacy* Levels for Ages 16 and Older, Provinces

1994 International Adult Literacy Survey (IALS)

The largest proportion of Canadians experience critical literacy at the moderate level (level 2). This pattern is consistent through much of the country. Just about one quarter of the population experiences the lowest level of critical literacy (level 1). Overall the West higher in critical literacy than the East.

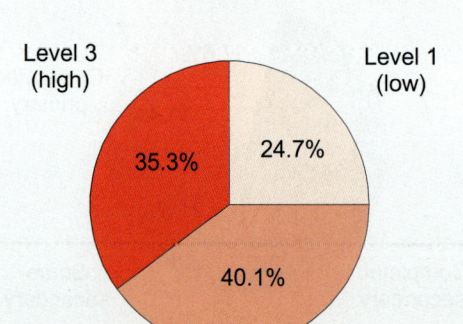

Canada

- Level 3 (high): 35.3%
- Level 1 (low): 24.7%
- Level 2: 40.1%

*Based on an alternative proxy for critical literacy derived from IALS.

Provincial pie charts (Level 3 / Level 1 / Level 2):
- British Columbia: 39% / 21% / 40%
- Alberta: 42% / 16% / 42%
- Saskatchewan: 45% / 16% / 39%
- Manitoba: 36% / 25% / 40%
- Ontario: 39% / 22% / 39%
- Quebec: 26% / 34% / 40%
- Newfoundland: 24% / 35% / 42%
- New Brunswick: 29% / 29% / 42%
- Nova Scotia: 32% / 22% / 46%
- Prince Edward Island: 34% / 24% / 42%

Map 3.14

III. THE GEOGRAPHY OF LITERACY | 43

Educational Attainment of Ages 16 to 64 with Low Critical Literacy Skills*, Provinces

1994 International Adult Literacy Survey (IALS)

The largest proportion of Canadian adults who experience low critical literacy have not completed high school (57%). This includes those with some high school and differing amounts of primary education. Less than one third have finished high school (30.8%) and 12% have completed college or university.

Canada

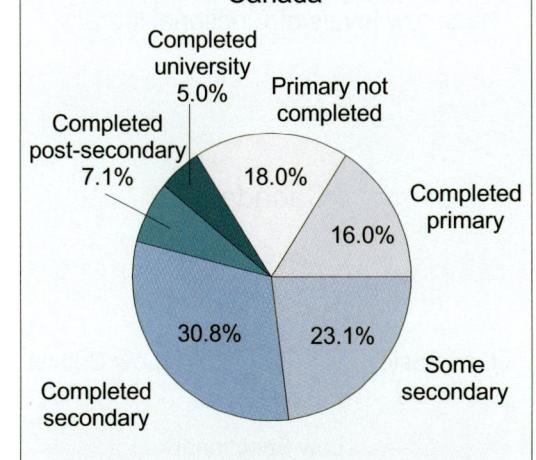

- Completed university: 5.0%
- Completed post-secondary: 7.1%
- Primary not completed: 18.0%
- Completed primary: 16.0%
- Some secondary: 23.1%
- Completed secondary: 30.8%

*Based on an alternative proxy for critical literacy derived from IALS. Low critical literacy skills are level 1. Not all educational levels are represented in each province due to small sample sizes.

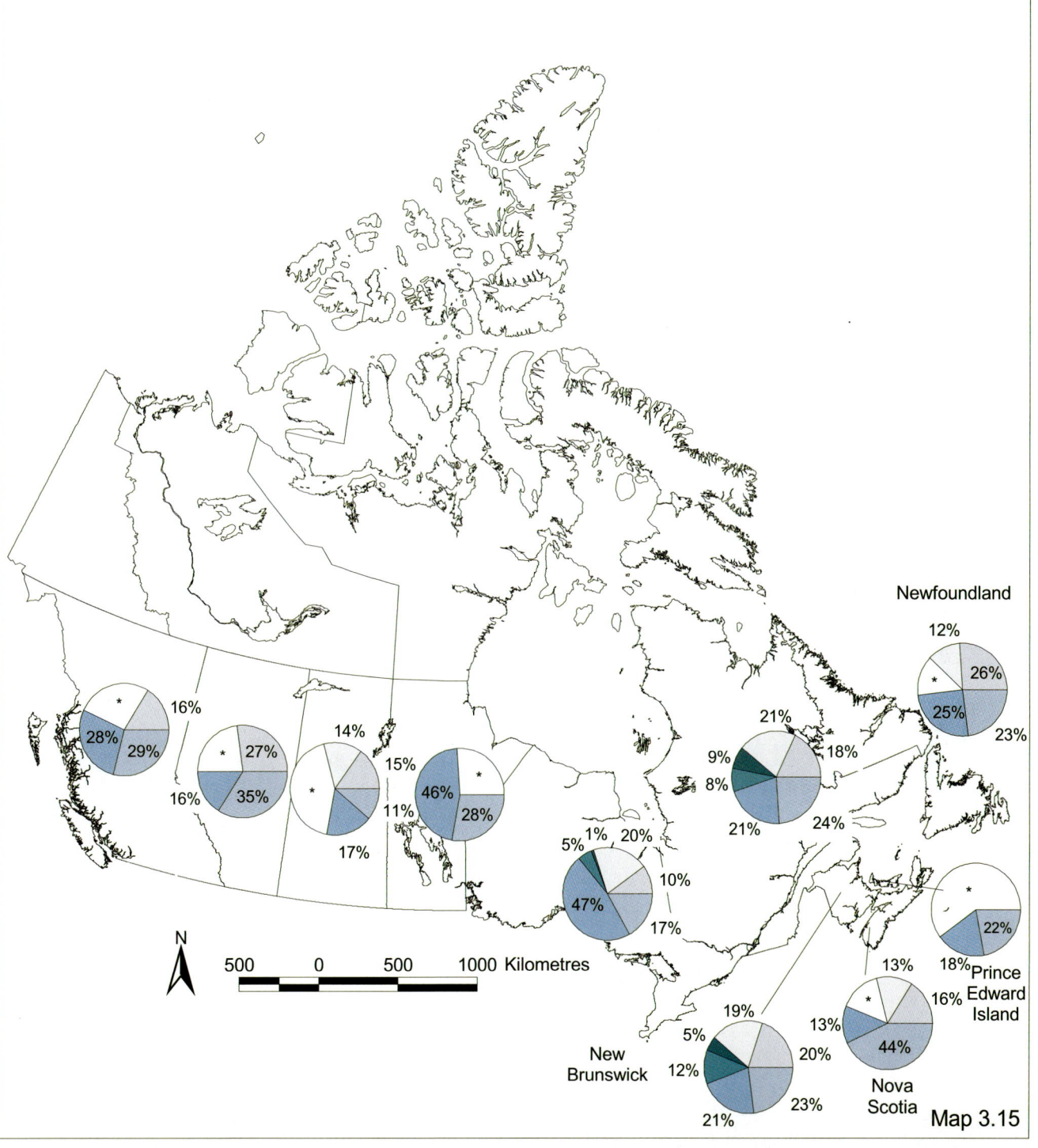

Newfoundland: 12%, 26%, 25%, 23%, *

Prince Edward Island: *, 22%, 18%

Nova Scotia: 13%, 16%, 44%, 20%, 13%, *

New Brunswick: 19%, 5%, 12%, 21%, 23%

Other provinces (west to east):
- 28%, 16%, 29%, *, 16%
- *, 27%, 35%, 17%
- 14%, 15%, 11%, *
- 46%, 28%, *
- 5%, 1%, 20%, 10%, 17%, 47%
- 21%, 9%, 8%, 21%, 24%, 18%

Map 3.15

ATLAS OF LITERACY AND DISABILITY

Low Basic, Functional and Critical Literacy Skills* for Ages 16 and Older, Provinces

1994 International Adult Literacy Survey (IALS)

Canadians overall are more likely to have low critical (24.7%) and low functional (24.5%) literacy than low basic literacy skills (16.3%), but this is not the case in every province. For example, in some areas the level of skill in the three types of literacy is very similar. In other parts of the country, higher numbers of people have low levels of functional literacy.

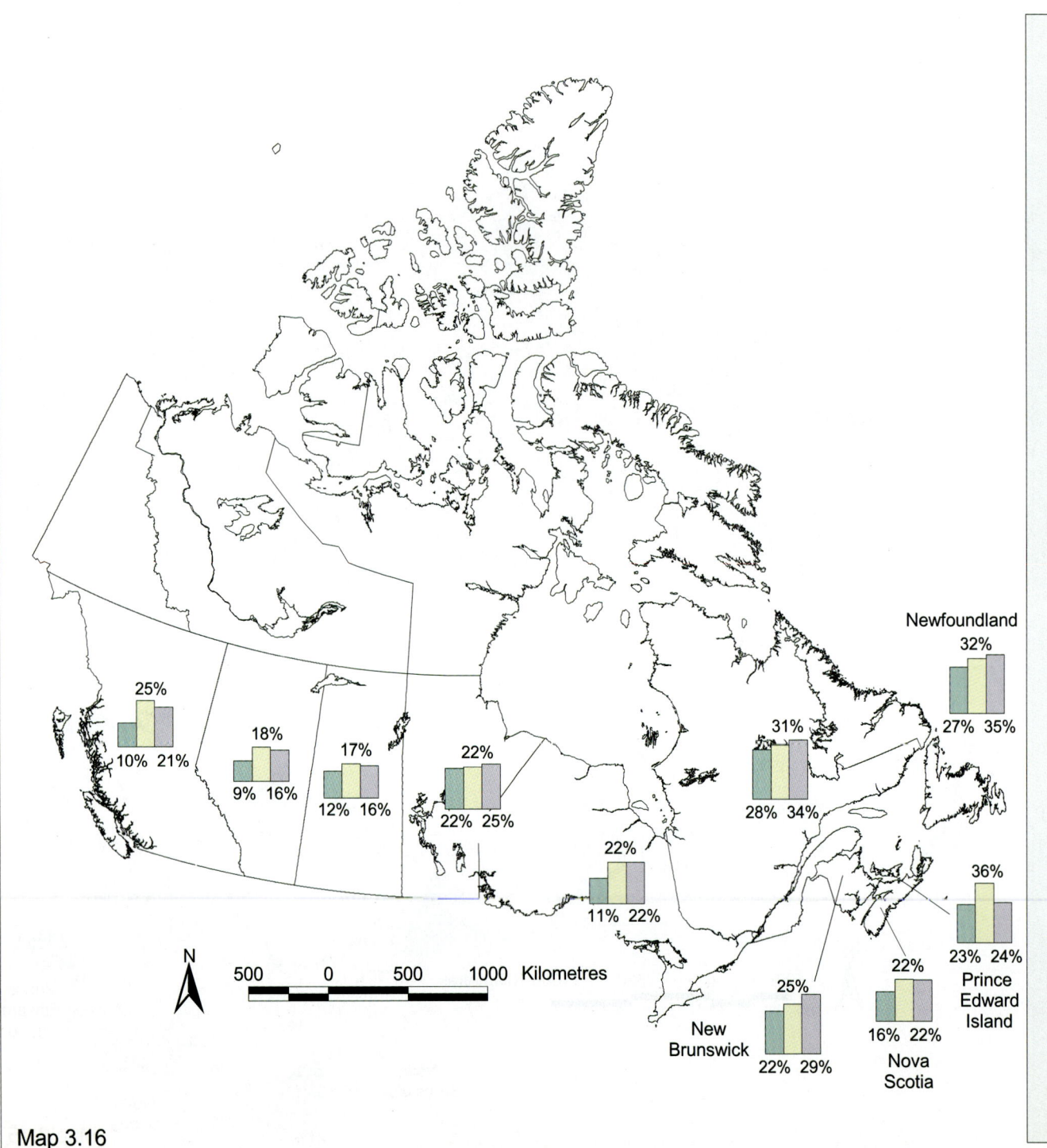

Canada

- Low Basic Literacy: 16.3%
- Low Functional Literacy: 24.5%
- Low Critical Literacy: 24.7%

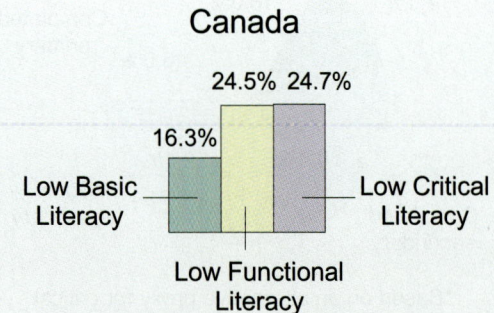

*Low literacy skills are less than grade 9 education for basic literacy. Low functional and critical literacy are represented as level 1.

Provincial data (Low Basic / Low Functional / Low Critical):

- Newfoundland: 27% / 32% / 35%
- Prince Edward Island: 23% / 36% / 24%
- Nova Scotia: 16% / 22% / 22%
- New Brunswick: 22% / 25% / 29%
- Quebec: 28% / 31% / 34%
- Ontario: 11% / 22% / 22%
- Manitoba: 22% / 22% / 25%
- Saskatchewan: 12% / 17% / 16%
- Alberta: 9% / 18% / 16%
- British Columbia: 10% / 25% / 21%

Map 3.16

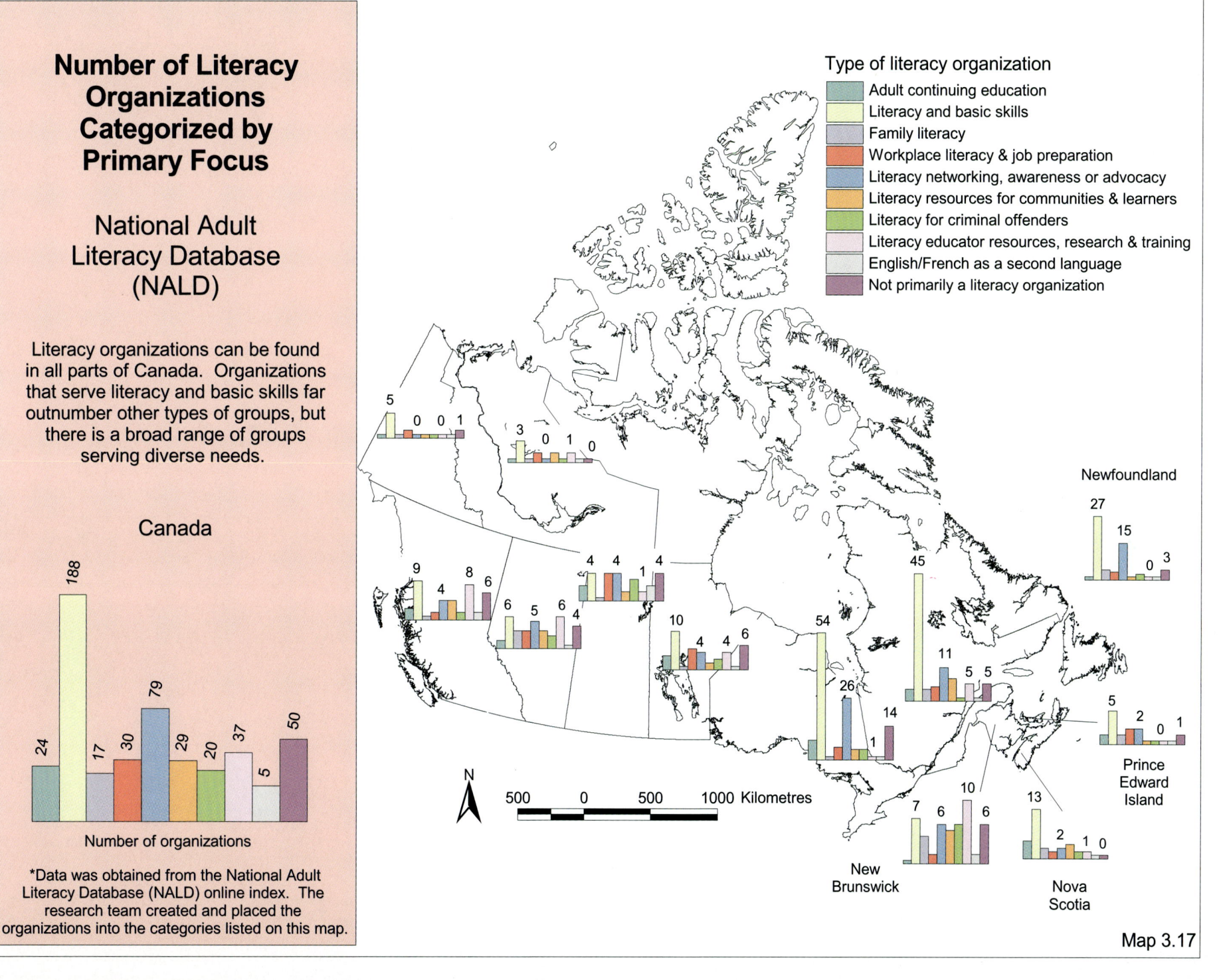

III. THE GEOGRAPHY OF LITERACY   45

Number of Literacy Organizations Categorized by Primary Focus

National Adult Literacy Database (NALD)

Literacy organizations can be found in all parts of Canada. Organizations that serve literacy and basic skills far outnumber other types of groups, but there is a broad range of groups serving diverse needs.

Type of literacy organization
- Adult continuing education
- Literacy and basic skills
- Family literacy
- Workplace literacy & job preparation
- Literacy networking, awareness or advocacy
- Literacy resources for communities & learners
- Literacy for criminal offenders
- Literacy educator resources, research & training
- English/French as a second language
- Not primarily a literacy organization

Canada

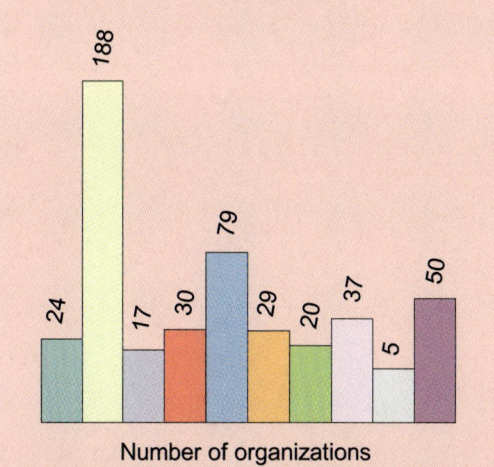

Number of organizations: 24, 188, 17, 30, 79, 29, 20, 37, 5, 50

*Data was obtained from the National Adult Literacy Database (NALD) online index. The research team created and placed the organizations into the categories listed on this map.

Map 3.17

IV. Geography of Disability

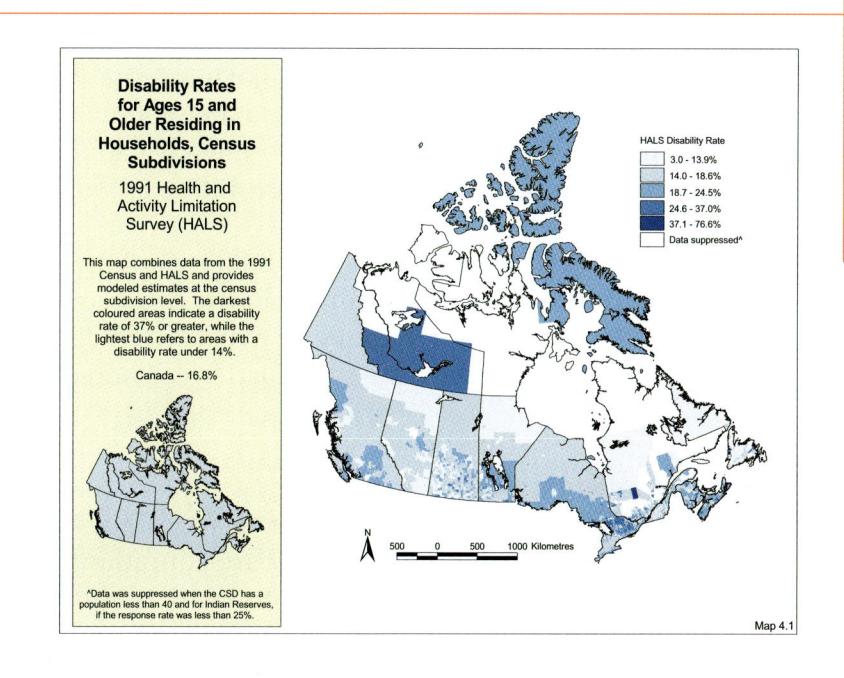

Disability Rates for Ages 15 and Older Residing in Households, Census Subdivisions

1991 Health and Activity Limitation Survey (HALS)

This map combines data from the 1991 Census and HALS and provides modeled estimates at the census subdivision level. The darkest coloured areas indicate a disability rate of 37% or greater, while the lightest blue refers to areas with a disability rate under 14%.

Canada -- 16.8%

^Data was suppressed when the CSD has a population less than 40 and for Indian Reserves, if the response rate was less than 25%.

HALS Disability Rate
- 3.0 - 13.9%
- 14.0 - 18.6%
- 18.7 - 24.5%
- 24.6 - 37.0%
- 37.1 - 76.6%
- Data suppressed^

Map 4.1

PROVINCIAL DISABILITY SCANS

Most of the maps comparing disability rates from various surveys are found in Chapter II. These show how different surveys produce different results. For example, HALS shows a disability rate of 17% (Map 2.5) and PALS shows a disability rate of 15% (Map 2.6). In these instances, the differences are likely due to survey methodologies. This chapter primarily focuses on disability data from HALS, because this is the most reliable disability survey to date. All the data was available during the making of this atlas, while PALS, though more up-to-date, is only slightly referenced. Not all of the data for PALS has been released yet.

There are a number of factors related to having a disability that affect people's experiences of their disability. The age a person was when he or she acquired a disability is one such factor. According to HALS, most Canadians acquire their disability when they are working-age adults, between 20 and 64 years old (60%). Age of onset affects education and employment opportunities, as well as access to supports and services.

HALS and PALS both look at type of disability. As shown in Maps 4.3 and 4.5, each survey reports mobility and agility as the most common types of disability. However, PALS shows more types of disability than did HALS. In PALS, pain is introduced as a frequently experienced disability. Patterns of disability type are similar throughout the country for both surveys. The same patterns emerge in major cities as well, according to HALS (Map 4.4).

Demographics and Disability

Some demographic factors have stronger relationships with disability than others. Two demographic factors that have a strong relationship with disability are educational attainment and age. HALS shows that people with disabilities tend to have lower levels of schooling than those without disabilities. They are less likely to go to grade school and less likely to attend college or university than those who do not have disabilities, as a comparison of Maps 4.6 and 4.7 reveals. As Map 4.8 shows, people are more likely to have a disability as they age. Close to half of Canadians over the age of 65 have a disability. On the other hand, less than one-fifth of those between the ages of 35 and 64, and less than one-tenth of young adults between 15 and 34, are people with disabilities.

In most parts of the country, The link between disability status and official language is less pronounced. Map 4.9 shows that the vast majority of adults with disabilities in the Canadian provinces speak either French or English (98.4%). The Yukon and Northwest Territories are exceptions. A larger proportion of these populations speak neither French nor English. Most likely this is because they are speaking one of the nine official native languages.[24]

Nor is the link between disability rate and gender very pronounced, as Map 4.10 reveals. In Canada, slightly more than half of the adult population are women, and just under half are men. The proportions of men and women with disabilities are similar. Likewise, as Map 4.11 makes clear, similar proportions of Canadians with disabilities

---

24 English, French, Inuktitut, Dogrib, Chipewayan, Gwich'in, North Slavey, South Slavey, Innuvialugtun and Cree.

are immigrants, compared to the population in general. In fact, a slightly higher percentage of immigrants acquired a disability at some point in their lives. Immigrants with disabilities, like other immigrants, are most likely to live in Ontario or British Columbia.

To establish disability rates for the Aboriginal population from 1991, HALS was combined with the Aboriginal Peoples Survey of the same year. Together, this includes people living on and off reserves who have official status as Indian, Métis or Inuit, or who report having an Aboriginal ancestor. Map 4.12 reveals that 21.5% of Aboriginal people in Canada had a disability in 1991. This suggests that First Nations people were more likely than the overall Canadian population to have a disability (the disability rate for the overall population was 16.8% in 1991, according to HALS). The HALS/APS data showed considerable variation in disability rates for Aboriginal people between provinces

Socio-Economic Factors and Disability

There are certain socio-economic impacts of disability, in which people with disabilities are disadvantaged in terms of labour force status and income. Map 4.13 shows that slightly over half of adults with disabilities were in the labour force (employed or looking for work) compared to three out of every four adults without disabilities. Income is represented on Maps 4.14 and 4.15. Those without disabilities tend to have higher incomes overall. According to HALS, more people without disabilities (56%) had a personal income of at least $15,000 a year, compared to people with disabilities (41%) in 1991.

ASSESSING ENVIRONMENTS, SUPPORTS AND INCLUSION

The *Barriers and Accommodations Index* (BAI) is a response to the need for indicators with an emphasis on social inclusion rather than the characteristics of individuals. It is an alternative to the index of severity of disability, used in other analyses of HALS. Map 4.16 illustrates findings from the Severity Index as a contrast to findings from the BAI. Nearly half of all Canadians with disabilities (49%) were classified as having "mild" disabilities, 33% with "moderate" disabilities and 18% with "severe" disabilities. The BAI looks instead at the numbers of barriers encountered by Canadians with disabilities in relation to the accommodations they receive. Map 4.17 shows that, in Canada, 13.5% of adults with disabilities reported that they encountered no barriers in their daily activities. An additional 10% stated that they experienced some barriers, but through accommodation, these had been removed. 49% of adults with disabilities reported that they experienced barriers and that some of those barriers had been removed. This means that 28% of adults with disabilities reported that no accommodations had been made to the barriers they experienced.

Maps 4.18 and 4.19 show the types of barriers and accommodations that are included in the BAI. The index includes four types of barriers in three domains of life. The most common type of barrier encountered is financial (48%), followed by transportation (31%), barriers related to personal care (18%), and, less frequently, structural barriers (9%). People encounter barriers in their communities (31%), in their daily lives (28%) and in their jobs (16%). Accommodations are likewise grouped into types and domains of life. HALS findings show that 36% receive accommodations in their daily lives, but only 3% receive them at work. Supports for personal care are the most common type of accommodation nationally, followed by structural adaptations (12%). Few receive transportation accommodations (3%).

The rest of the maps in this section of the atlas measure the numbers of barriers and accommodations people with disabilities encounter. Map 4.20 reveals that 23% of adults with disabilities report no barriers at all.[25] When a person with a disability encounters barriers, he or she will most likely experience 5 or fewer (nearly 40%). About half that many encounter 6 to 10 barriers, and 16.4% reported 11 or more barriers. The pattern of accommodations is similar, although there is a trend toward lower accommodations and higher barriers. Most people with disabilities report having only a few, if any, accommodations in their daily lives. Map 4.21 shows that 42% receive no accommodations, and close to half (49.2%) receive between 1 and 5 accommodations.

Generally, in Canada, the higher the reported age of onset of disability, the higher the proportion of people who faced between 1 and 5 barriers. People who became disabled before 5 years of age were the least likely to report 1 to 5 barriers, and those aged 45 to 64 were the most likely. Among people who said their age of onset of disability was 65 to 99 years, nearly 60% reported between 1 and 5 accommodations. In Canada overall, except for those who acquired a disability between birth and 4 years, as the age of onset increased, the proportion receiving accommodations also increased.

Gender is correlated with numbers of barriers and accommodations in Maps 4.24 and 4.25. Women with disabilities encounter higher numbers of barriers than men with disabilities, and are more likely to be receiving accommodations. Men (25%) are more likely to live barrier-free lives than women (21%). Over 10% more women than men report receiving accommodations. Women are also more likely to experience higher numbers of barriers that impede their inclusion in the community, and to receive higher numbers of accommodations.

The pattern of barriers of people who are in the labour force is similar to those in the overall population of people with disabilities. As with the general population of people with disabilities, about 77% of those who are in the labour force report experiencing at least one barrier, while around 54% report not receiving any accommodations.

The experience of barriers among people with disabilities is tied to their economic marginalization. There is a strong relationship between the number of barriers experienced and the risk of being a member of an economic family whose income is classified as low, using the Statistics Canada Low Income Cutoff (LICO). The more barriers

---

25 The categories "zero barriers" and "zero accommodations" each include two types of persons. The "zero barriers" category includes those who have experienced no barriers and as a result have required no accommodations, and it includes those who are currently experiencing no barriers because all of their barriers have been removed. Likewise, the "zero accommodation" category includes individuals who require no accommodation because they have experienced no barriers, as well as those individuals who are experiencing one or more barriers but for whom no accommodation has been received.

a person experiences, the greater the likelihood they are living in poverty. The population of people with disabilities who are living in poverty are more likely to experience high numbers of barriers than low numbers. 36.5% encountered 11 or more and 26% encountered between 6 and 10 barriers. In contrast, only 17.5% encountered 1 to 5 barriers.

As Map 4.29 shows, people who are both disabled and living in poverty do not receive high numbers of accommodations to address the high numbers of disability-related barriers they experience. Only 29% receive more than 6 accommodations, 21% receive between 1 and 5, and 21% receive no accommodations at all.

GEOGRAPHY OF DISABILITY ORGANIZATIONS

Canada's infrastructure for disability services and organizations involves non-governmental organizations and federal, provincial and territorial governments. The diverse array of disability organizations play many different roles in relation to the disability community and Canadian society. Map 4.30 shows the distribution of over 5,000 disability organizations included in the Canadian Abilities Foundation's database of disability organizations. Ten broad categories of disability organizations were designated by the research team. The most common types found in Canada are cross-disability and those related to mental disabilities, followed by organizations that are health and illness-related. The provinces with the largest populations have the most disability organizations. These are Ontario, Quebec and British Columbia.

IV. THE GEOGRAPHY OF DISABILITY

Disability Rates for Ages 15 and Older Residing in Households, Census Subdivisions

1991 Health and Activity Limitation Survey (HALS)

This map combines data from the 1991 Census and HALS and provides modeled estimates at the census subdivision level. The darkest coloured areas indicate a disability rate of 37% or greater, while the lightest blue refers to areas with a disability rate under 14%.

Canada -- 16.8%

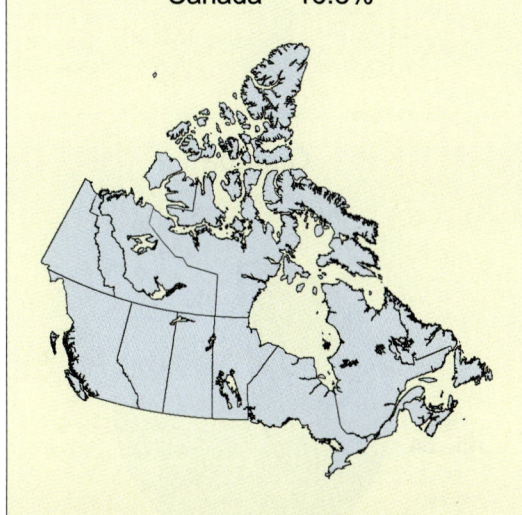

^Data was suppressed when the CSD has a population less than 40 and for Indian Reserves, if the response rate was less than 25%.

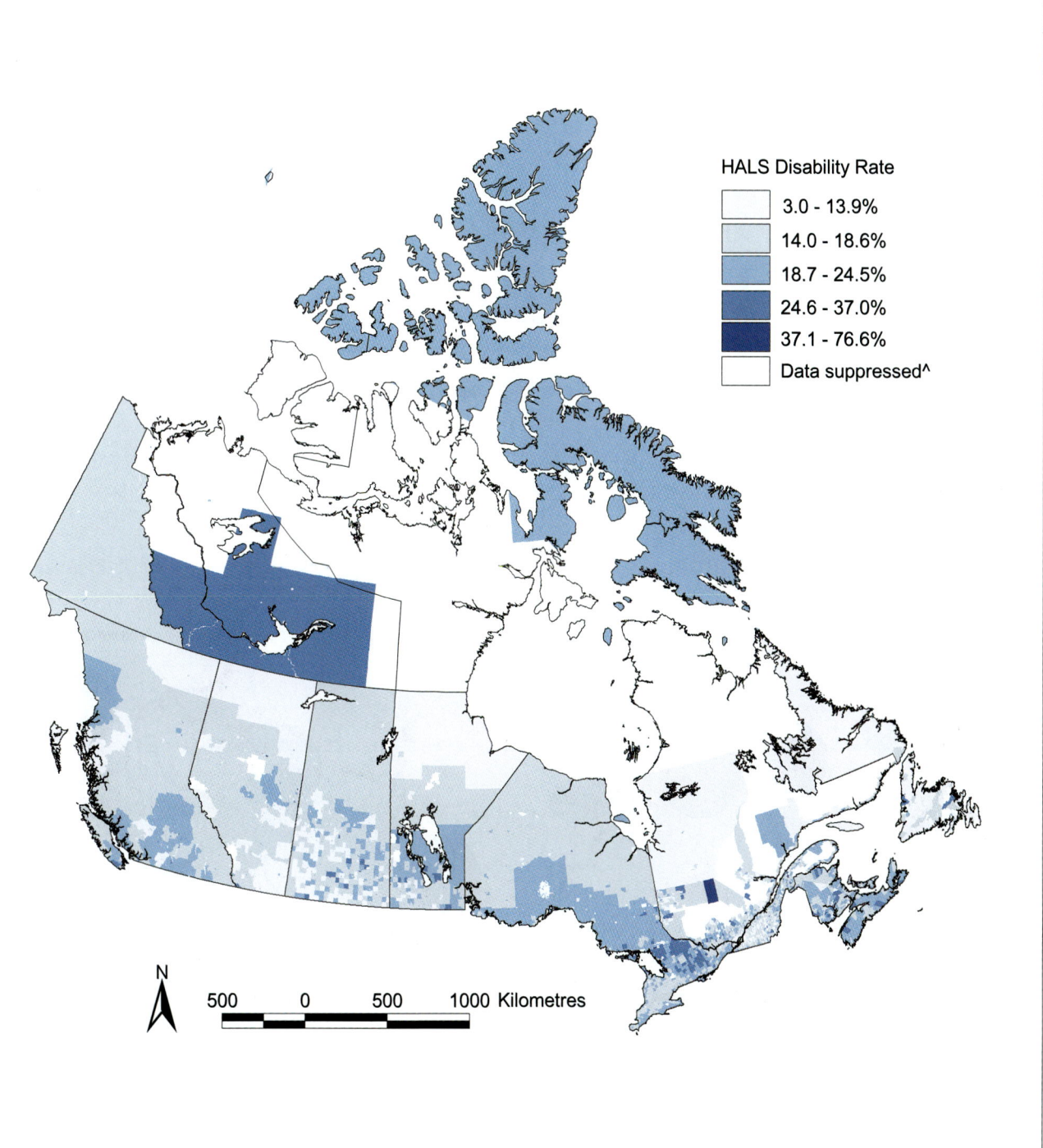

HALS Disability Rate
- 3.0 - 13.9%
- 14.0 - 18.6%
- 18.7 - 24.5%
- 24.6 - 37.0%
- 37.1 - 76.6%
- Data suppressed^

Map 4.1

ATLAS OF LITERACY AND DISABILITY

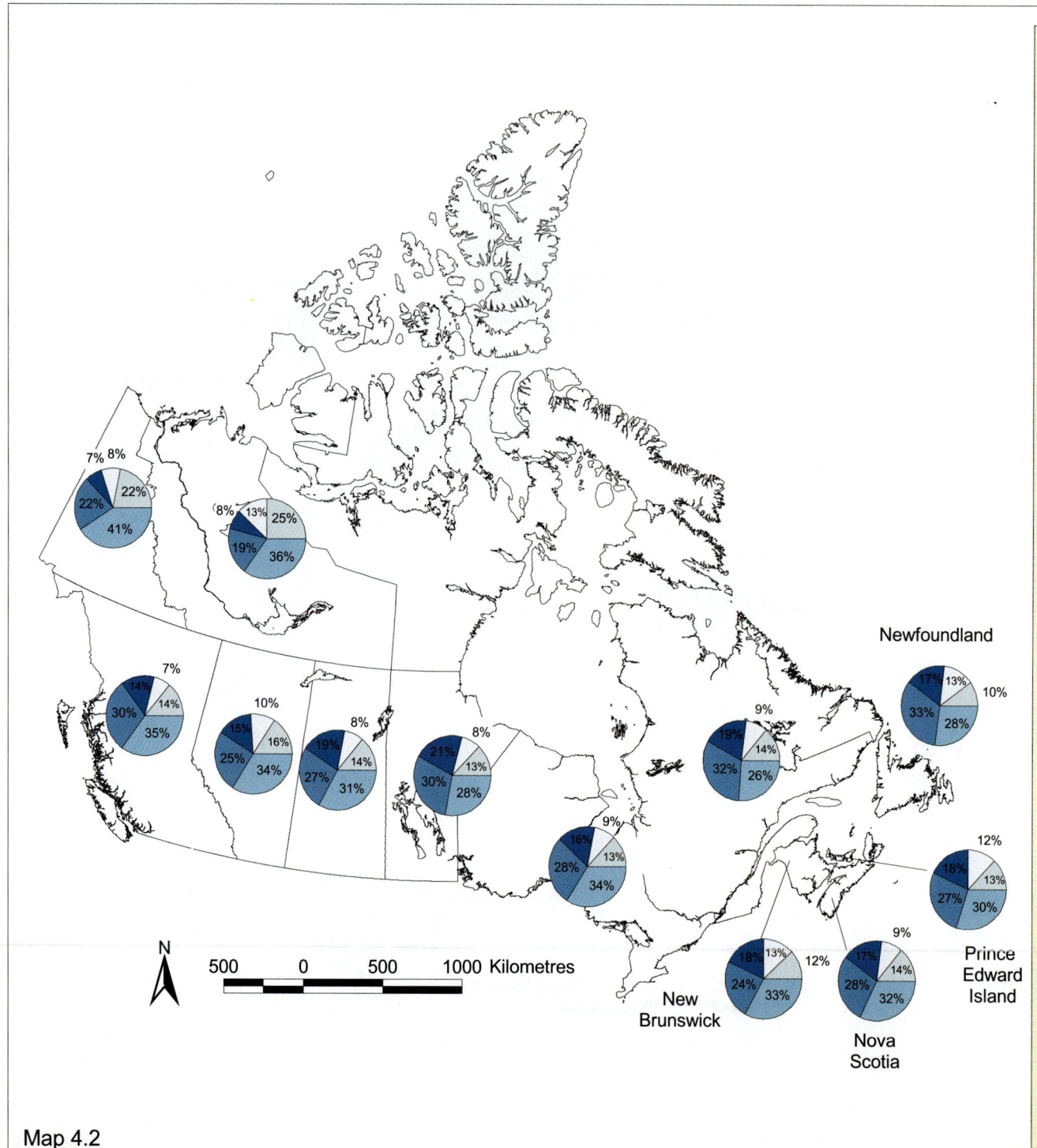

Earliest Age of Onset of Disability for Ages 15 and Older Residing in Households, Provinces and Territories

1991 Health and Activity Limitation Survey (HALS)

Most Canadians become disabled after they have reached adulthood. Across the country a relatively low percentage are disabled between birth and four years (average of 9%). In every region, the most likely period for onset of disability is during the working years (20-64 years).

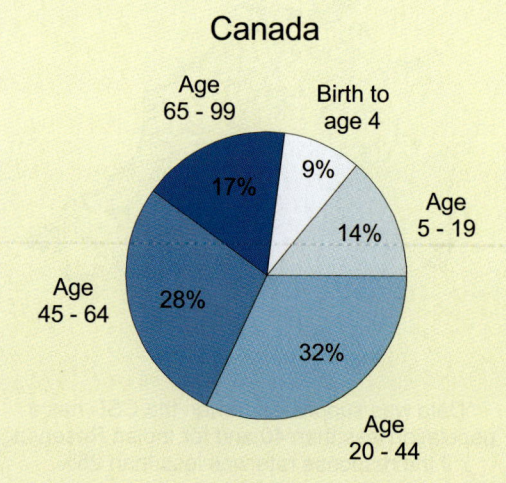

Canada

- Birth to age 4: 9%
- Age 5 - 19: 14%
- Age 20 - 44: 32%
- Age 45 - 64: 28%
- Age 65 - 99: 17%

Map 4.2

IV. THE GEOGRAPHY OF DISABILITY | 55

Type of Disability* for Ages 15 and Older Residing in Households, Provinces and Territories

1991 Health and Activity Limitation Survey (HALS)

Mobility and agility disabilities are the most common types of disabilities reported by adults living in households. Almost one third of adults reported disabilities that were classified as 'other' - these included disabilities related to learning, development and mental health. One in ten adults reported a general limitation in activity - type of disability was classified as 'unknown'.

Canada

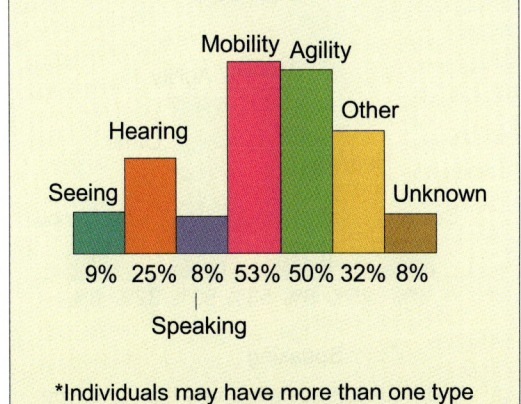

Seeing 9% | Hearing 25% | Speaking 8% | Mobility 53% | Agility 50% | Other 32% | Unknown 8%

*Individuals may have more than one type of disability.

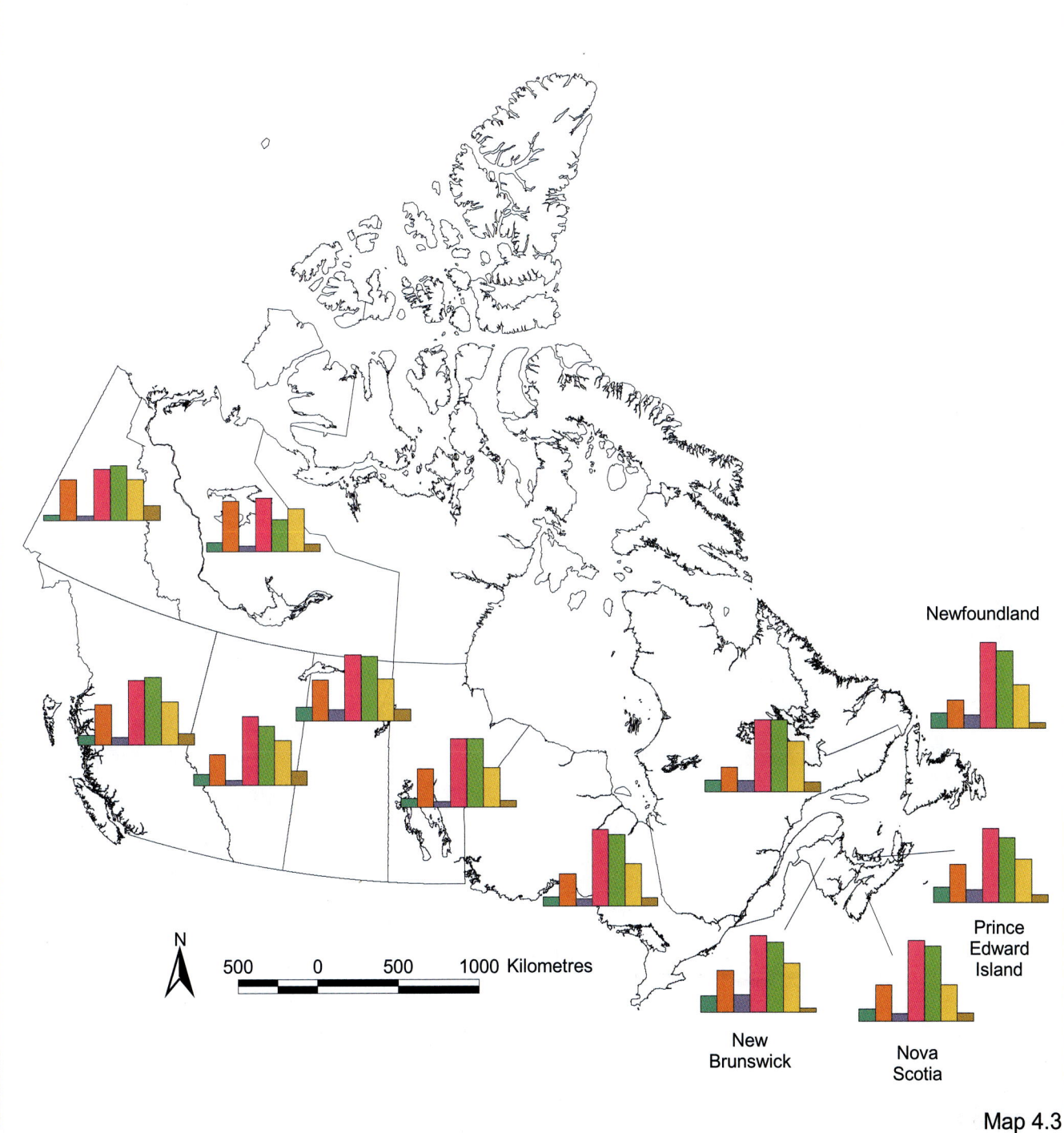

Map 4.3

ATLAS OF LITERACY AND DISABILITY

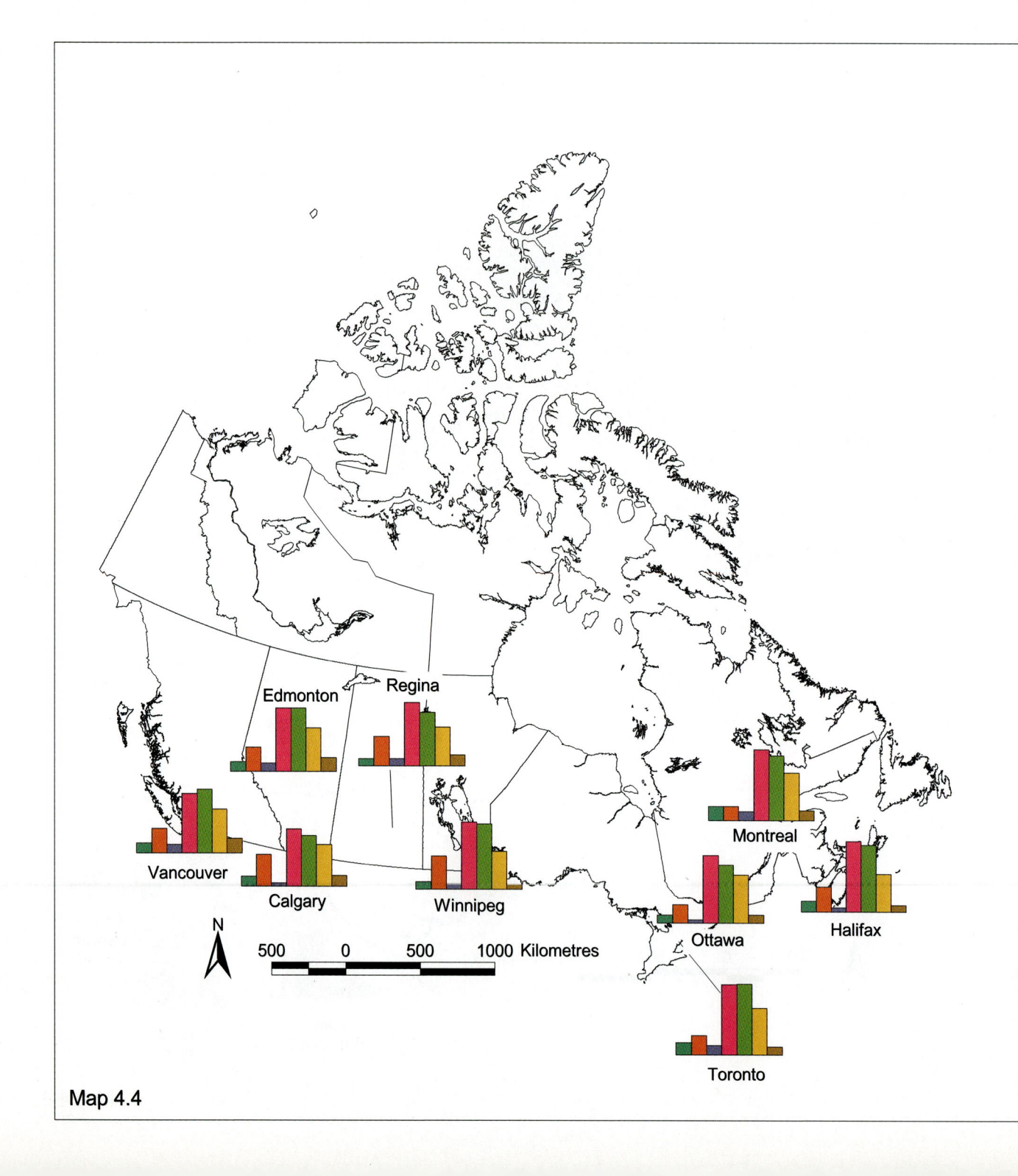

Map 4.4

Type of Disability* for Ages 15 and Older Residing in Households, Census Metropolitan Areas

1991 Health and Activity Limitation Survey (HALS)

Major cities in Canada show patterns of disability type that are similar to the provinces. In major cities throughout the country, the most common types of disability are mobility and agility, followed by 'other' and hearing. The least common types of disability are speaking, seeing, and unknown.

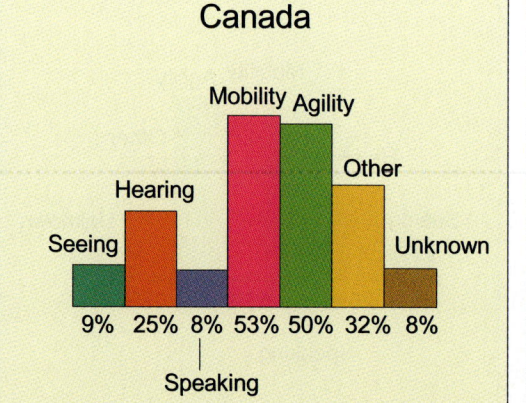

Canada

Seeing 9% | Hearing 25% | Speaking 8% | Mobility 53% | Agility 50% | Other 32% | Unknown 8%

*Individuals may have more than one type of disability.

IV. THE GEOGRAPHY OF DISABILITY

Type of Disability* for Ages 15 and Older, Provinces

2001 Participation and Activity Limitation Survey (PALS)

PALS gives more detail for disability type than HALS did. In every province mobility, agility, and pain stand out as the most common types of disability. The next most common are hearing, seeing and psychological disabilities. Learning, memory, speech, developmental and unknown disabilities are the least common.

Canada

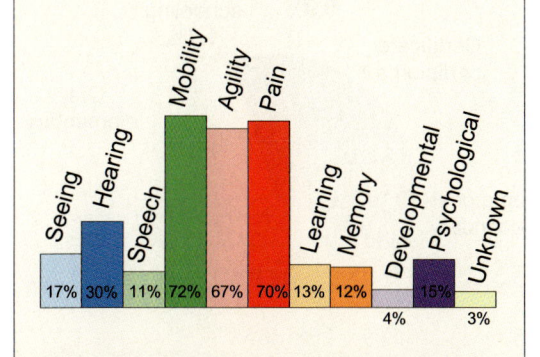

Seeing	Hearing	Speech	Mobility	Agility	Pain	Learning	Memory	Developmental	Psychological	Unknown
17%	30%	11%	72%	67%	70%	13%	12%	4%	15%	3%

*Individuals may have more than one type of disability.

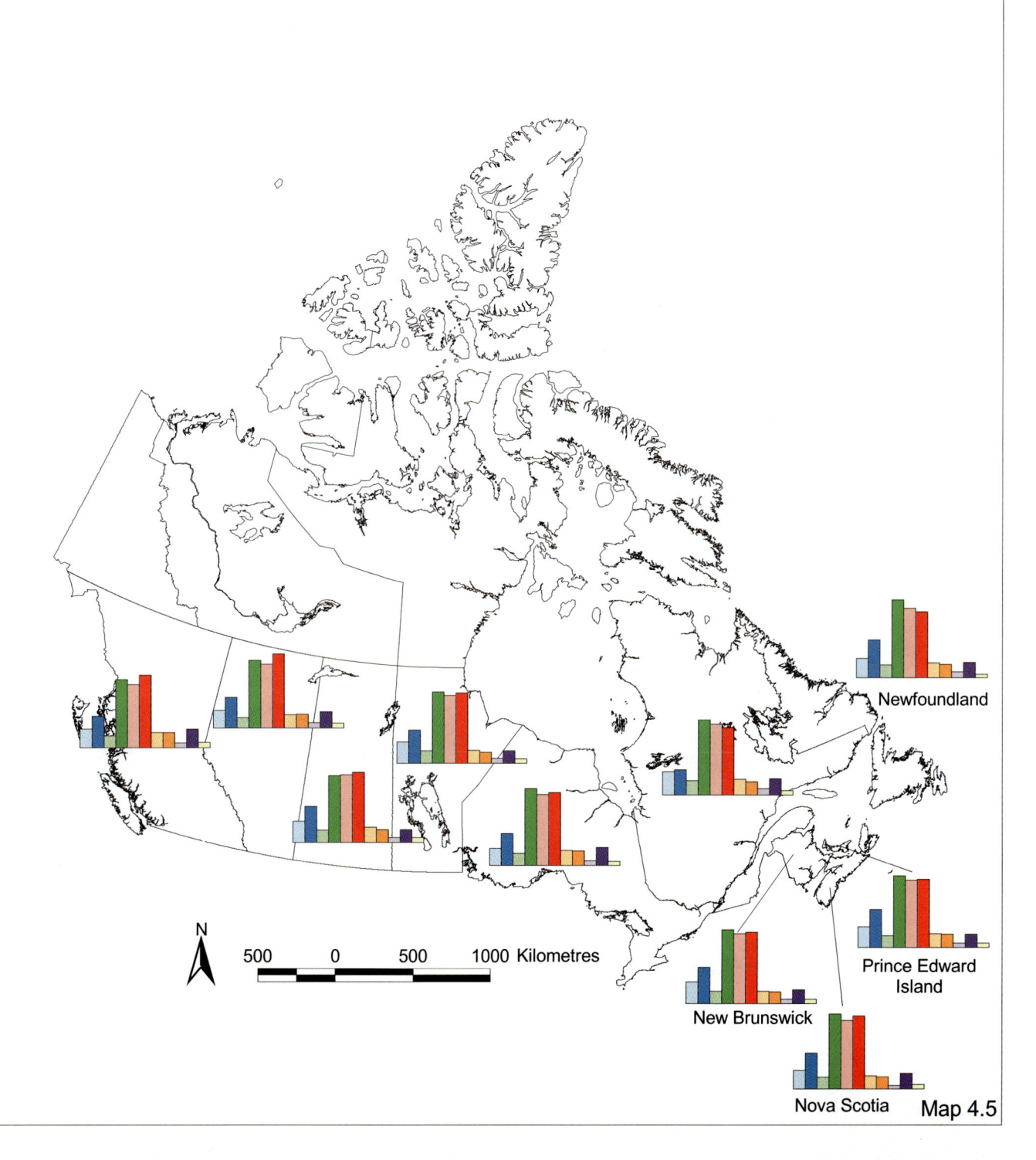

Map 4.5

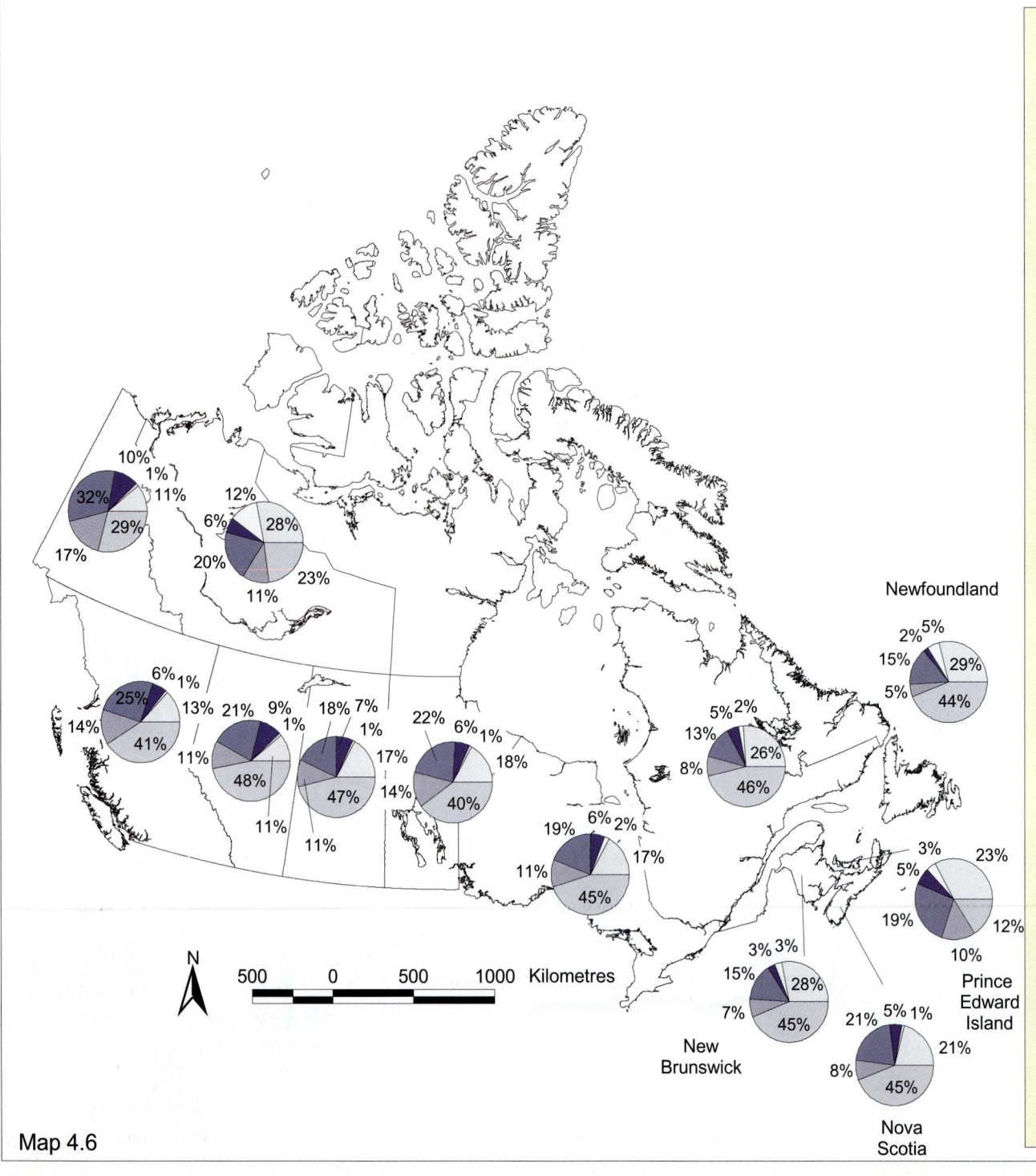

ATLAS OF LITERACY AND DISABILITY

Map 4.6

Educational Attainment for Ages 15 to 64 with Disabilities Residing in Households, Provinces and Territories

1991 Health and Activity Limitation Survey (HALS)

Almost 20% of adults with disabilities have less than grade 9 education and almost 25% have a post-secondary certificate or diploma (18.7%) or a university degree (5.9%). However, the majority (44.9%) reports that their highest level of education is either high school graduation or some secondary education. This percentage is similar to the population without disabilities (see next map).

Canada

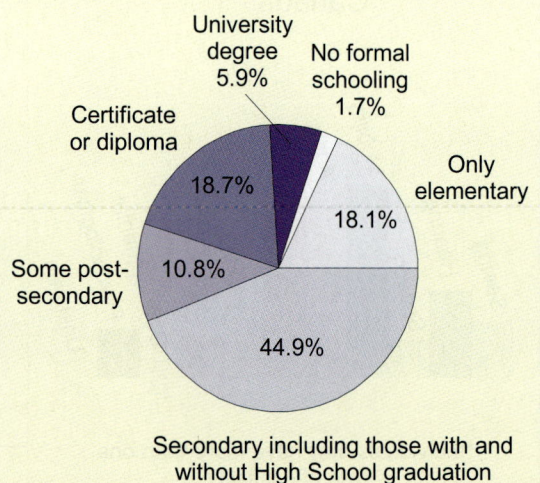

- University degree: 5.9%
- No formal schooling: 1.7%
- Only elementary: 18.1%
- Secondary including those with and without High School graduation: 44.9%
- Some post-secondary: 10.8%
- Certificate or diploma: 18.7%

IV. THE GEOGRAPHY OF DISABILITY | 59

Educational Attainment for Ages 15 to 64 without Disabilities Residing in Households, Provinces and Territories

1991 Health and Activity Limitation Survey (HALS)

In contrast to the adult population with disabilities ages 15 to 64, only 8.1% of adults without disabilities in this same age group report having less than grade 9 education. Almost 40% report having a post-secondary certificate or diploma (22.3%) or a university degree (13.6%). This pattern is fairly consistent across the country.

Canada

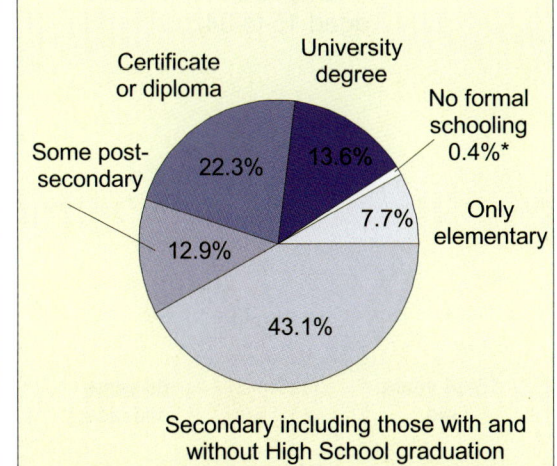

- University degree: 13.6%
- Certificate or diploma: 22.3%
- Some post-secondary: 12.9%
- Secondary including those with and without High School graduation: 43.1%
- Only elementary: 7.7%
- No formal schooling: 0.4%*

*In many provinces, less than 1% of the population has no formal schooling.

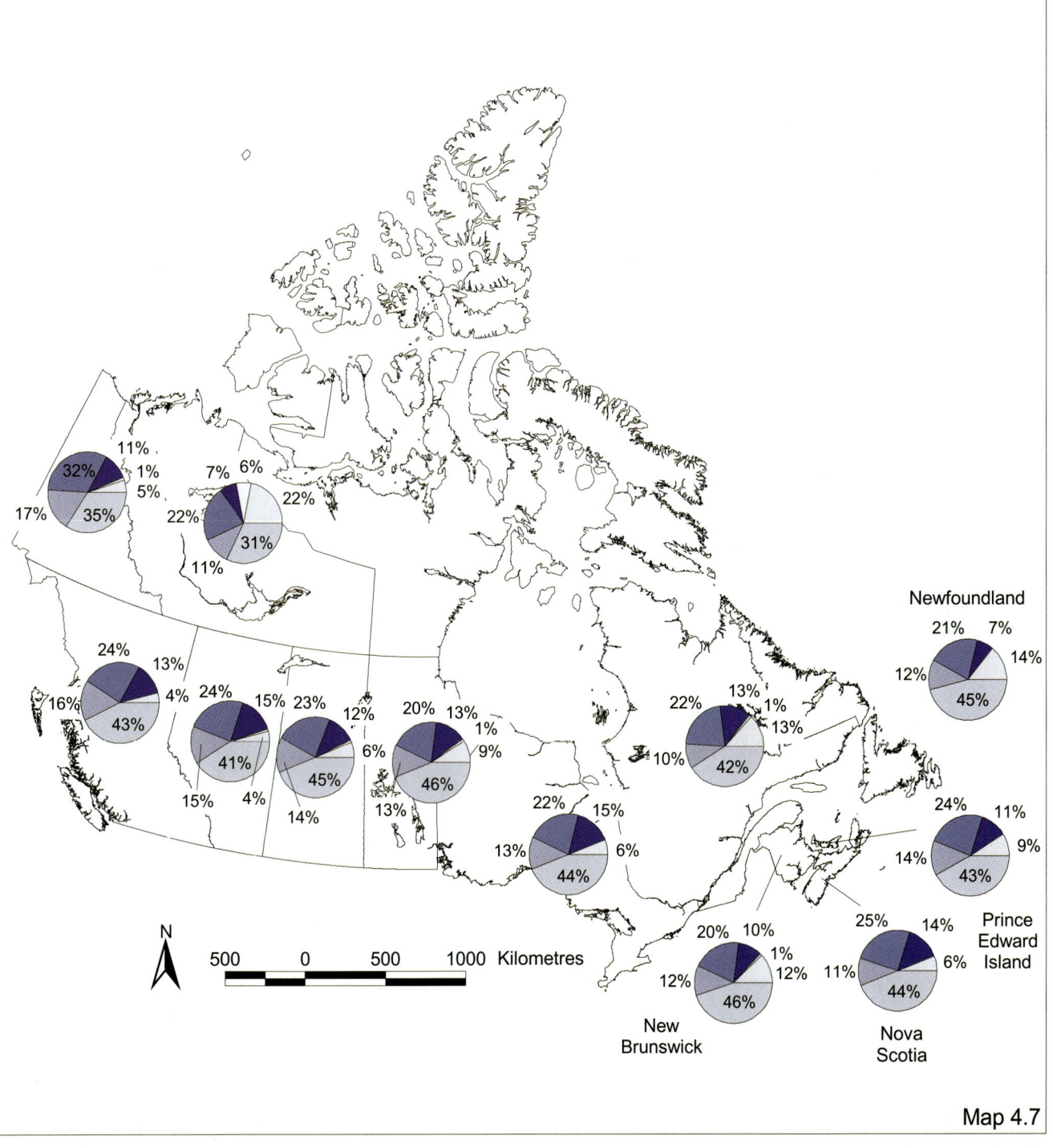

Map 4.7

Newfoundland: 21%, 7%, 14%, 45%, 12%
Prince Edward Island: 24%, 11%, 9%, 43%, 14%
Nova Scotia: 25%, 14%, 6%, 44%, 11%
New Brunswick: 20%, 10%, 1%, 12%, 46%, 12%

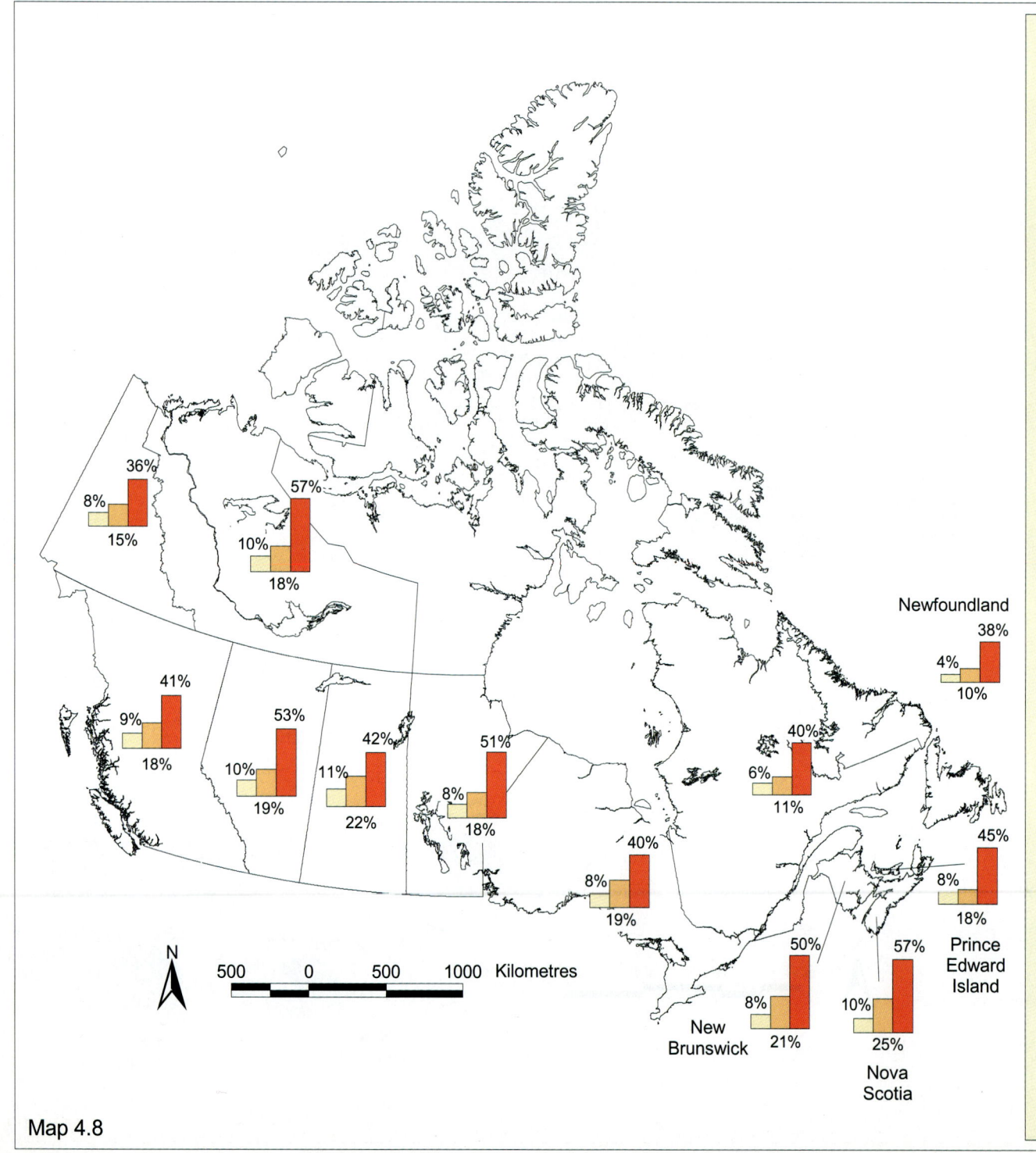

60 ATLAS OF LITERACY AND DISABILITY

Age Distribution of Ages 15 and Older with Disabilities Residing in Households, Provinces and Territories

1991 Health and Activity Limitation Survey (HALS)

People are more likely to have a disability as they age. Just over four out of every ten Canadians aged 65 and older who live in private households report having some limitation in activity because of a health problem or health condition. This number drops to almost two out of ten for persons aged 35 to 64 and to less than one in ten (7.9%) for persons aged 15 to 34.

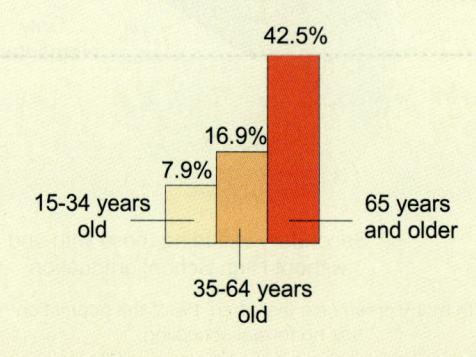

Canada

- 15-34 years old: 7.9%
- 35-64 years old: 16.9%
- 65 years and older: 42.5%

Provinces and Territories

- Yukon: 8%, 15%, 36%
- Northwest Territories: 10%, 18%, 57%
- British Columbia: 9%, 18%, 41%
- Alberta: 10%, 19%, 53%
- Saskatchewan: 11%, 22%, 42%
- Manitoba: 8%, 18%, 51%
- Ontario: 8%, 19%, 40%
- Quebec: 6%, 11%, 40%
- Newfoundland: 4%, 10%, 38%
- New Brunswick: 8%, 21%, 50%
- Nova Scotia: 10%, 25%, 57%
- Prince Edward Island: 8%, 18%, 45%

Map 4.8

IV. THE GEOGRAPHY OF DISABILITY | 61

Use of Official Language by Ages 15 and Older with Disabilities Residing in Households, Provinces and Territories

1991 Health and Activity Limitation Survey (HALS)

Most adults with disabilities in Canada (98.4%) speak either French or English. The few who do not speak either official language are more like to live in the Yukon and Northwest Territories than any other part of Canada.

Canada

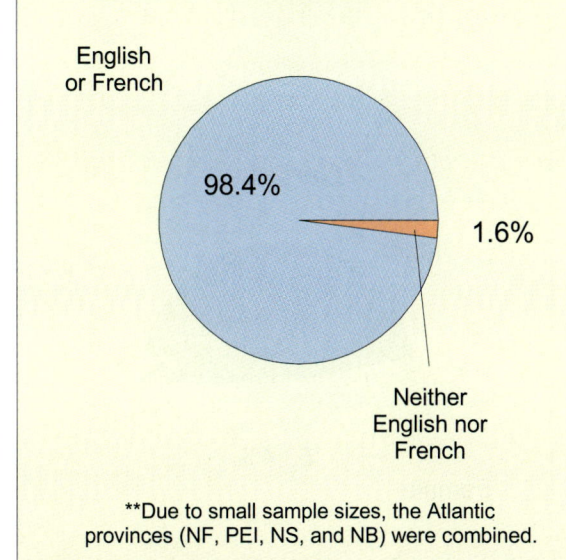

English or French: 98.4%
Neither English nor French: 1.6%

Territories/Provinces:
- Yukon/NWT: 88%
- BC: 99%
- AB: 98%
- SK: 99%
- MB: 100%
- ON: 98%
- QC: 98%
- Atlantic**: 100%

**Due to small sample sizes, the Atlantic provinces (NF, PEI, NS, and NB) were combined.

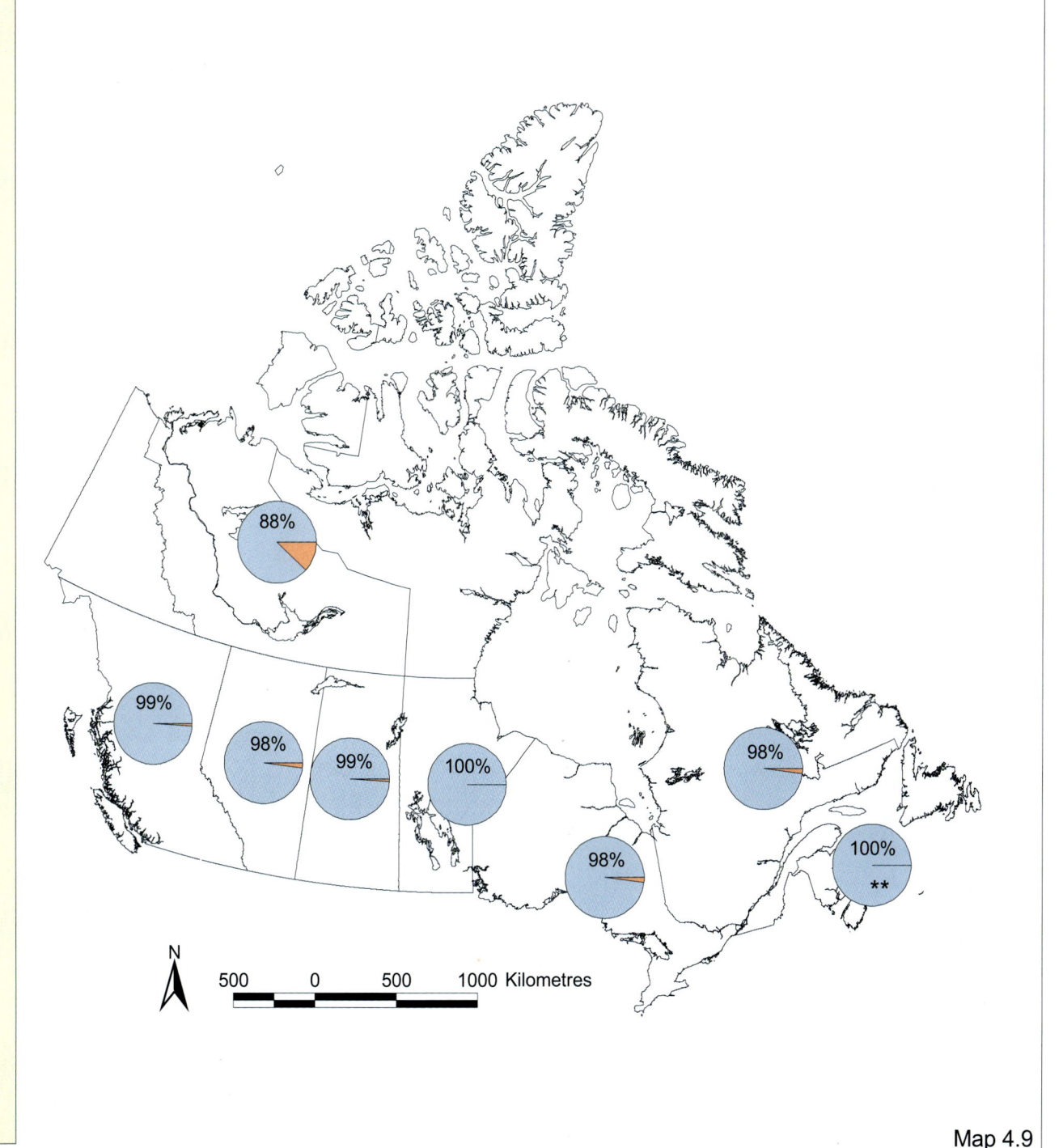

Map 4.9

ATLAS OF LITERACY AND DISABILITY

Gender Distribution for Ages 15 and Older with Disabilities Residing in Households, Provinces and Territories

1991 Health and Activity Limitation Survey (HALS)

Gender differences in rates of disability are slight in Canada. Overall, slightly more than half of the adult population with disabilities is women (53.4%) and just under half are men (46.6%). In most provinces there is a higher percentage of women with disabilities than men with disabilities.

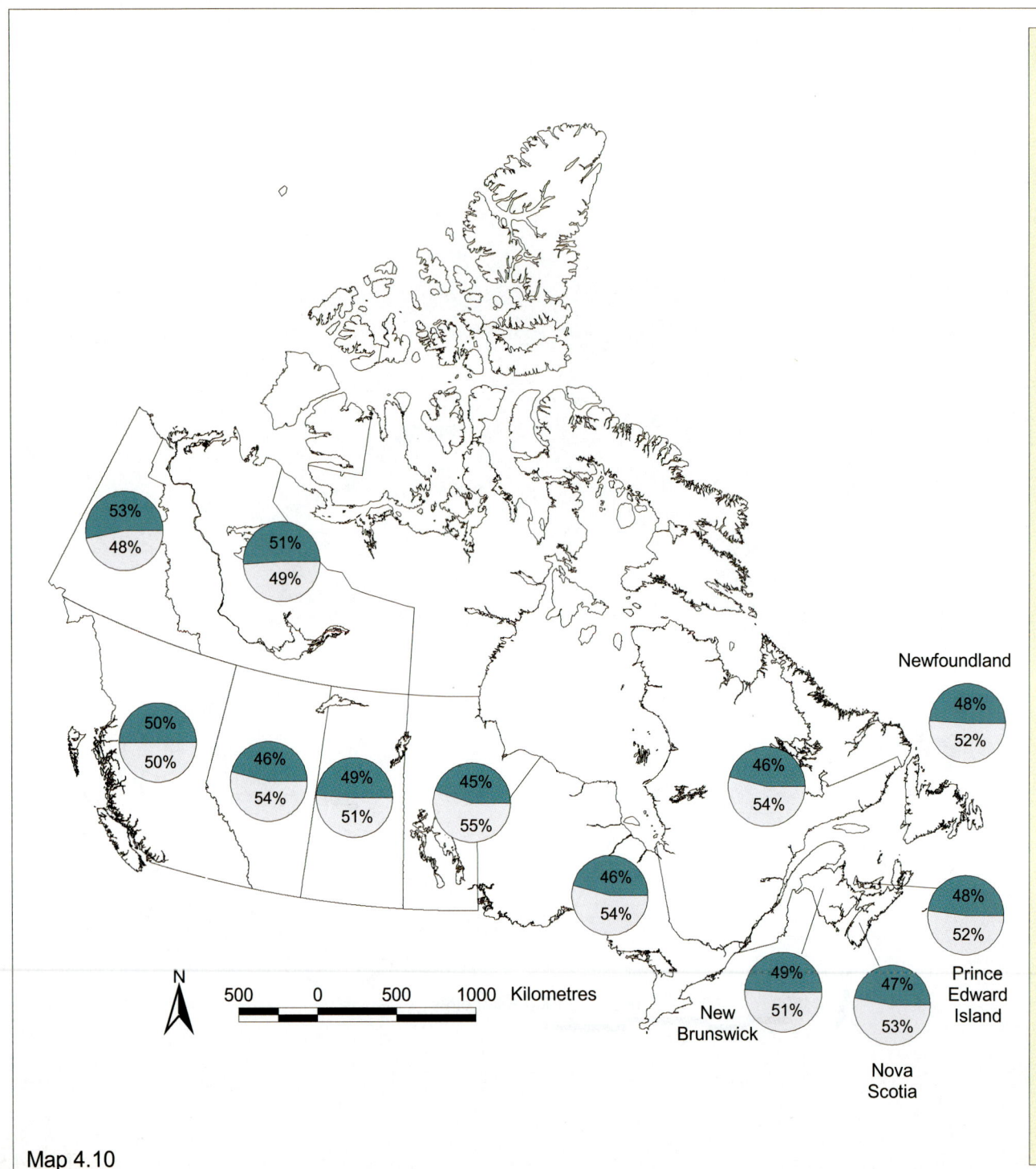

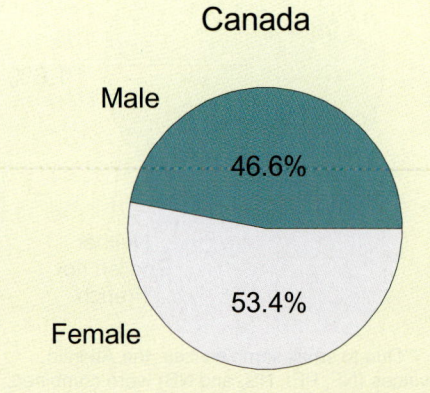

Canada
- Male: 46.6%
- Female: 53.4%

Provincial/Territorial distribution (Male/Female):
- Yukon: 53% / 48%
- Northwest Territories: 51% / 49%
- British Columbia: 50% / 50%
- Alberta: 46% / 54%
- Saskatchewan: 49% / 51%
- Manitoba: 45% / 55%
- Ontario: 46% / 54%
- Quebec: 46% / 54%
- Newfoundland: 48% / 52%
- New Brunswick: 49% / 51%
- Nova Scotia: 47% / 53%
- Prince Edward Island: 48% / 52%

Map 4.10

IV. THE GEOGRAPHY OF DISABILITY | 63

Immigration Status of Ages 15 and Older with Disabilities Residing in Households, Provinces and Territories

1991 Health and Activity Limitation Survey (HALS)

The vast majority of Canadians with disabilities were born in Canada (81.2%). Only 18.8% immigrated from other countries. Immigrants with disabilities are most likely to live in British Columbia (27%) and Ontario (25%).

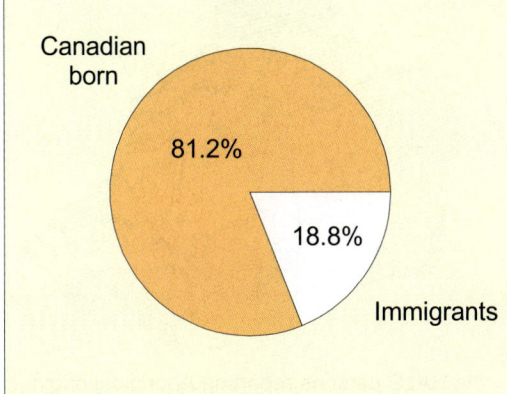

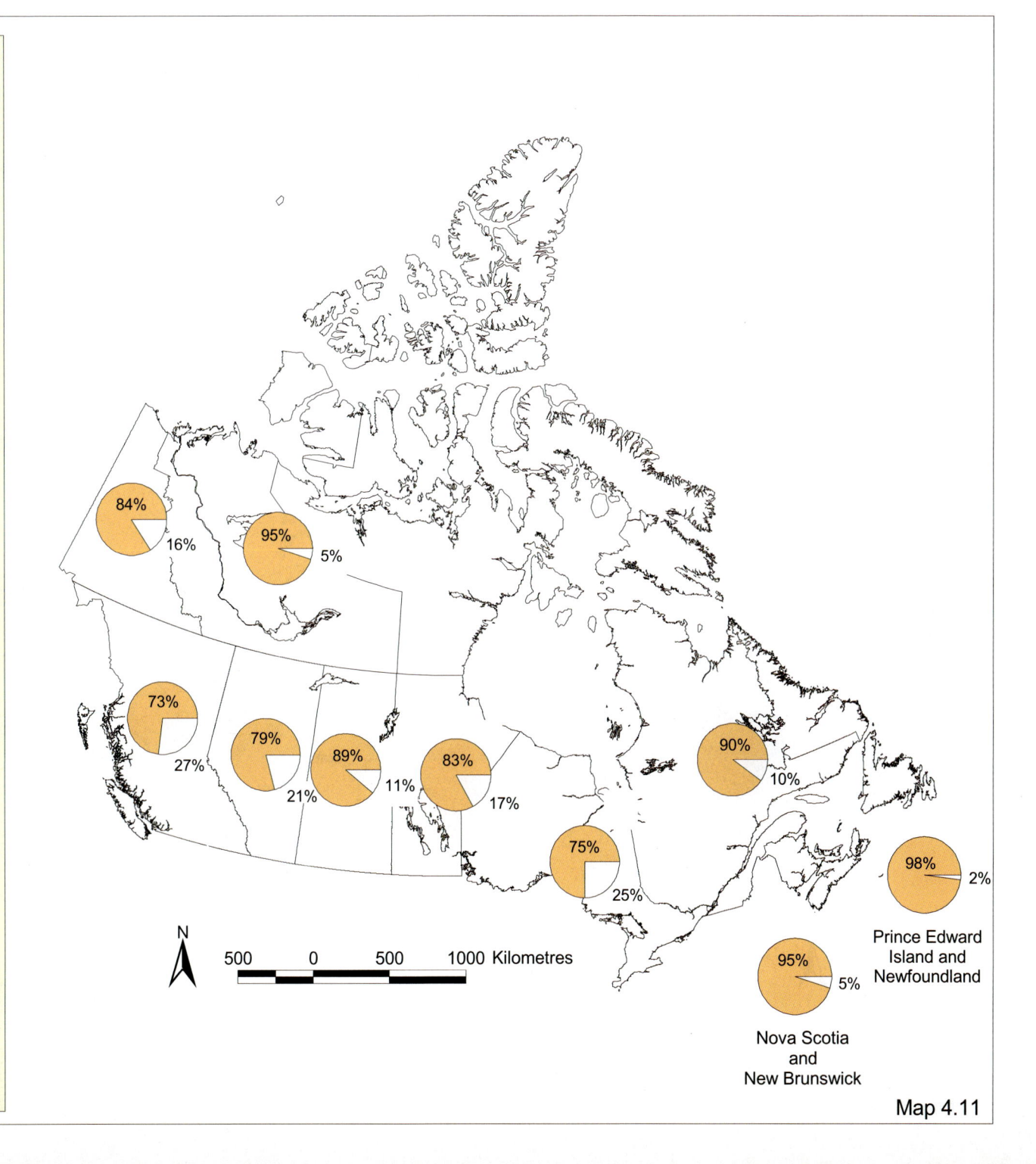

Canada

Canadian born: 81.2%
Immigrants: 18.8%

Yukon: 84% / 16%
Northwest Territories: 95% / 5%
British Columbia: 73% / 27%
Alberta: 79% / 21%
Saskatchewan: 89% / 11%
Manitoba: 83% / 17%
Ontario: 75% / 25%
Quebec: 90% / 10%
Prince Edward Island and Newfoundland: 98% / 2%
Nova Scotia and New Brunswick: 95% / 5%

Map 4.11

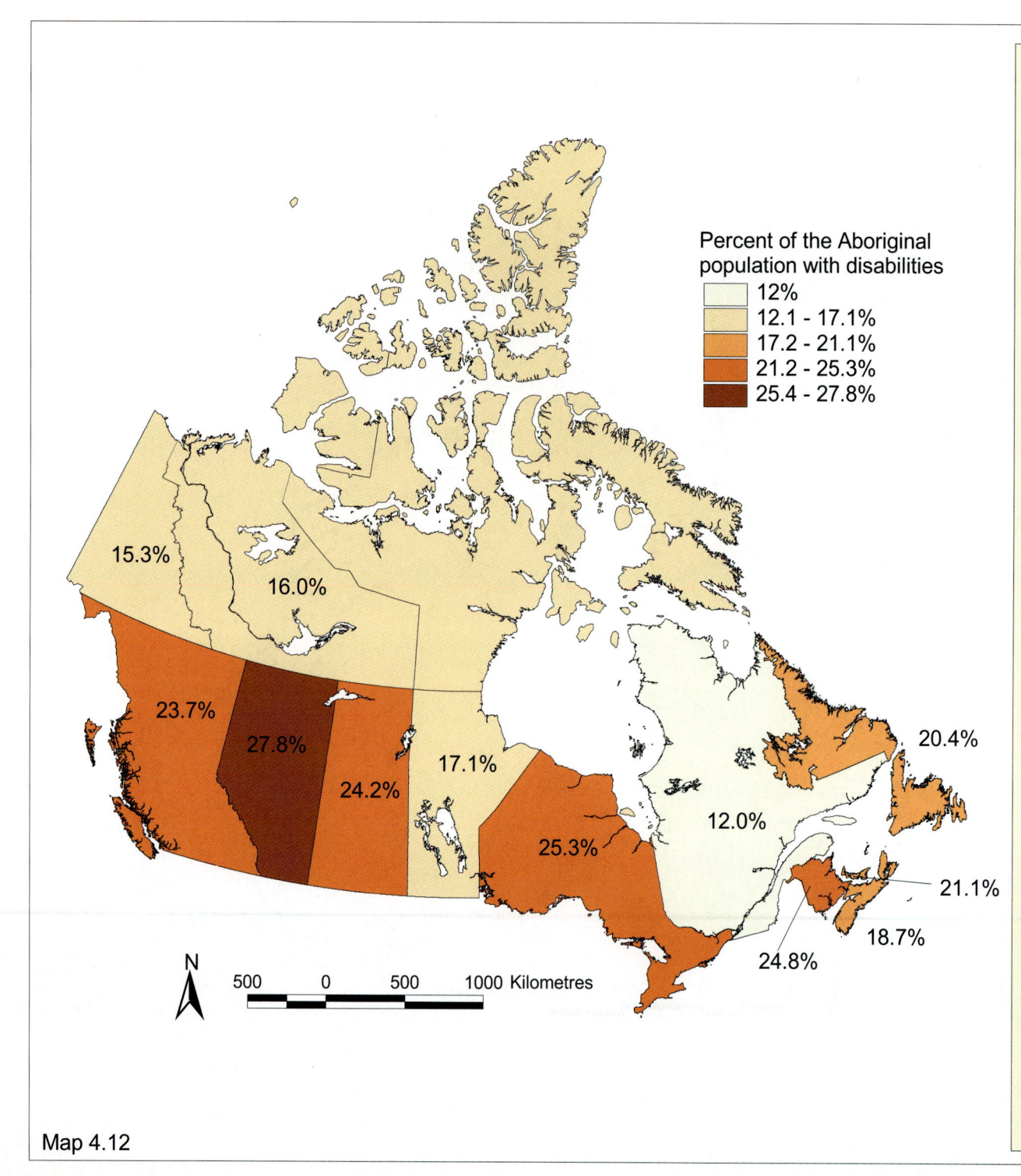

64 ATLAS OF LITERACY AND DISABILITY

Disability Rates for the Aboriginal Population* Ages 15 and Older, Provinces and Territories

1991 Health and Activity Limitation Survey (HALS) and 1991 Aboriginal Peoples Survey (APS)

One in five Aboriginal people ages 15 and older have a disability. Rates of disability for this population tend to be higher in the West compared to the East. Disability rates among Native people are lowest in Quebec, the Yukon and Northwest Territories and Manitoba.

Canada -- 21.5%

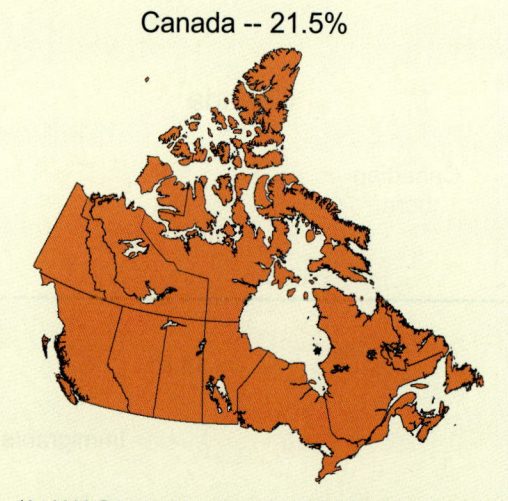

Percent of the Aboriginal population with disabilities
- 12%
- 12.1 - 17.1%
- 17.2 - 21.1%
- 21.2 - 25.3%
- 25.4 - 27.8%

Values shown on map:
- 15.3%
- 16.0%
- 23.7%
- 27.8%
- 24.2%
- 17.1%
- 25.3%
- 12.0%
- 20.4%
- 21.1%
- 18.7%
- 24.8%

*In HALS persons reporting Aboriginal origin and in APS persons residing on Indian Reserves were defined as Aboriginal persons.

Map 4.12

IV. THE GEOGRAPHY OF DISABILITY | 65

Adults with and without Disabilities Who are Active in the Labour Force*, Provinces and Territories

1991 Health and Activity Limitation Survey (HALS)

Three out of every four non-disabled adults were either employed or looking for work. Among the population with disabilities, only slightly over half (56.3%) were employed or looking for work and the rest had opted out of the labour force - either because they were unable to work or because they had experienced barriers that prevented or impeded them from looking for work.

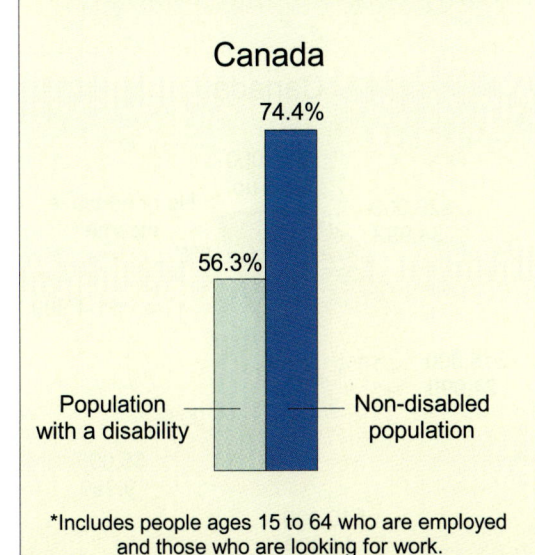

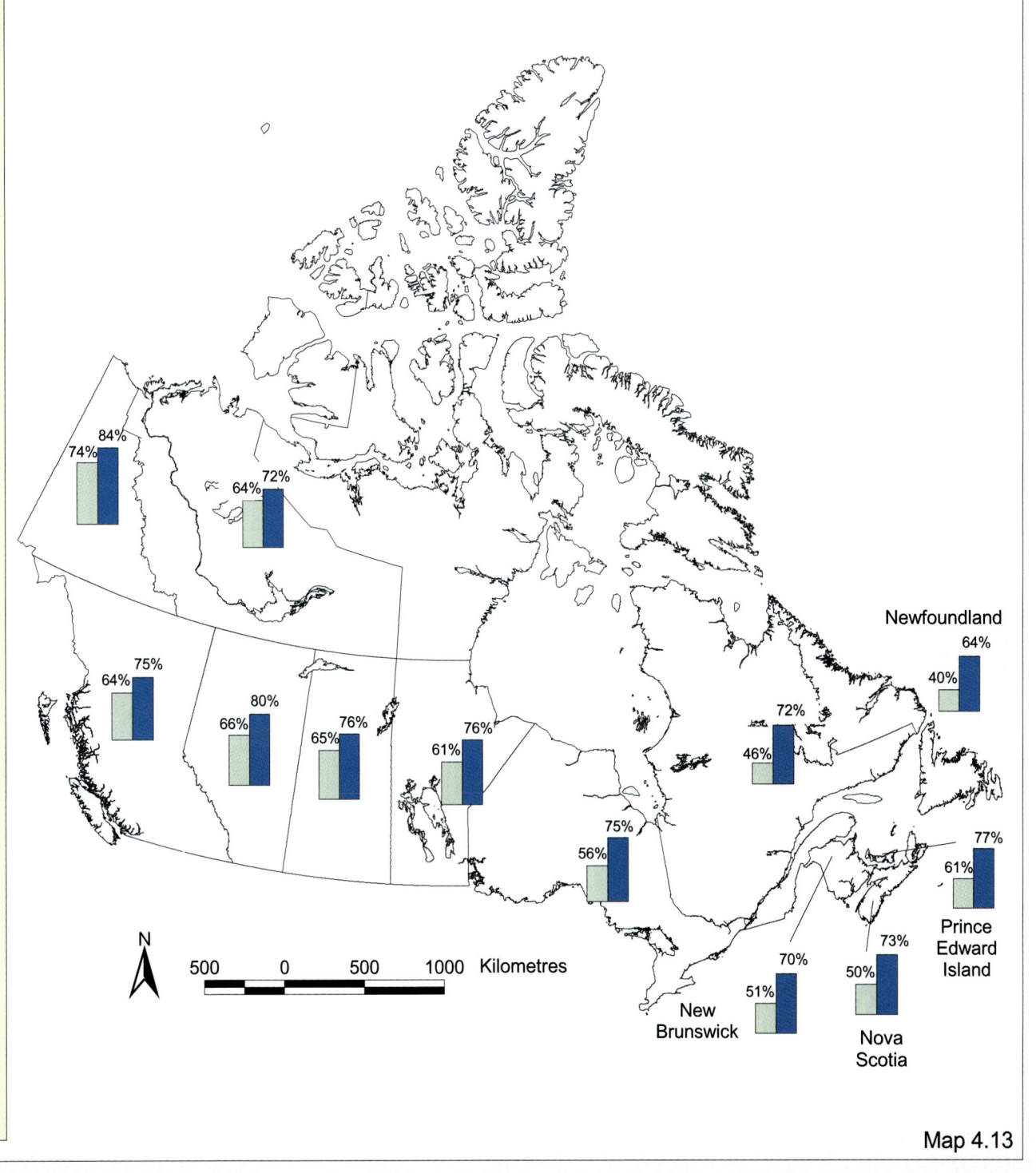

Canada

- Population with a disability: 56.3%
- Non-disabled population: 74.4%

*Includes people ages 15 to 64 who are employed and those who are looking for work.

Yukon: 74% / 84%
Northwest Territories: 64% / 72%
British Columbia: 64% / 75%
Alberta: 66% / 80%
Saskatchewan: 65% / 76%
Manitoba: 61% / 76%
Ontario: 56% / 75%
Quebec: 46% / 72%
Newfoundland: 40% / 64%
New Brunswick: 51% / 70%
Nova Scotia: 50% / 73%
Prince Edward Island: 61% / 77%

Map 4.13

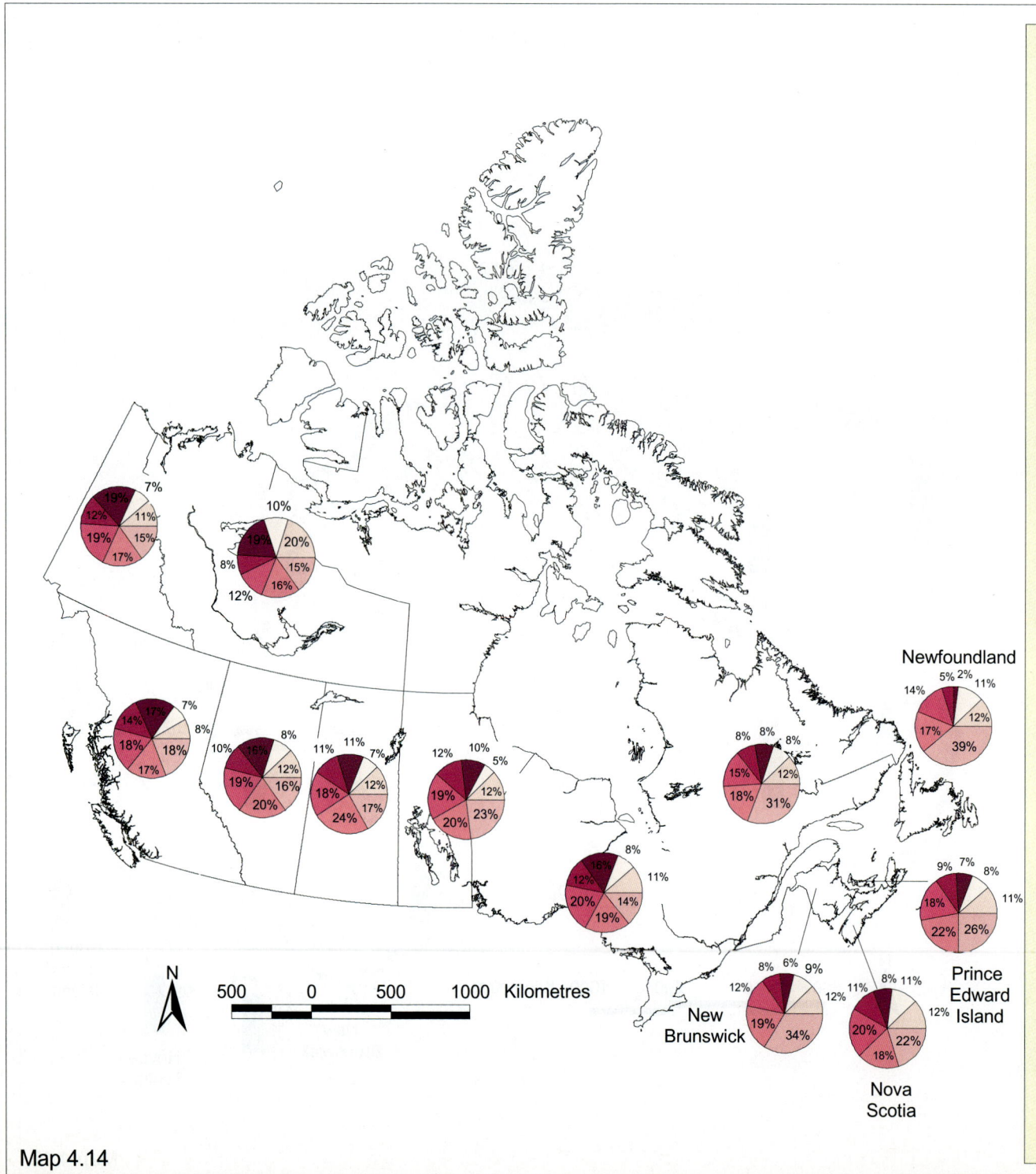

66　ATLAS OF LITERACY AND DISABILITY

Personal Income Levels for Ages 15 and Older with Disabilities Residing in Households, Provinces and Territories

1991 Health and Activity Limitation Survey (HALS)

In every province and territory a consistently high proportion of adults with disabilities have incomes that would generally be considered low. Nearly 40% have incomes lower than $10,000 per year. Notably 8% report no income at all and nearly 20% report personal income that is les than $5,000 per year.

Canada

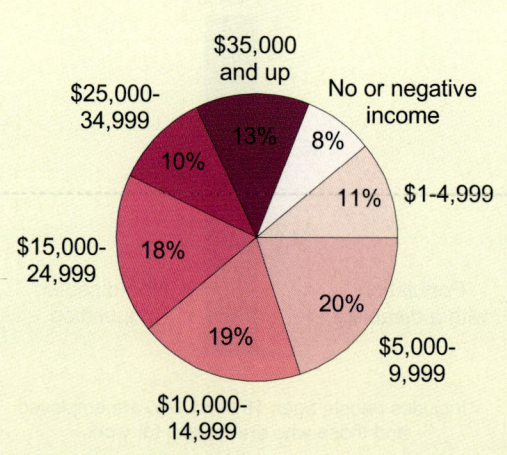

Pie chart categories:
- $35,000 and up: 13%
- No or negative income: 8%
- $1-4,999: 11%
- $5,000-9,999: 20%
- $10,000-14,999: 19%
- $15,000-24,999: 18%
- $25,000-34,999: 10%

Map 4.14

IV. THE GEOGRAPHY OF DISABILITY | 67

Personal Income Levels for Ages 15 and Older without Disabilities, Provinces and Territories

1991 Health and Activity Limitation Survey (HALS)

In general, adults without disabilities are less likely to be poor than their disabled peers. Almost 40% of adults without disabilities reported personal income in 1990 of $25,000 or more; in contrast, only 23% of adults with disabilities reported personal income at that level.

Canada

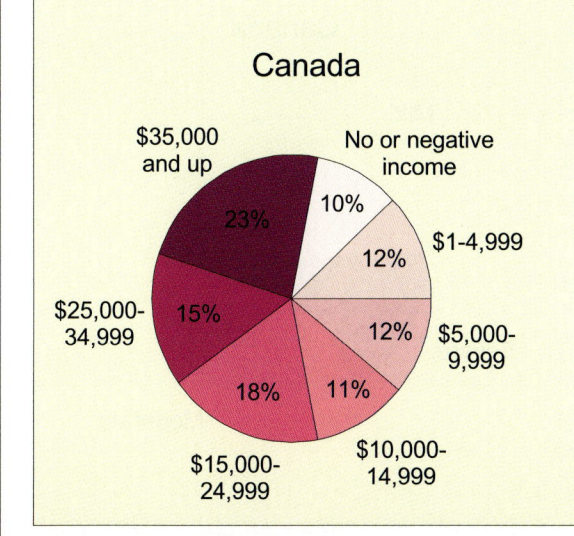

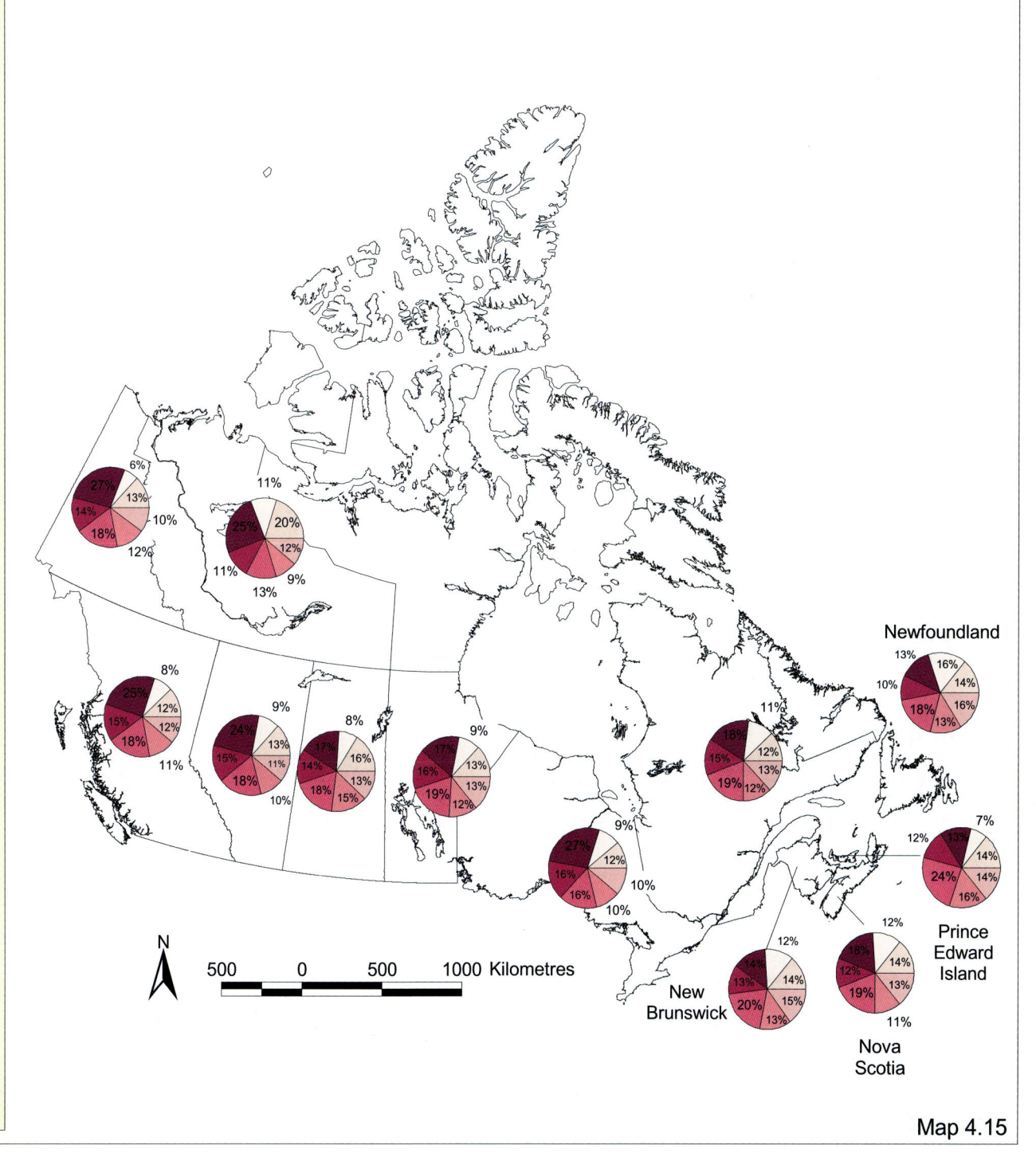

- $35,000 and up: 23%
- No or negative income: 10%
- $1-4,999: 12%
- $5,000-9,999: 12%
- $10,000-14,999: 11%
- $15,000-24,999: 18%
- $25,000-34,999: 15%

Map 4.15

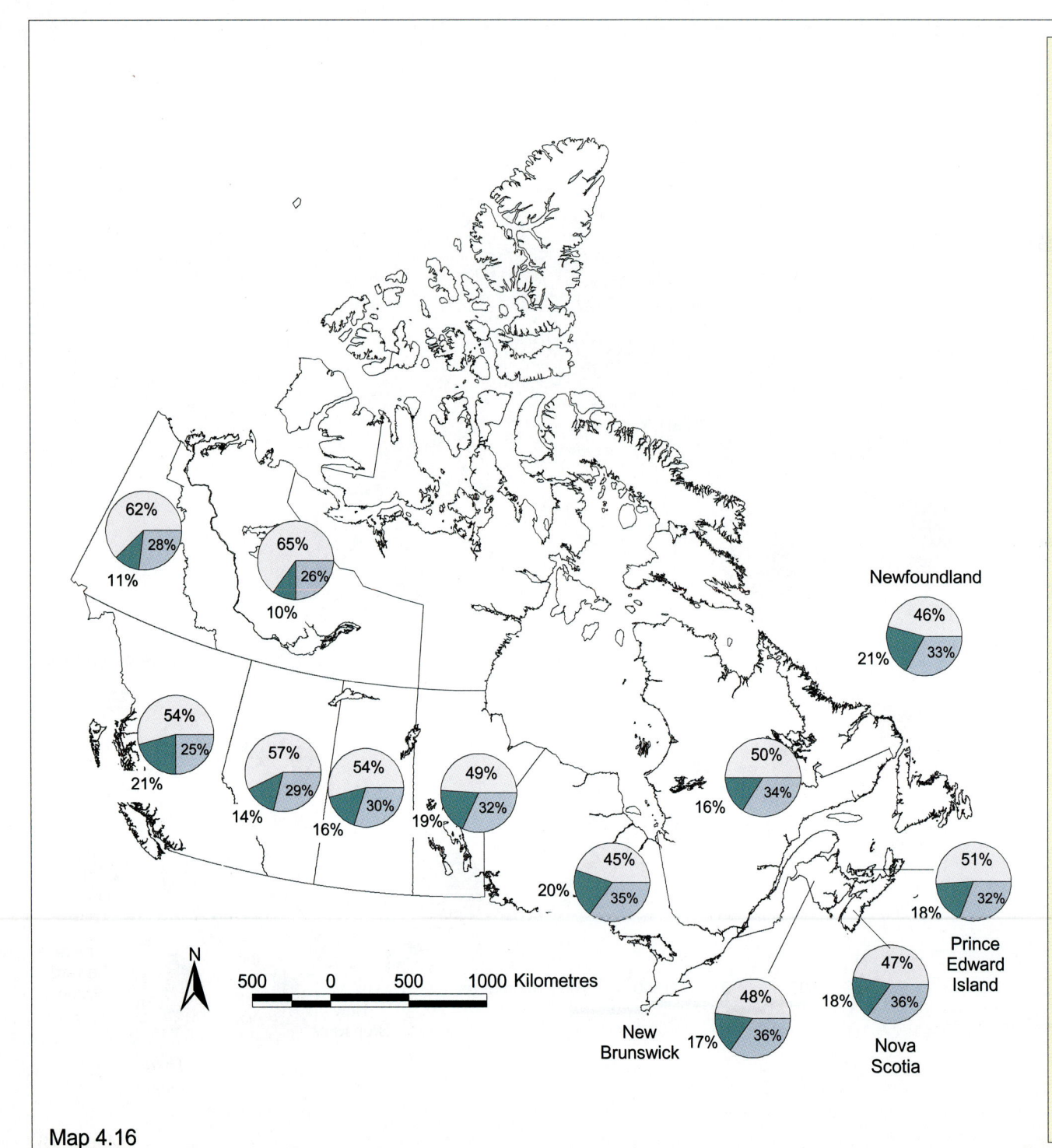

Severity of Limitation in Activity for Ages 15 and Older Residing in Households, Provinces and Territories

1991 Health and Activity Limitation Survey (HALS)

Severity of disability is an index based on the frequency of positive responses to the HALS screening questions combined with the extent of the limitation. Based on this measure, nearly half of Canadians with disabilities were found to have mild disabilities. 33% have moderate disabilities and 18% have severe disabilities.

Canada

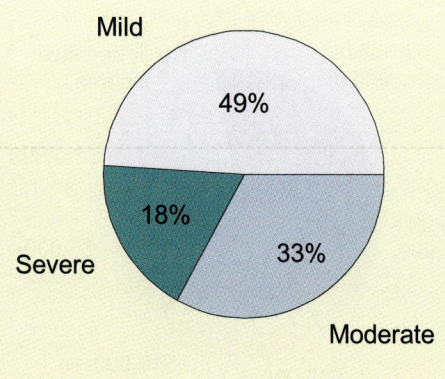

- Mild: 49%
- Moderate: 33%
- Severe: 18%

Provincial and Territorial Data (Mild / Moderate / Severe)

- Yukon: 62% / 28% / 11%
- Northwest Territories: 65% / 26% / 10%
- British Columbia: 54% / 25% / 21%
- Alberta: 57% / 29% / 14%
- Saskatchewan: 54% / 30% / 16%
- Manitoba: 49% / 32% / 19%
- Ontario: 45% / 35% / 20%
- Quebec: 50% / 34% / 16%
- Newfoundland: 46% / 33% / 21%
- New Brunswick: 48% / 36% / 17%
- Nova Scotia: 47% / 36% / 18%
- Prince Edward Island: 51% / 32% / 18%

Map 4.16

IV. THE GEOGRAPHY OF DISABILITY | 69

Barriers and Accommodations Index for Ages 15 and Older with Disabilities Residing in Households, Provinces and Territories

1991 Health and Activity Limitation Survey (HALS)

At the time of the HALS survey, almost half (49%) of all adults with disabilities reported that they encountered barriers in their everyday activities and some, but not all of those barriers had been removed. A further 28% reported that they faced barriers and none of the barriers had been removed. The remaining 23% were barrier-free - either because they had never experienced any barriers (13.5%) or because all barriers had been removed (9.5%).

Canada

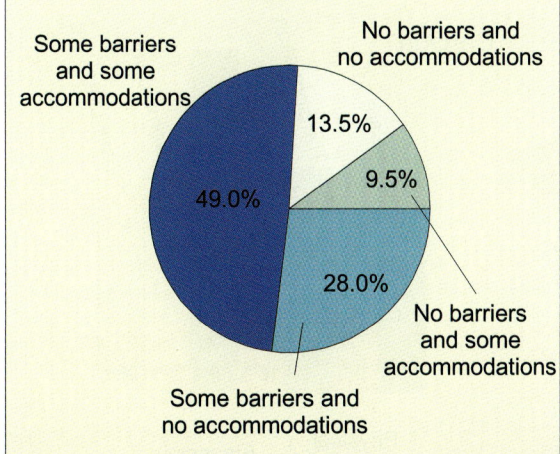

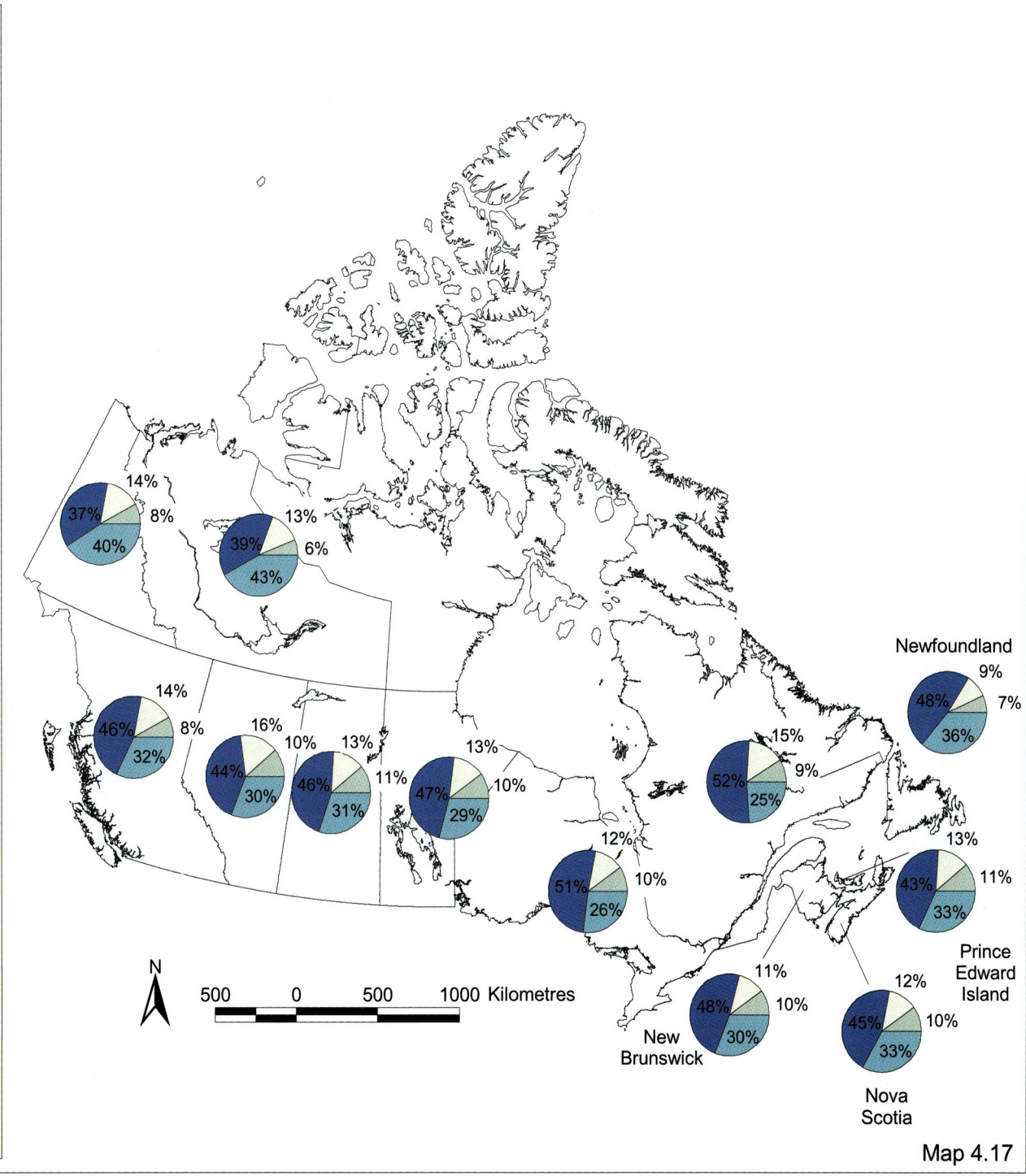

- Some barriers and some accommodations: 49.0%
- No barriers and no accommodations: 13.5%
- No barriers and some accommodations: 9.5%
- Some barriers and no accommodations: 28.0%

Map 4.17

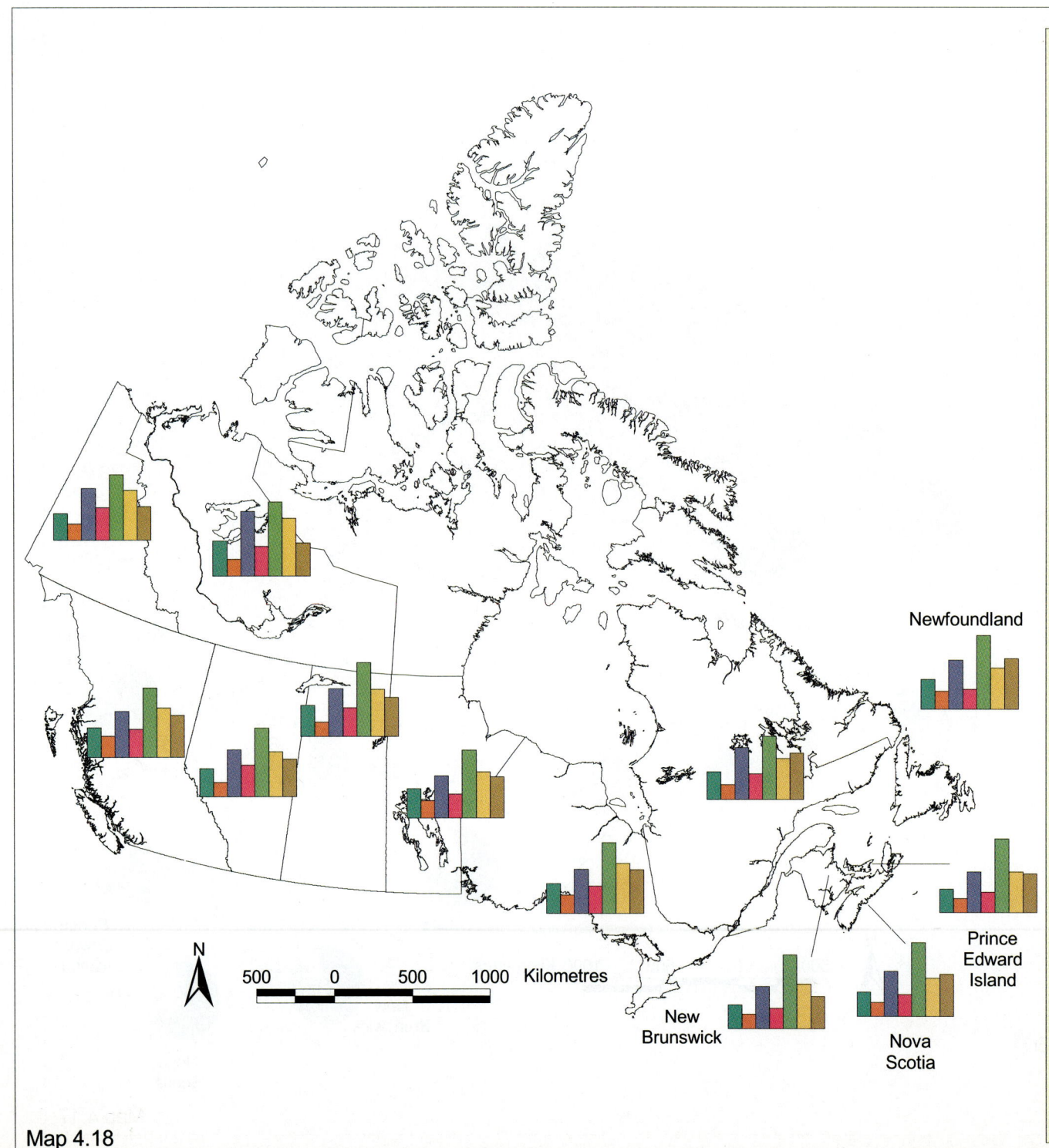

ATLAS OF LITERACY AND DISABILITY

Map 4.18

Type of Barriers Encountered for Ages 15 and Older with Disabilities Residing in Households, Provinces and Territories

1991 Health and Activity Limitation Survey (HALS)

Almost half (48%) of adults with disabilities reported barriers based on lack of financial resources. Almost one third (31%) reported barriers in transportation and one third (31%) also reported community barriers - attitudes. People also report experiencing barriers in daily activities such as preparing meals (28%), personal care barriers such as the unavailability of aids or support (18%), and barriers from inaccessible structures (9%). Barriers encountered in the workplace were identified by 16% of adults with disabilities.

Canada

Personal Care	Physical Structures	Transportation	Workplace	Financial	Community	Daily Life
18%	9%	31%	16%	48%	31%	28%

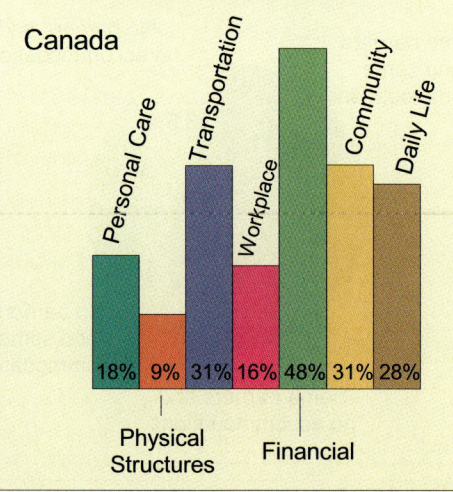

IV. THE GEOGRAPHY OF DISABILITY | 71

Type of Accommodations Received for Ages 15 and Older with Disabilities Residing in Households, Provinces and Territories

1991 Health and Activity Limitation Survey (HALS)

Almost four out of every ten adults with disabilities (38%) reported receiving some accommodations to remove personal barriers such as getting the aids that they need. 36% reported receiving accommodations to remove barriers in daily activities such as help with preparing meals, shopping for groceries and personal care, while only 3% received them at work. A scant 3% report receiving transportation accommodations.

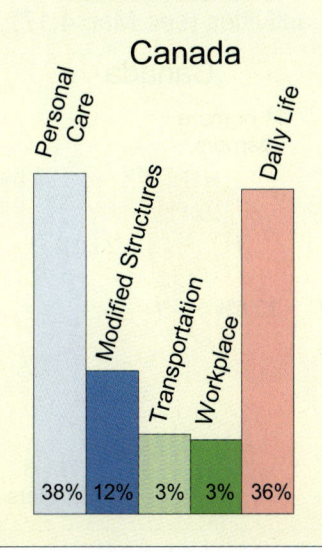

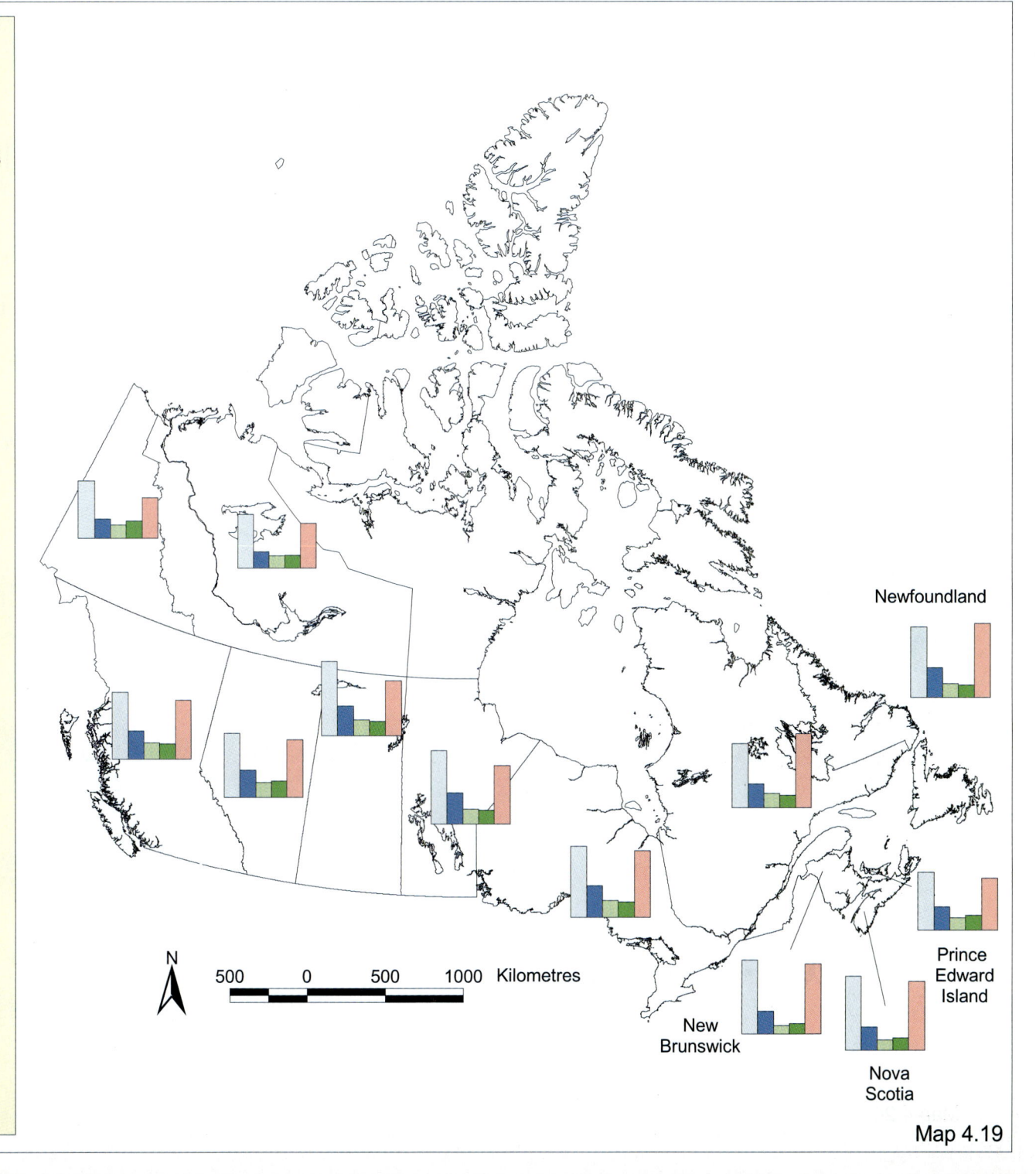

Canada

Personal Care: 38%
Modified Structures: 12%
Transportation: 3%
Workplace: 3%
Daily Life: 36%

Newfoundland
Prince Edward Island
New Brunswick
Nova Scotia

Map 4.19

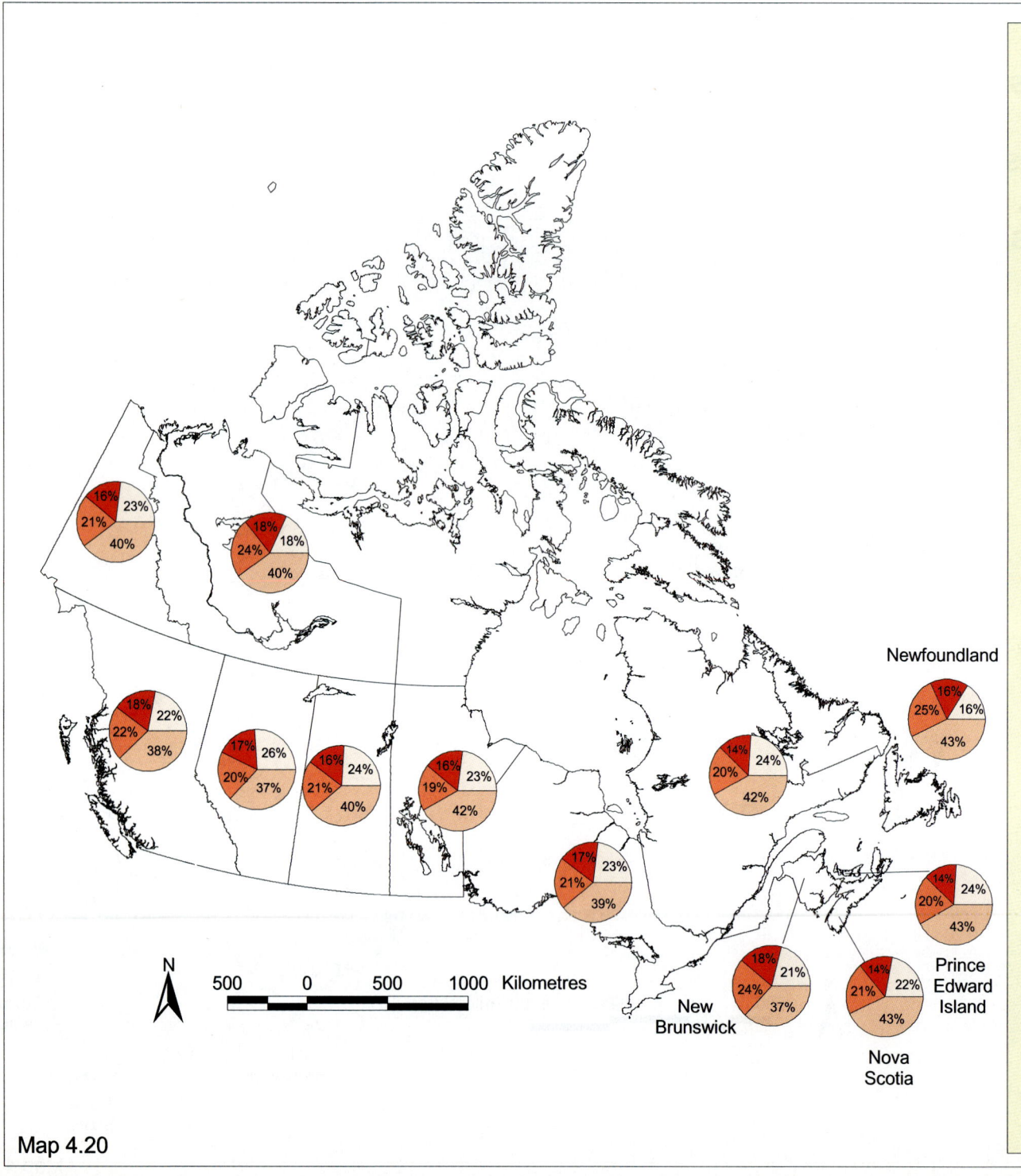

ATLAS OF LITERACY AND DISABILITY

Barriers Encountered by Ages 15 and Older with Disabilities Residing in Households, Provinces and Territories

1991 Health and Activity Limitation Survey (HALS)

The largest proportion of Canadians with disabilities (39.7%) experience between 1 and 5 barriers in their daily lives. Nearly one quarter of all adults with disabilities reported encountering no barriers at the time of the survey. This group includes two types of individuals - those who have encountered barriers in the past and all barriers had been removed through accommodations (see Map 4.17) and those who have never experienced any barriers at all in their everyday activities (see Map 4.17).

Canada

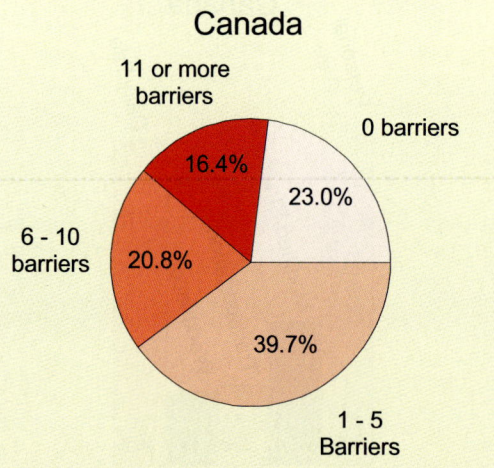

- 11 or more barriers: 16.4%
- 6 - 10 barriers: 20.8%
- 1 - 5 Barriers: 39.7%
- 0 barriers: 23.0%

Map 4.20

IV. THE GEOGRAPHY OF DISABILITY | 73

Accommodations Received for Ages 15 and Older with Disabilities Residing in Households, Provinces and Territories

1991 Health and Activity Limitation Survey (HALS)

Four out of every ten adults with disabilities reported receiving no accommodations to remove barriers. This group includes two types of individuals - those who required no accommodations (13.5% - see Map 4.17) and those who were encountering some barriers but had received no accommodations (28% - see Map 4.17). Almost half of all adults with disabilities reported having received 1 to 5 accommodations to remove barriers that they had encountered in their everyday activities.

Canada

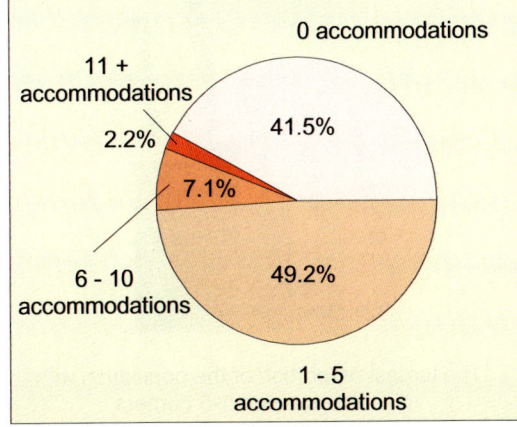

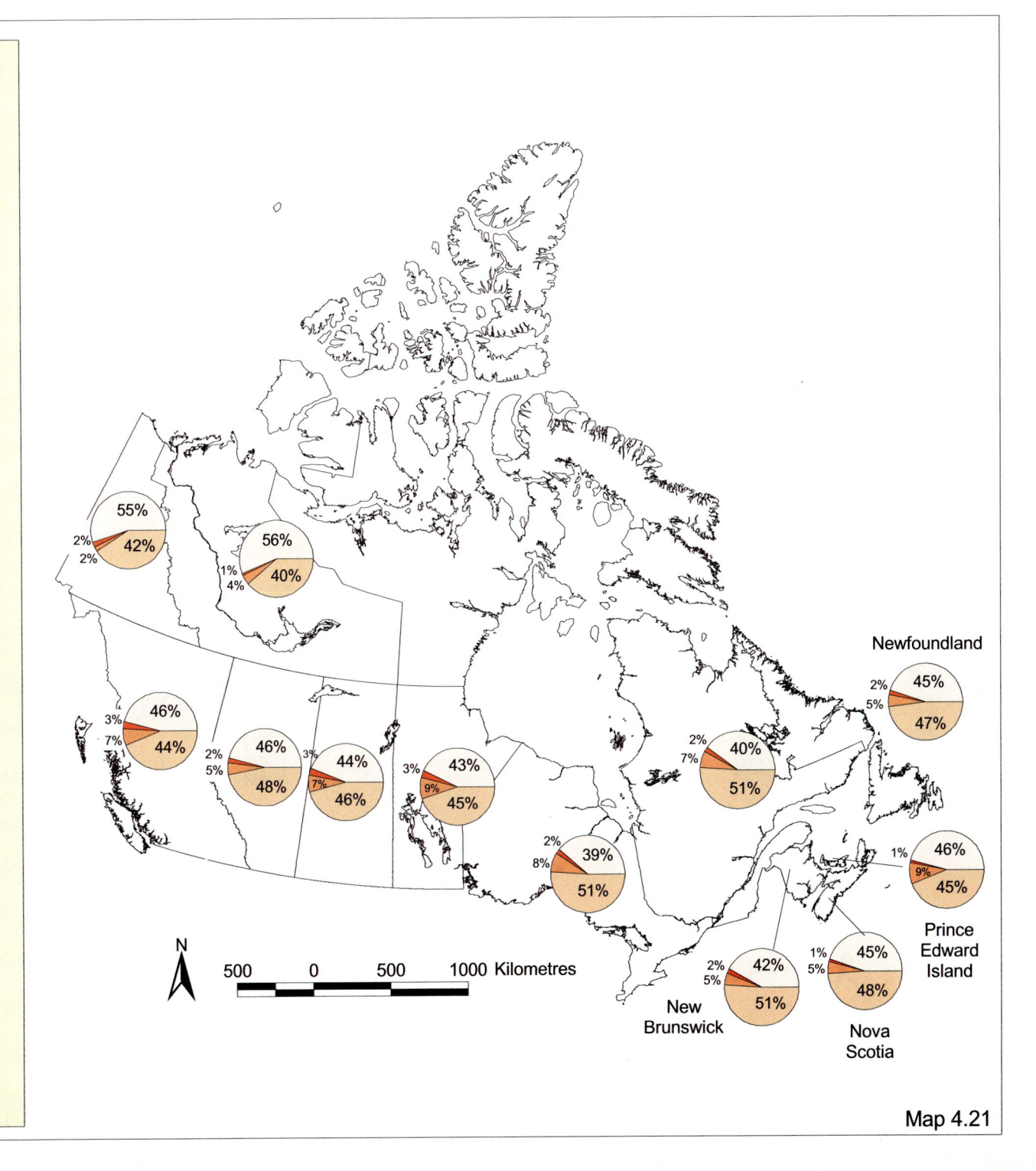

- 0 accommodations: 41.5%
- 11 + accommodations: 2.2%
- 6 - 10 accommodations: 7.1%
- 1 - 5 accommodations: 49.2%

Map 4.21

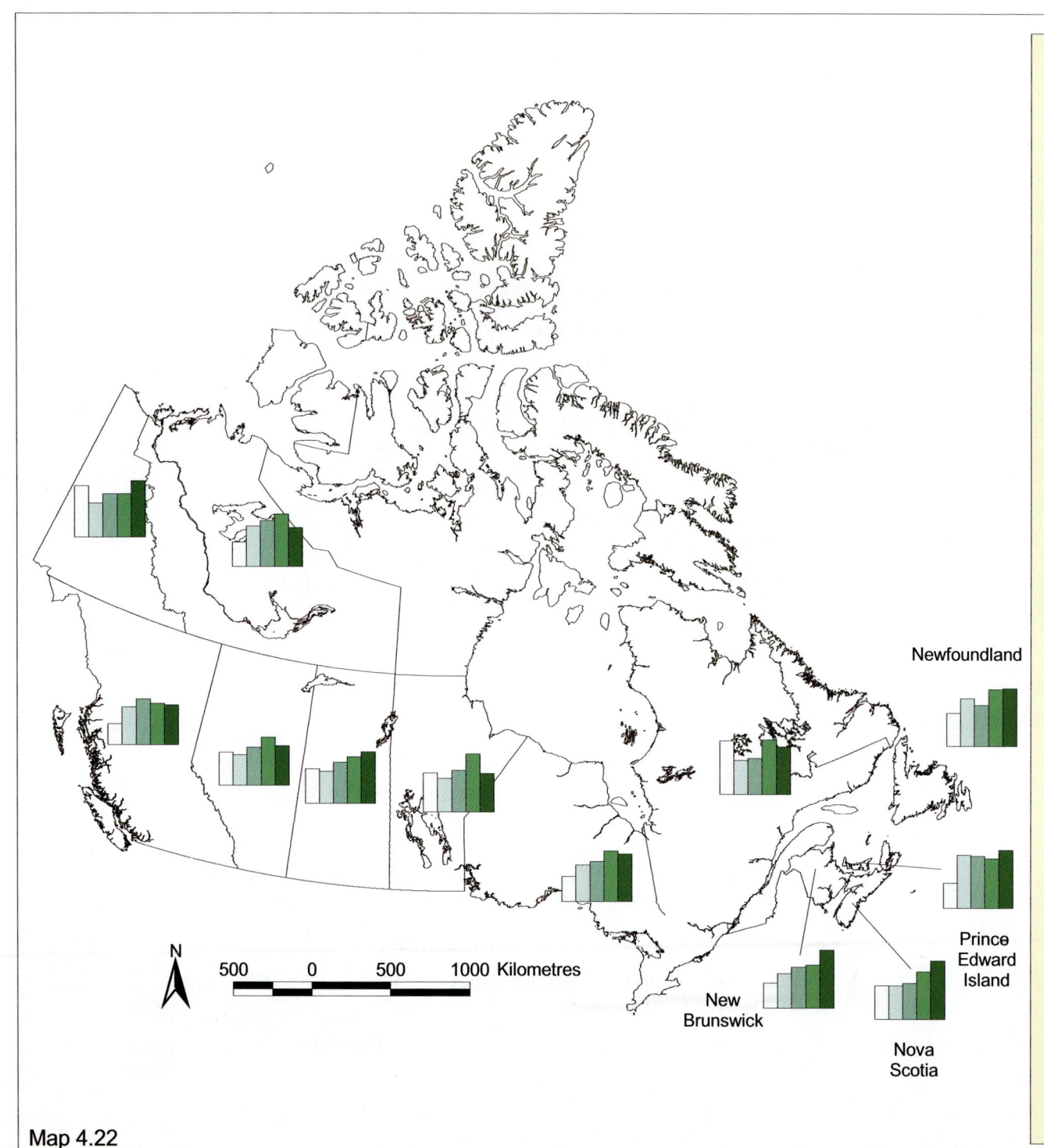

ATLAS OF LITERACY AND DISABILITY

Age of Onset of Disability for Ages 15 and Older with One to Five Barriers* Encountered, Provinces and Territories

1991 Health and Activity Limitation Survey (HALS)

Generally in Canada, the higher the reported age of onset of disability, the higher the proportion of people who faced 1 to 5 barriers. People who became disabled before 4 years of age were the least likely to report 1 to 5 barriers, and those ages 45 to 64 were the most likely.

Canada

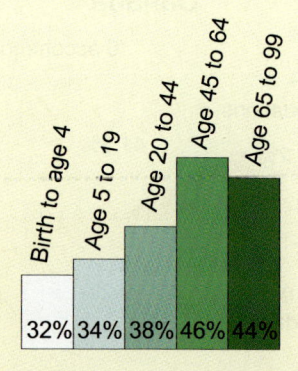

Birth to age 4: 32%
Age 5 to 19: 34%
Age 20 to 44: 38%
Age 45 to 64: 46%
Age 65 to 99: 44%

*The largest proportion of the population with disabilities report 1-5 barriers.

Map 4.22

IV. THE GEOGRAPHY OF DISABILITY | 75

Age of Onset of Disability for Ages 15 and Older with One to Five Accommodations*, Received, Provinces and Territories

1991 Health and Activity Limitation Survey (HALS)

Among people who said their ages of onset of disability was 65-99 years, nearly 60% reported 1 to 5 accommodations. In Canada overall, except for those whose onset occurred before four years, as the age of onset increased, the proportion receiving accommodations also increased.

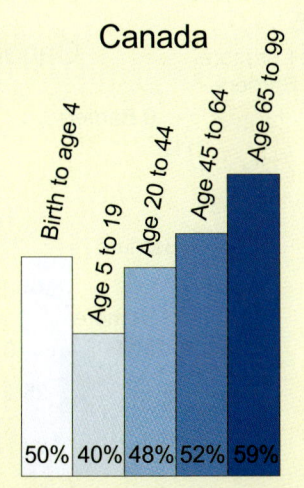

Canada

Birth to age 4	Age 5 to 19	Age 20 to 44	Age 45 to 64	Age 65 to 99
50%	40%	48%	52%	59%

* The largest proportion of the population with disabilities report 1-5 accommodations.

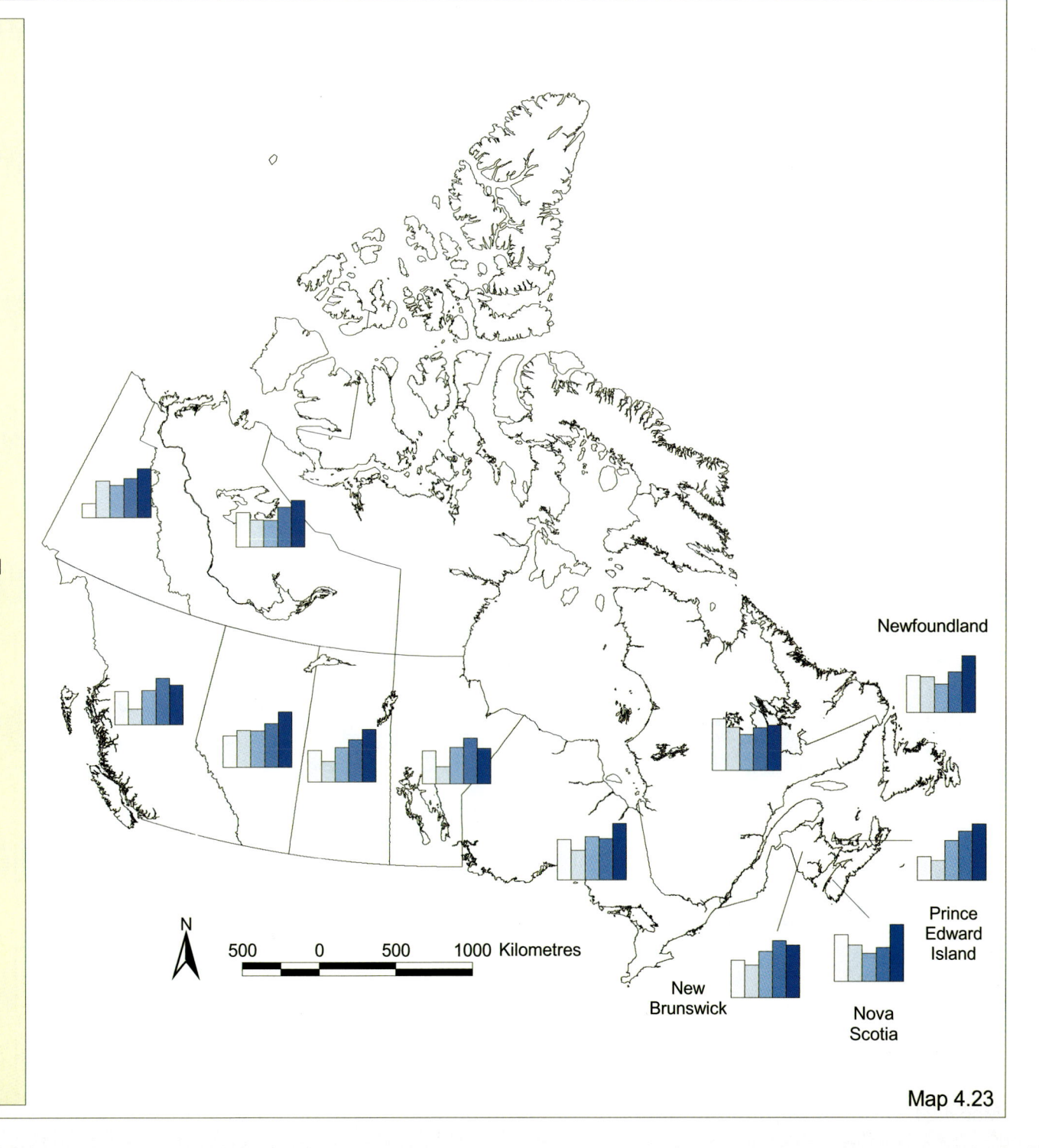

Map 4.23

ATLAS OF LITERACY AND DISABILITY

Number of Barriers Encountered by Ages 15 and Older with Disabilities Residing in Households by Gender, Provinces and Territories

1991 Health and Activity Limitation Survey (HALS)

There is only a slight gender difference noted in the population with disabilities experiencing no barriers. Women experience higher numbers of barriers than men. They are more likely to deal with over 11 barriers than men (18% compared to 14%). Men are more likely to face fewer barriers. 41% of men experience 1 to 5 barriers, compared to 39% of women. Men (25%) are more likely to live barrier-free lives than women (21%).

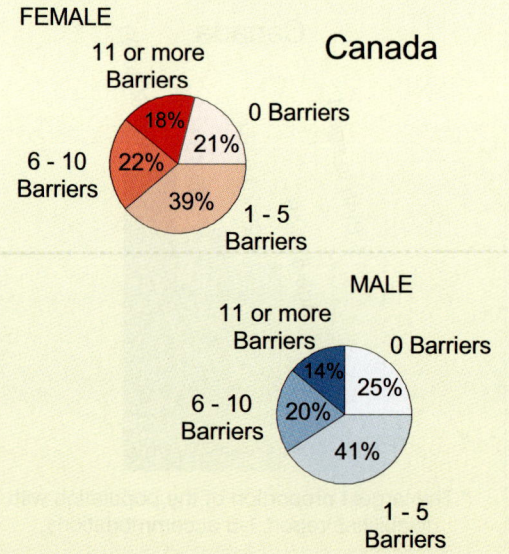

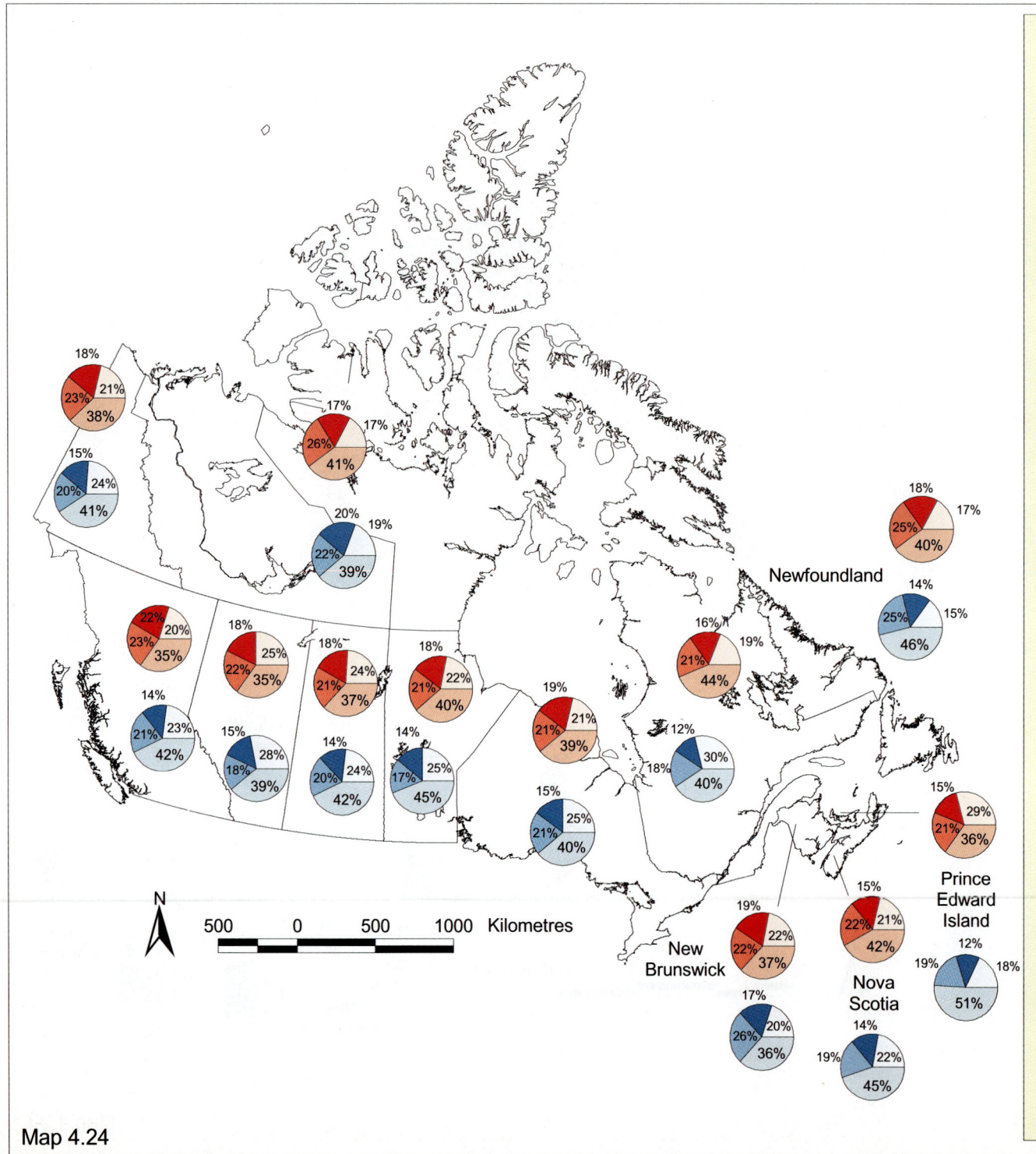

Canada

FEMALE
- 11 or more Barriers: 18%
- 6 - 10 Barriers: 22%
- 1 - 5 Barriers: 39%
- 0 Barriers: 21%

MALE
- 11 or more Barriers: 14%
- 6 - 10 Barriers: 20%
- 1 - 5 Barriers: 41%
- 0 Barriers: 25%

Map 4.24

IV. THE GEOGRAPHY OF DISABILITY   77

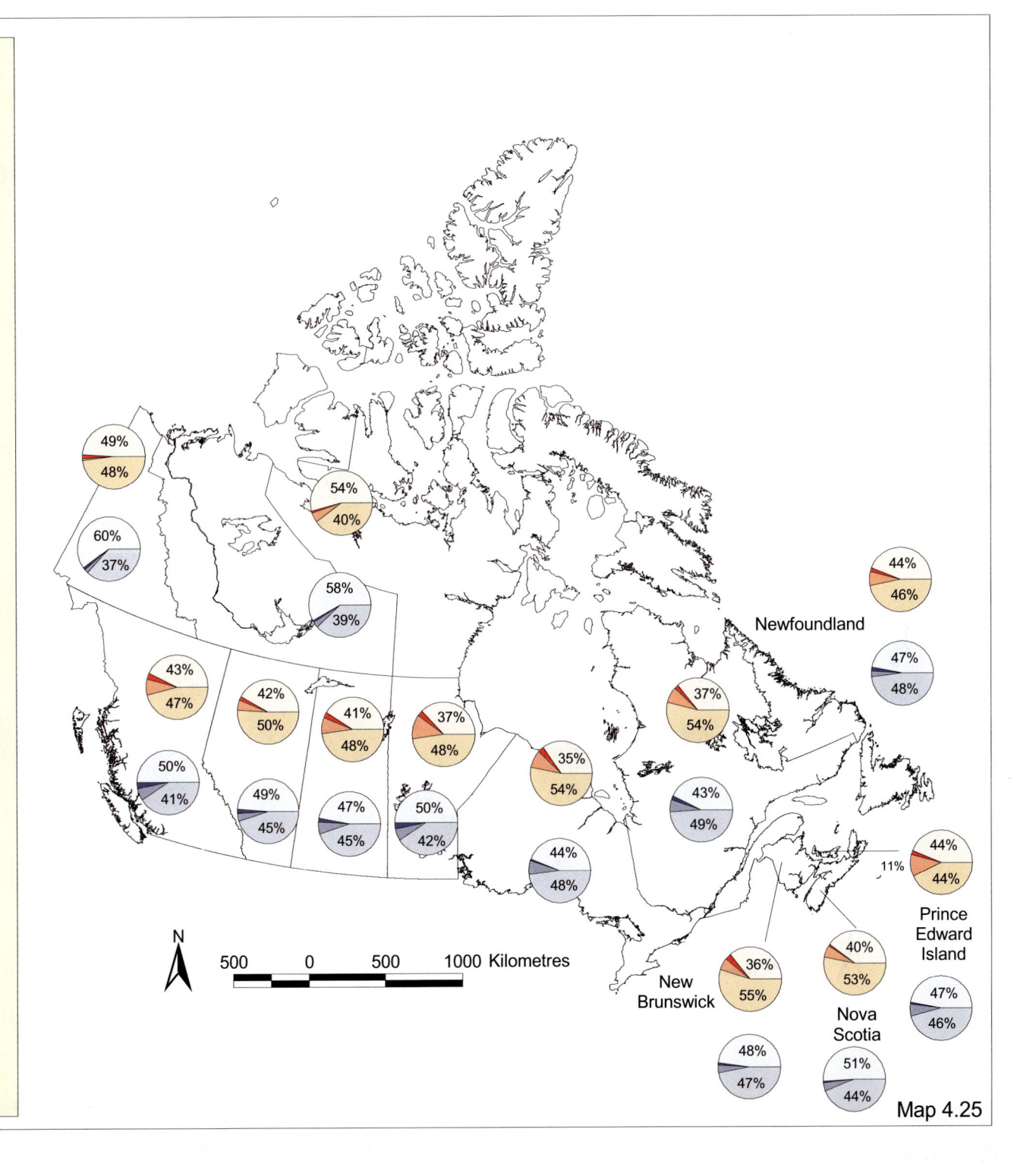

Number of Accommodations Received by Ages 15 and Older with Disabilities Residing in Households by Gender, Provinces and Territories

1991 Health and Activity Limitation Survey (HALS)

Women with disabilities are more likely than men to be receiving accommodations. Only 38% of women compared to 46% of men received no accommodations at all. Just over 6 out of every 10 women (62.5%) with disabilities have received at least one accommodation while only 54% of men have received at least one accommodation.

FEMALE
- 0 Accommodations: 37.6%
- 1 - 5 Accommodations: 51.7%
- 6 - 10: 8.2%
- 11 or more: 2.6%

Canada

MALE
- 0 Accommodations: 46.0%
- 1 - 5 Accommodations: 46.2%
- 6 - 10: 6.0%
- 11 or more: 1.8%

Map 4.25

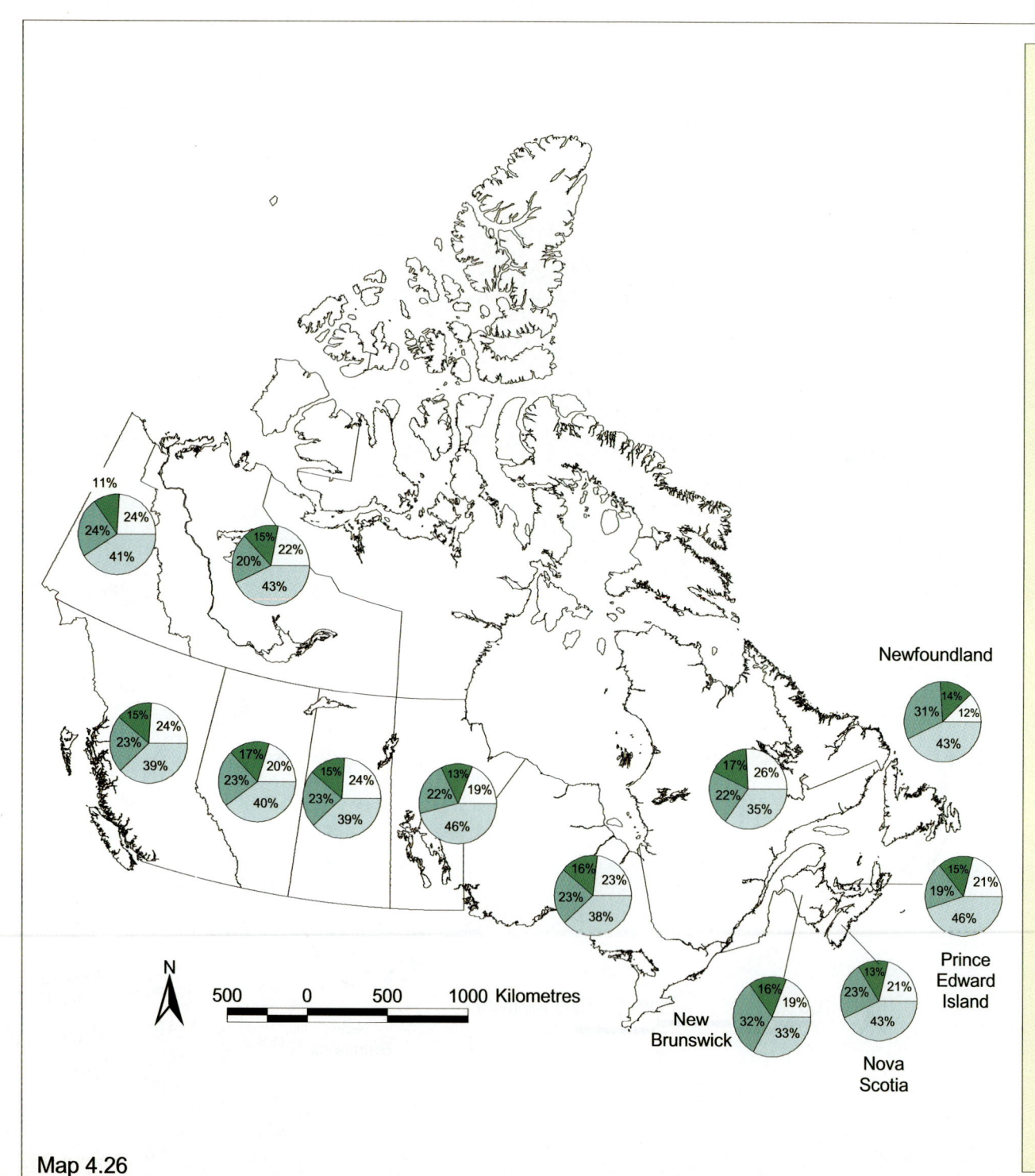

ATLAS OF LITERACY AND DISABILITY

Number of Barriers Encountered for Ages 15 and Older with Disabilities Residing in Households who are in the Labour Force, Provinces and Territories

1991 Health and Activity Limitation Survey (HALS)

Almost one quarter of adults (22.8%) who are in the labour force (either employed or looking for work) reported experiencing no barriers in their everyday activities. The remaining reported some barriers with the majority (38.5%) reporting 1 to 5 barriers. This pattern is similar across the provinces and both territories.

Canada

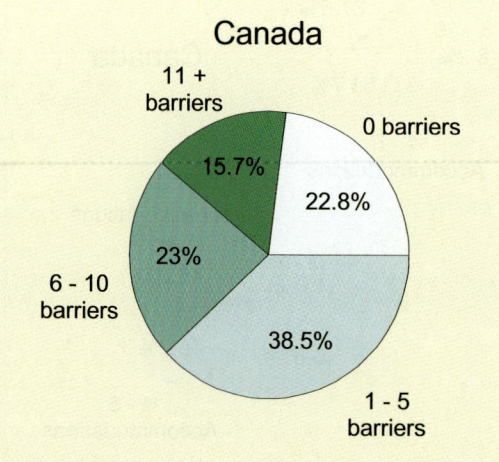

- 11 + barriers: 15.7%
- 0 barriers: 22.8%
- 6 - 10 barriers: 23%
- 1 - 5 barriers: 38.5%

Yukon: 11%, 24%, 24%, 41%
Northwest Territories: 15%, 22%, 20%, 43%
British Columbia: 15%, 24%, 23%, 39%
Alberta: 17%, 20%, 23%, 40%
Saskatchewan: 15%, 24%, 23%, 39%
Manitoba: 13%, 19%, 22%, 46%
Ontario: 16%, 23%, 23%, 38%
Quebec: 17%, 26%, 22%, 35%
Newfoundland: 14%, 12%, 31%, 43%
New Brunswick: 16%, 19%, 32%, 33%
Nova Scotia: 13%, 21%, 23%, 43%
Prince Edward Island: 15%, 21%, 19%, 46%

Map 4.26

IV. THE GEOGRAPHY OF DISABILITY | 79

Number of Accommodations Received for Ages 15 and Older with Disabilities who are in the Labour Force, Provinces and Territories

1991 Health and Activity Limitation Survey (HALS)

The majority of people with disabilities in Canada who are in the labour force (either employed or looking for work) report that they do not receive any accommodations (54.3%). Almost half of adults (45.7%) reported receiving at least one accommodation with the majority (41%) reporting between 1 and 5 accommodations. This pattern s similar across the provinces and both territories.

Canada

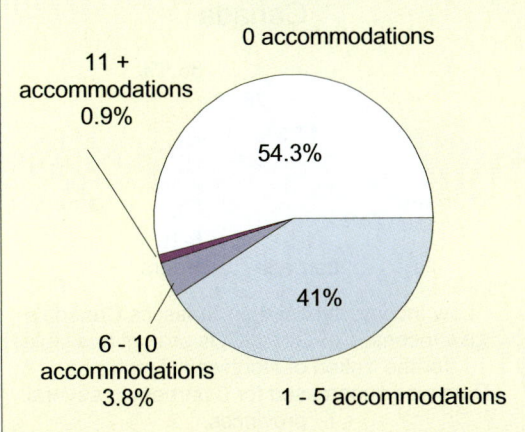

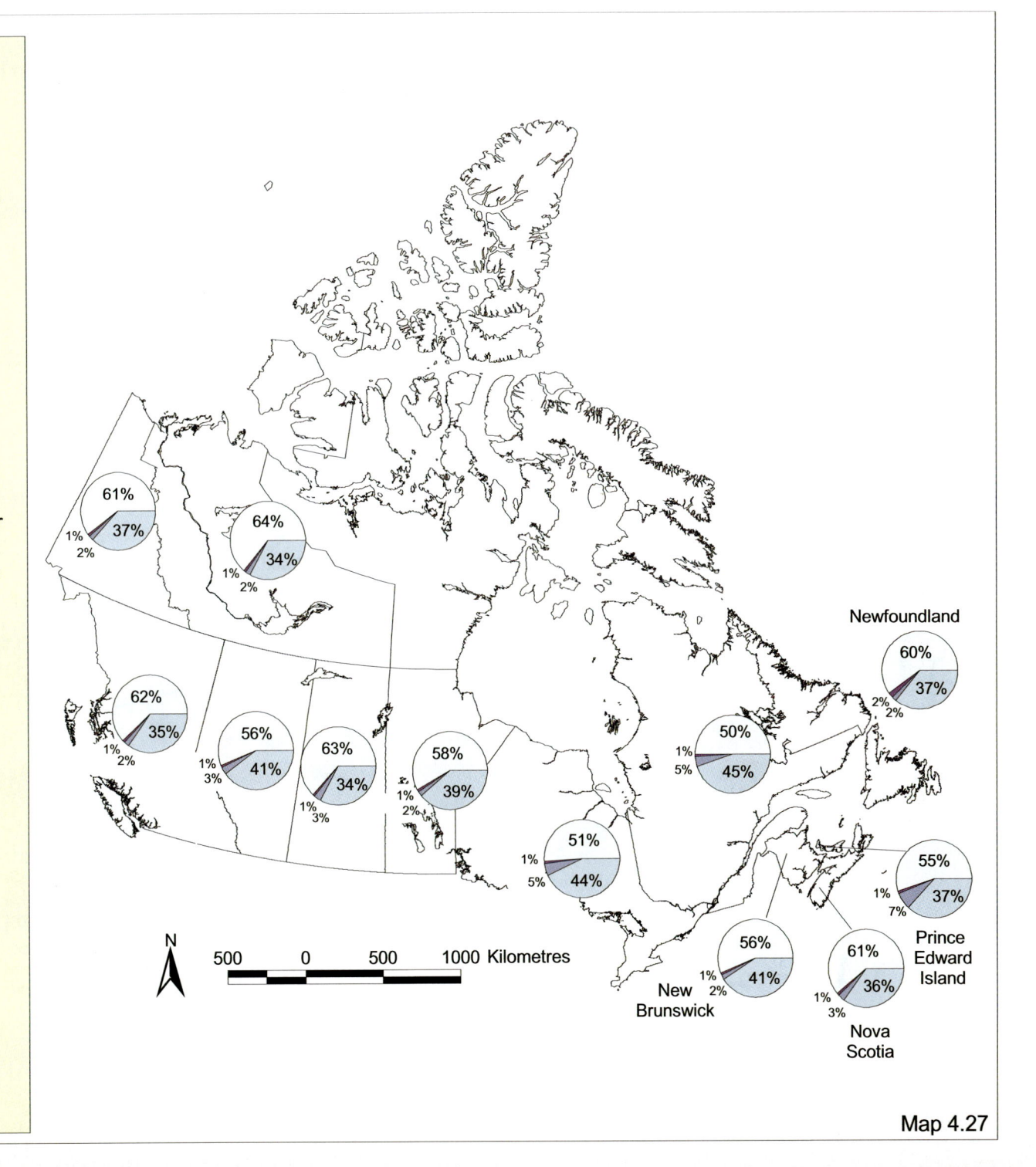

- 0 accommodations: 54.3%
- 1 - 5 accommodations: 41%
- 6 - 10 accommodations: 3.8%
- 11 + accommodations: 0.9%

Map values by province/territory:

- Yukon: 61%, 37%, 1%, 2%
- Northwest Territories: 64%, 34%, 1%, 2%
- British Columbia: 62%, 35%, 1%, 2%
- Alberta: 56%, 41%, 1%, 3%
- Saskatchewan: 63%, 34%, 1%, 3%
- Manitoba: 58%, 39%, 1%, 2%
- Ontario: 51%, 44%, 1%, 5%
- Quebec: 50%, 45%, 1%, 5%
- Newfoundland: 60%, 37%, 2%, 2%
- New Brunswick: 56%, 41%, 1%, 2%
- Nova Scotia: 61%, 36%, 1%, 3%
- Prince Edward Island: 55%, 37%, 1%, 7%

Map 4.27

ATLAS OF LITERACY AND DISABILITY

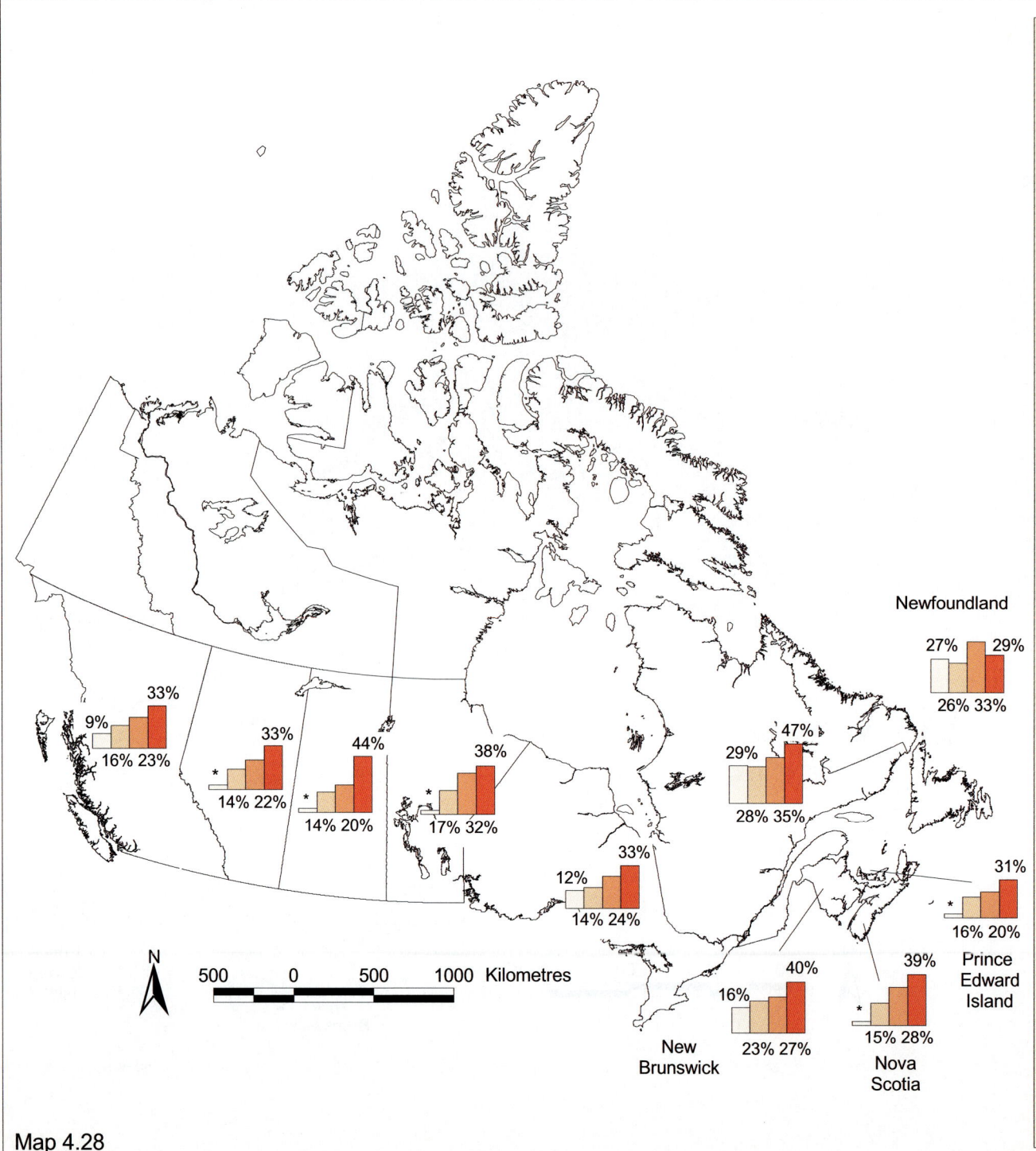

Number of Barriers Encountered for Ages 15 and Older with Disabilities Residing in Households whose Family Incomes are Low*, Provinces

1991 Health and Activity Limitation Survey (HALS)

One out of five adults with a disability is a member of a family whose income in 1990 was classified as low*. Just over one third (36.5%) of adults who experienced 11 or more barriers in their everyday activities were members of low income families. This map shows that adults with disabilities who are members of low income families are more likely to face barriers than those who are not members of low income families.

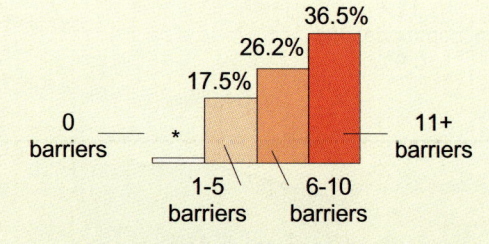

Canada

Canada bar chart:
- 0 barriers: *
- 1-5 barriers: 17.5%
- 6-10 barriers: 26.2%
- 11+ barriers: 36.5%

Provincial data (0, 1-5, 6-10, 11+ barriers):
- British Columbia: 9%, 16%, 23%, 33%
- Alberta: *, 14%, 22%, 33%
- Saskatchewan: *, 14%, 20%, 44%
- Manitoba: *, 17%, 32%, 38%
- Ontario: 29%, 28%, 35%, 47%
- Quebec: 12%, 14%, 24%, 33%
- Newfoundland: 27%, 26%, 33%, 29%
- Prince Edward Island: *, 16%, 20%, 31%
- Nova Scotia: *, 15%, 28%, 39%
- New Brunswick: 16%, 23%, 27%, 40%

*Low Income is based on Statistics Canada's Low Income Cut-Off. LICOs are not available for the Yukon or Northwest Territories. Data was suppressed for 0 barriers in several provinces.

Map 4.28

IV. THE GEOGRAPHY OF DISABILITY | 81

Number of Accommodations Received for Ages 15 and Older with Disabilities Residing in Housholds whose Family Incomes are Low*, Provinces

1991 Health and Activity Limitation Survey (HALS)

One out of five adults with a disability is a member of a family whose income in 1990 was classified as low*. Among adults with disabilities who reported receiving 6 or more accommodations, 28.7% were members of a low income family. This map shows that adults who are members of low income families are slightly more likely to have received accommodations to remove barriers.

Canada

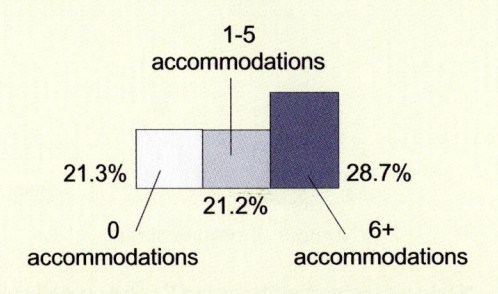

- 0 accommodations: 21.3%
- 1-5 accommodations: 21.2%
- 6+ accommodations: 28.7%

*Low income is based on Statistics Canada's Low Income Cut-Off. LICOs are not available for the Yukon or Northwest Territories.

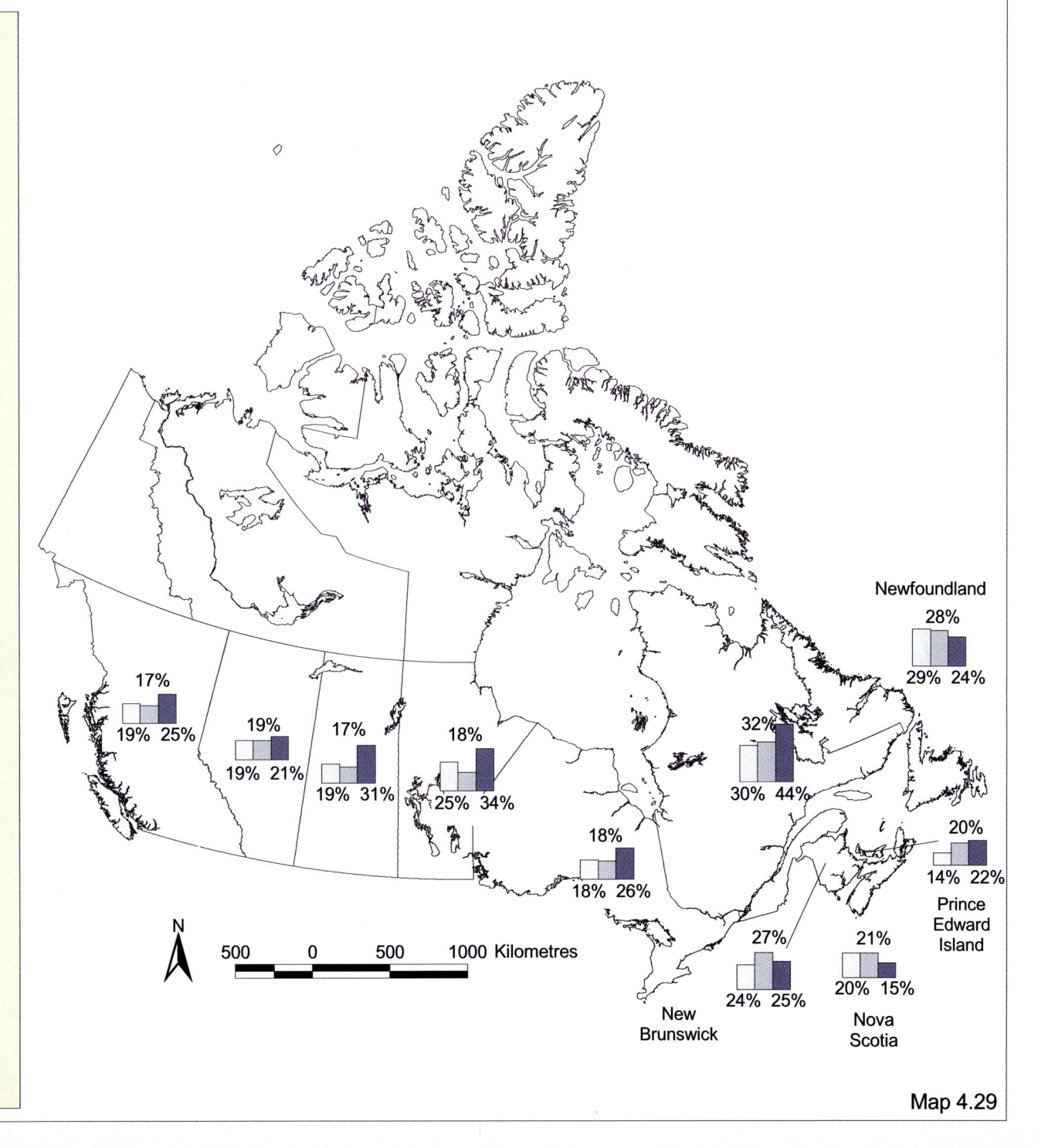

Newfoundland: 28% / 29% / 24%
17% / 19% / 25%
19% / 19% / 21%
17% / 19% / 31%
18% / 25% / 34%
32% / 30% / 44%
20% / 14% / 22% — Prince Edward Island
18% / 18% / 26%
27% / 24% / 25% — New Brunswick
21% / 20% / 15% — Nova Scotia

Map 4.29

ATLAS OF LITERACY AND DISABILITY

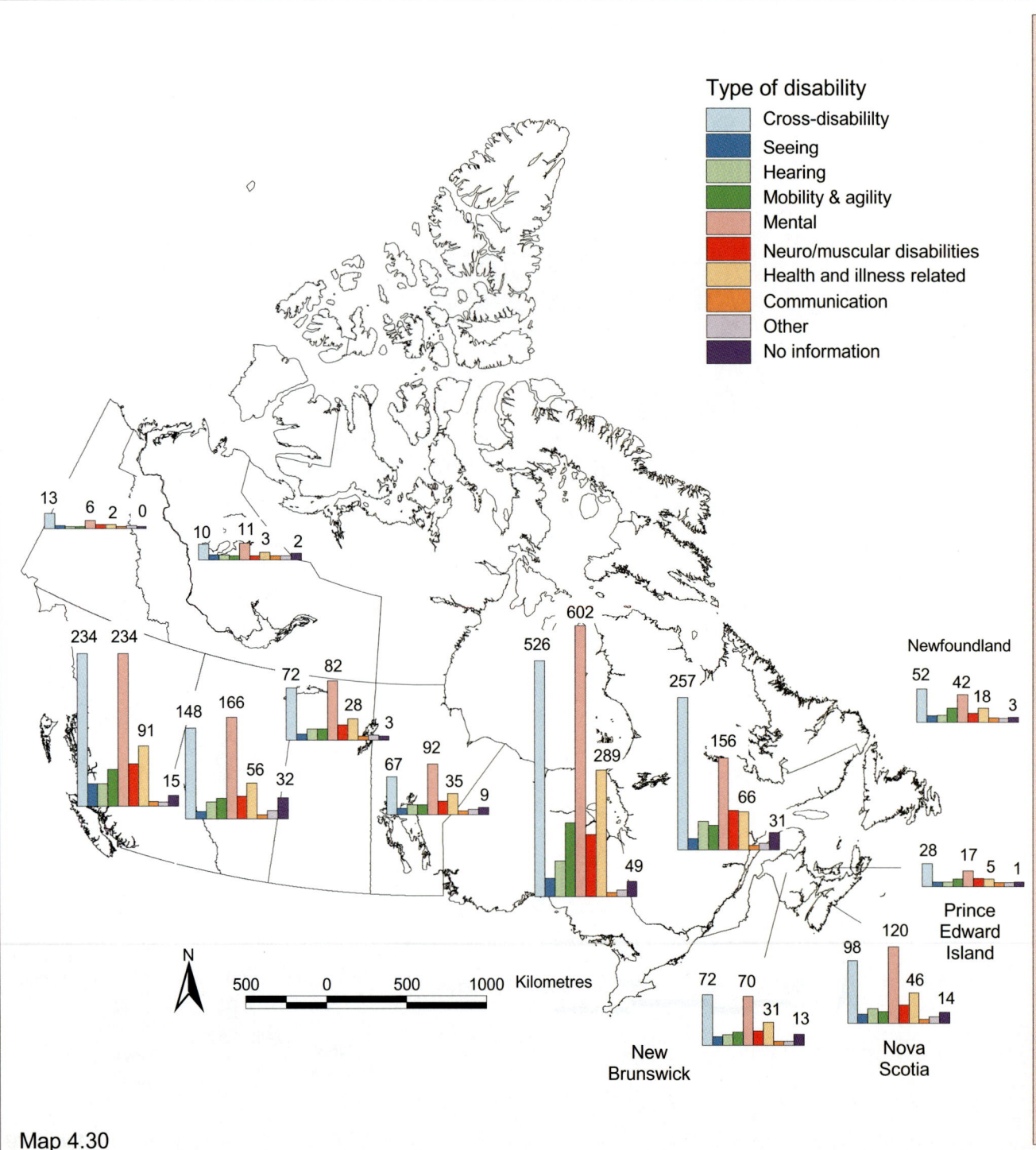

Number of Disability Organizations Categorized by Primary Type of Disability Served

Canadian Abilities Foundation

There are a significant number of disability organizations throughout the country that serve a wide array of types of disability. The two most common types of disability organizations are cross-disability and those that are related to mental disabilities, followed by organizations that are health and illness related.

Type of disability
- Cross-disability
- Seeing
- Hearing
- Mobility & agility
- Mental
- Neuro/muscular disabilities
- Health and illness related
- Communication
- Other
- No information

Canada

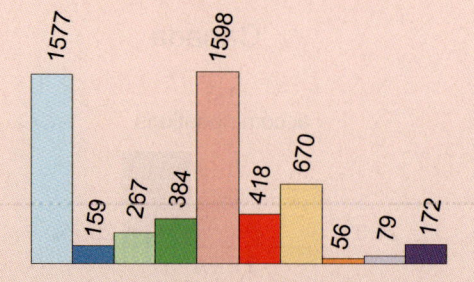

Totals: 1577, 159, 267, 384, 1598, 418, 670, 56, 79, 172

Number of organizations

*Data was obtained from the Canadian Abilities Foundation organization database. The research team created and placed the organizations into the categories listed on this map.

Map 4.30

Regional values shown on map:

- Yukon area: 13, 6, 2, 0
- Northwest Territories area: 10, 11, 3, 2
- British Columbia: 234, 234, 91, — , 15 (with bars 148, 166, 56, 32)
- Alberta: 72, 82, 28, 3
- Saskatchewan/Manitoba: 67, 92, 35, 9
- Ontario: 526, 602, 289, 49
- Quebec: 257, 156, 66, 31
- Newfoundland: 52, 42, 18, 3
- New Brunswick: 72, 70, 31, 13
- Nova Scotia: 98, 120, 46, 14
- Prince Edward Island: 28, 17, 5, 1

V. Literacy and Disability at the Crossroads

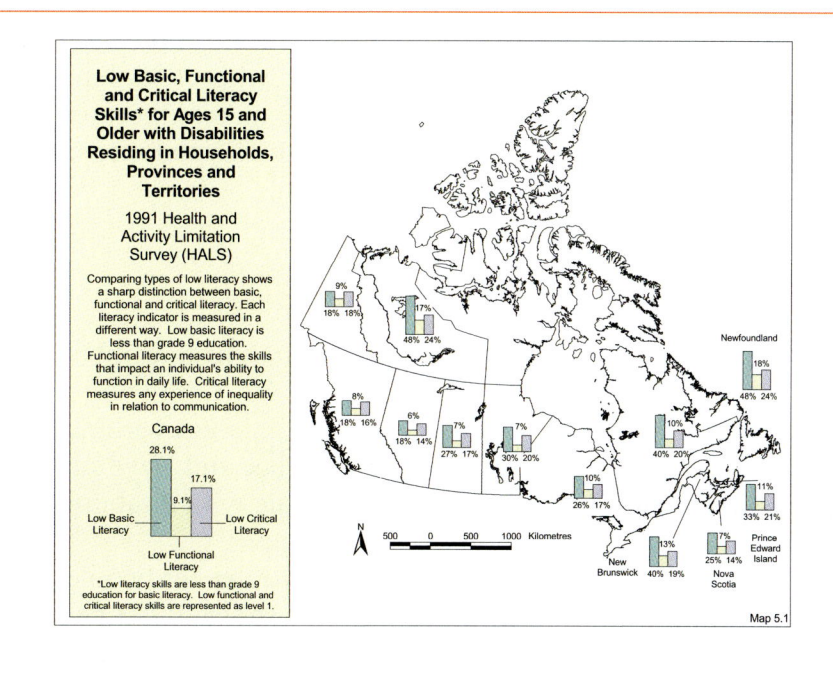

Low Basic, Functional and Critical Literacy Skills* for Ages 15 and Older with Disabilities Residing in Households, Provinces and Territories

1991 Health and Activity Limitation Survey (HALS)

Comparing types of low literacy shows a sharp distinction between basic, functional and critical literacy. Each literacy indicator is measured in a different way. Low basic literacy is less than grade 9 education. Functional literacy measures the skills that impact an individual's ability to function in daily life. Critical literacy measures any experience of inequality in relation to communication.

Canada
- Low Basic Literacy: 28.1%
- Low Functional Literacy: 9.1%
- Low Critical Literacy: 17.1%

*Low literacy skills are less than grade 9 education for basic literacy. Low functional and critical literacy skills are represented as level 1.

Map 5.1

The maps in this chapter explore the intersection of literacy and disability, drawing primarily from HALS data, but also in some instances using IALS. Differing perspectives of both literacy and disability are highlighted through the application of functional and critical literacy proxies, and the Barriers and Accommodations Index. The HALS functional and critical proxies are similar to the IALS functional and critical literacy proxies, but they are not directly comparable. They measure the same ideas, but use different questions from different surveys to do so. Like the IALS proxies, they have not been tested for reliability or validity, and should be considered exploratory.

Map 5.1, drawn from HALS, compares basic, functional and critical literacy rates for the population with disabilities. It shows differences in the rates of these three interpretations of literacy. Twenty-eight percent of Canadians with disabilities have low basic literacy, while 17% have low critical literacy. The percentage with low functional literacy is 9%. These differences were expected, because each of these indicators measures something different. The first measures level of education, the second measures functionality in daily life, and the third equality in communication and social participation.

BASIC LITERACY AND DISABILITY

Map 5.2 moves the yardstick in data analysis to combine the HALS and Census datasets, allowing for greater geographical detail than HALS alone provides. Grade nine completion rates are shown at the Census subdivision level, so we can see differences in literacy rates within provinces and territories. The map shows that large sections in the Northwest Territories, Quebec and Newfoundland and Labrador have very high proportions (between 46 and 75%) of the population of people with disabilities who have not gone to high school.

Map 5.3 and 5.4 compare basic literacy rates for people with disabilities in the NPHS and HALS at the level of provinces and territories. Both surveys showed that people with disabilities were considerably less likely than people without disabilities to be literate, according to measures of basic literacy. According to HALS, people with disabilities were nearly three times as likely to have less than a grade nine education (28.1%) compared to other Canadians (10.8%). NPHS has similar findings. Both surveys show that people in the western provinces were more likely to have gone on to high school than those in the eastern provinces, whether or not they were people with disabilities.

FUNCTIONAL LITERACY AND DISABILITY

This section relies primarily on data from HALS to explore the functional literacy of people with disabilities. However, a map drawn from IALS is also included, as it allows a comparison with the population without disabilities. IALS findings for functional literacy in the population with disabilities, shown in Map 5.5, were very different from HALS. IALS found much higher proportions of the population with disabilities at the lowest level of functional literacy (29%), and much lower proportions at the highest level (32%) compared to HALS. In contrast, the

HALS proxy shown in Map 5.6 revealed that only about 1 in 10 adults with disabilities has functional literacy skills at the lowest level in most regions of Canada (9.1%). Around a third of the population with disabilities (32.7%) is at the middle level, and more than half score at the highest level of functional literacy (58.2%). These findings suggest that nearly half of Canadians with disabilities face barriers related to functional literacy.

HALS data shows that the age at which a person acquired his or her disability is correlated to his or her level of functional literacy. Map 5.7 shows that a large proportion of people with disabilities who have low functional literacy skills (one-quarter each) became disabled before age 5. Among those with medium and high levels of functional literacy, most acquired their disability during the working years.

Functional Literacy, Disability and Socio-Economic Status
As with the overall population, functional literacy is related to the socio-economic opportunities of people with disabilities. Adults with disabilities are more likely to have high levels of functional literacy when they are in the labour force than when they are not. As Map 5.8 shows, according to HALS, 63% of working-age Canadian adults with disabilities who are in the labour force have functional literacy skills at the highest level. There is also a clear link between poverty, low literacy skills and disability. People with disabilities who have low and medium literacy skills are more likely to be living in a low-income household than those with high functional literacy (Map 5.9). People with disabilities are considerably less likely to be living in poverty if they have high functional literacy skills (62% compared to 50%).

Functional Literacy, Disability and the Social Determinants of Disadvantage
When the Barriers and Accommodation Index is cross-tabulated with our functional literacy proxy, a relationship between disability-related barriers and accommodations and functional literacy level emerges, as seen in Maps 5.10 and 5.11. The higher the level of functional literacy, the fewer the barriers and accommodations experienced. Conversely, the lower the level of functional literacy, the higher the numbers of disability-related barriers and accommodations experienced. A comparison of these two maps reveals that a sizeable proportion of people at all levels of literacy encounter high numbers of non-accommodated barriers. This disparity is particularly pronounced for people at low levels of literacy who encounter more than 11 barriers. The more disability-related barriers a person experiences, whether or not they are accommodated, the lower their functional literacy is likely to be. This suggests that there is a relationship between disability-related disadvantage and literacy-related disadvantage. When a person is marginalized in the one sphere, they are more likely to be marginalized in the other.

Social determinants, such as barriers and accommodations, in relation to functional literacy have an impact on the economic opportunities of people with disabilities. About 66% of adults with disabilities who are in the labour force and have low functional literacy skills face more than 6 barriers in their everyday activities (Map 5.12). Yet only about 7% of this group receive accommodations (Map 5.13), suggesting that even though they are labour force participants, this group experiences significant disability-related disadvantage as well as literacy-related disadvantage. Map 5.14 shows that of the adults with disabilities who face 6 or more barriers, 17.4% live in low-income households and have low functional literacy skills. Of those who encounter 1 to 5 barriers, only 9% are in this low-income, low-literacy group. The pattern of decreasing numbers of people facing smaller numbers of barriers is consistent across the nation. Map 5.15 shows the corresponding accommodations. Of the people with disabilities who receive 6 or more accommodations, one out of five have both low income and low functional literacy skills. Of those who received 1 to 5 accommodations, less than 15% were in this group. The pattern of decreasing percentages of adults corresponding to smaller numbers of accommodations is seen in the eastern and western provinces but not the central provinces.

Critical literacy: Literate Citizenship for People with Disabilities

Maps 5.16 and 5.17 reveal very different patterns of critical literacy in IALS compared to HALS. In IALS, the highest proportion of people with disabilities experience medium levels of critical literacy (43.6%), followed by high levels (29.8%) and low levels (26.5%). In contrast, according to HALS, almost 60% of adult Canadians with disabilities report experiencing high critical literacy. Another 17% experience low critical literacy and only about 24% have moderate literacy. These differences are likely because these surveys are measuring different things, and have a different target population.

Critical literacy levels by earliest age of onset of disability, 1991 HALS

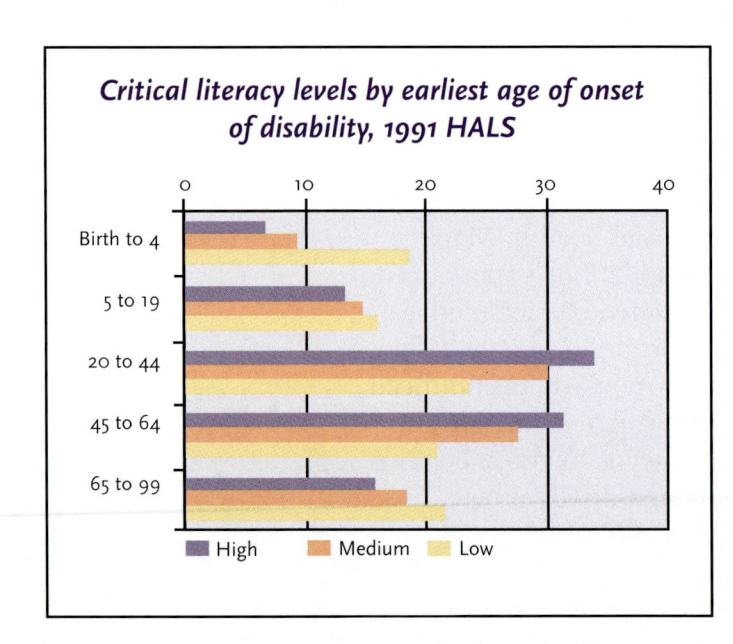

Map 5.18 suggests that the age of onset of disability does not make a large difference in terms of low critical literacy. Of note is the fact that the map does not show a comparison to people with medium and high levels of literacy. As the chart shows, those who acquired a disability during childhood, up to age 19, and in their senior years tend to have lower levels of literacy than those who became disabled as working-age adults.

Critical Literacy, Disability and Socio-Economic Status

The critical literacy level of adults with disabilities has a bearing on their socio-economic status. Those who experience higher levels of critical literacy are also more likely to be in the labour force, and to have incomes above the low-income cutoff (Map 5.20). As Map 5.19 shows, according to HALS, only 13% of adults aged 15 to 64 found to have low critical literacy were active labour force participants – either employed or unemployed – at the time of the survey. This is compared to 63% of the same group who were classified as having high critical literacy.

Although a majority of Canadians with disabilities were found to have high critical literacy, whether or not they were poor, those with low incomes were more likely to have low and medium levels of literacy than those who were not poor. Likewise, a higher proportion of financially comfortable families had high critical literacy.

Critical Literacy, Disability and the Social Determinants of Disadvantage
This section applies a human rights perspective of disability with a critical perspective of literacy. In effect, it looks at the social determinants of both literacy and disability, and the relationship between the two. People who experience high critical literacy are the most likely not to encounter disability-related barriers and receive accommodations. Those who experience low critical literacy are the most likely to experience high numbers of barriers and accommodations. To rephrase this, when people with disabilities experience disability-related barriers, they are more likely to experience barriers to equitable communication and participation in social discourse. An alarming 32% of people with disabilities who have low levels of critical literacy face more than 11 barriers in their daily lives (map 5.21). This indicates that these people are simply not participating in social discourse and the public sphere and are likely isolated and disenfranchised. The proportion of people receiving more than 6 accommodations increases as literacy levels get lower (Map 5.22). However, there remains a large gap for this population, where many people with low critical literacy encounter more barriers than those for which they receive accommodations. Only 19% of those with the lowest level of critical literacy received more than six accommodations.

Maps 5.23 and 5.24 show barriers and accommodations for people with disabilities who have low critical literacy and are in the labour force. The lower the level of critical literacy, the greater the likelihood that the labour force participant will experience a higher number of disability-related barriers. Among labour force participants, close to 60% of those experiencing low critical literacy say they face more than 6 disability-related barriers. Only 6.9% of this group report zero disability-related barriers, a much lower proportion than in the overall population with disabilities.

Maps 5.25 and 5.26 show the numbers of barriers and accommodations encountered by people with disabilities who have low critical literacy and also have low incomes. Map 5.25 shows a relationship among income, critical literacy and barriers that people face. Of the adults with disabilities facing 6 or more barriers in their daily lives, 40% reside in households with low income and have low critical literacy. Sixteen percent of people with between 1 and 5 barriers have low income and low critical literacy. Map 5.26 shows the corresponding relationship with accommodations. Of those people with disabilities who report receiving 1 to 5 accommodations, 34.6 % live in poverty and experience low critical literacy. These maps identify this population as a group experiencing critical levels of marginalization. They are living in poverty, and are restricted by high numbers of disability-related barriers that are not being accommodated. Further, they are isolated, and report diminished control over their lives and minimal participation in public discourse.

Finally, Maps 6.1, 6.2 and 6.3 return to the issue of geographic location of Canadians with disabilities today, post-2001, in the third millennium. The 2001 relative indices of barriers shows at all scales that Canadians with disabilities cannot find large number of contiguous areas where there are low barriers. In other words, areas of strong barriers abut areas of low barriers (Map 6.1). So, if one lives in an area of low barriers, the probability is very high that in your daily life you will need to go to areas of strong barriers. The same is true for accommodations (Map 6.2). However, if one was an optimist, one would hope that in areas where there are high numbers of barriers there would also be strong numbers of accommodations. This would alleviate the problem of the high degree of variation in the contiguous areas. Unfortunately, as Map 6.3 shows, this is not the case. In short, one may expect Canadians with disabilities to continue to face a type of geographic discrimination until such time as planning falls into line with the facts as we now understand them.

V. LITERACY AND DISABILITY AT THE CROSSROADS | 89

Low Basic, Functional and Critical Literacy Skills* for Ages 15 and Older with Disabilities Residing in Households, Provinces and Territories

1991 Health and Activity Limitation Survey (HALS)

Comparing types of low literacy shows a sharp distinction between basic, functional and critical literacy. Each literacy indicator is measured in a different way. Low basic literacy is less than grade 9 education. Functional literacy measures the skills that impact an individual's ability to function in daily life. Critical literacy measures any experience of inequality in relation to communication.

Canada

- Low Basic Literacy: 28.1%
- Low Functional Literacy: 9.1%
- Low Critical Literacy: 17.1%

*Low literacy skills are less than grade 9 education for basic literacy. Low functional and critical literacy skills are represented as level 1.

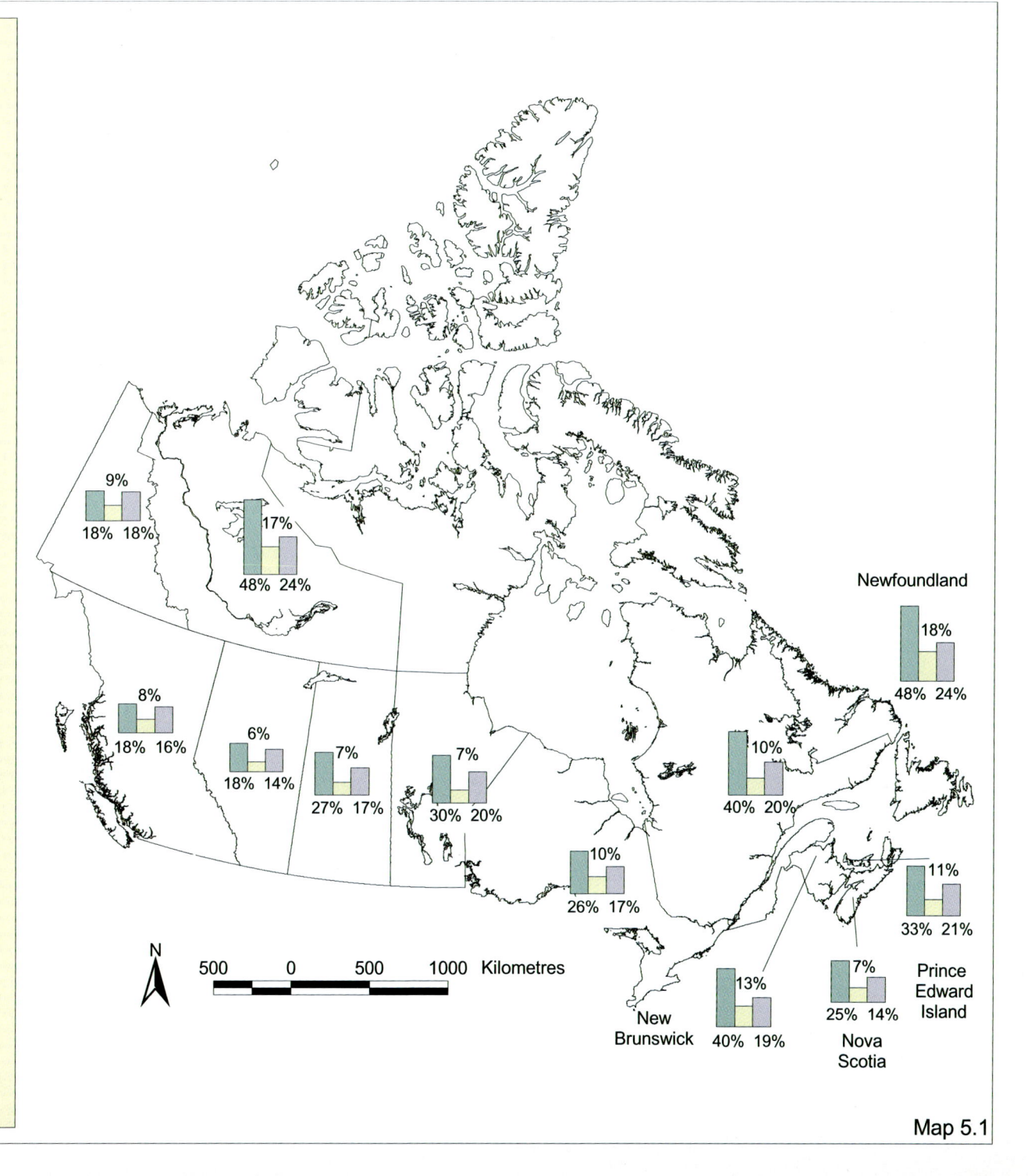

Yukon: 9% / 18% / 18%
NWT: 17% / 48% / 24%
British Columbia: 8% / 18% / 16%
Alberta: 6% / 18% / 14%
Saskatchewan: 7% / 27% / 17%
Manitoba: 7% / 30% / 20%
Ontario: 10% / 26% / 17%
Quebec: 10% / 40% / 20%
Newfoundland: 18% / 48% / 24%
New Brunswick: 13% / 40% / 19%
Nova Scotia: 7% / 25% / 14%
Prince Edward Island: 11% / 33% / 21%

Map 5.1

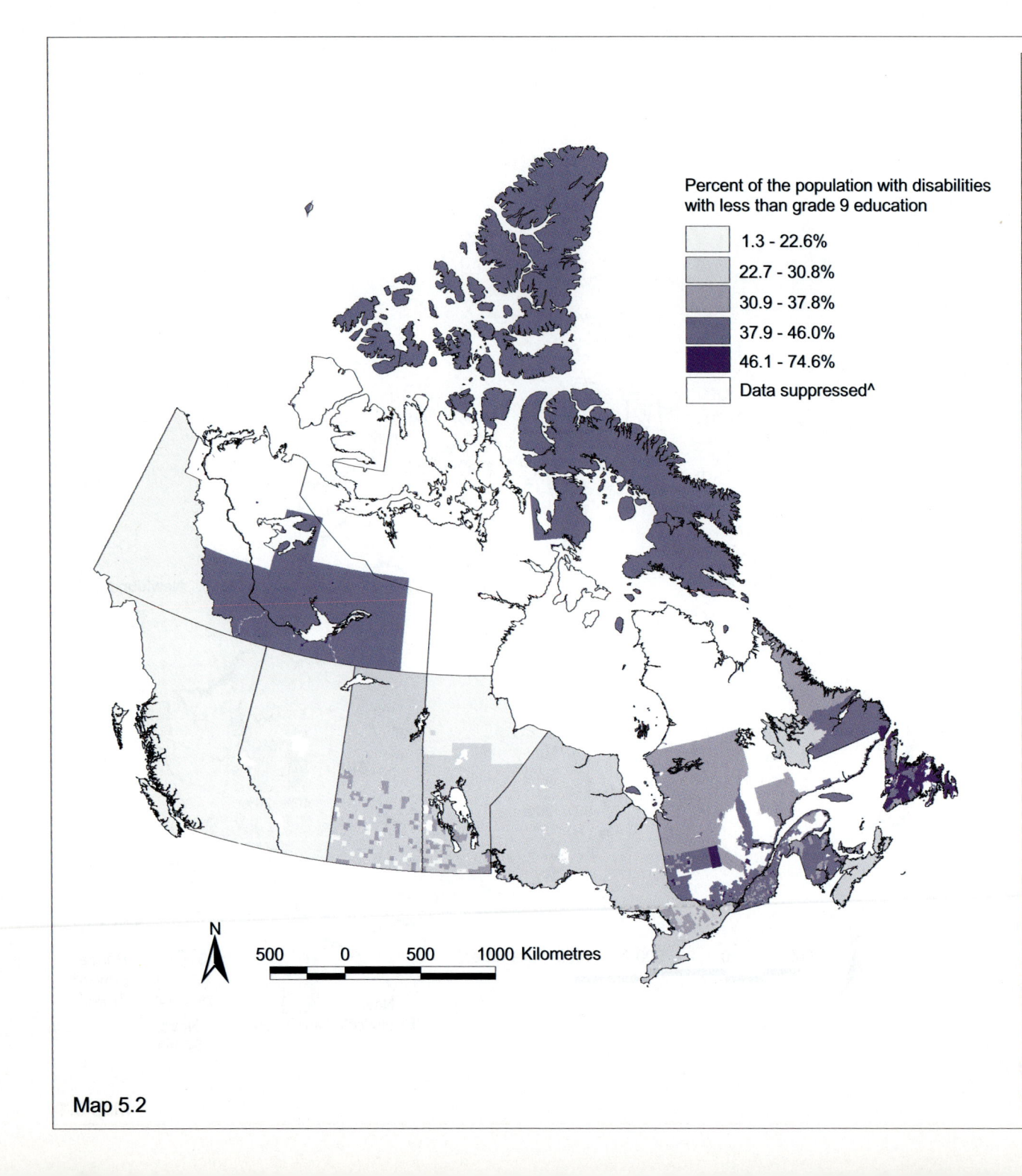

ATLAS OF LITERACY AND DISABILITY

Percent of the Population with Disabilities with Less than Grade 9 Education*, Census Subdivisions

1991 Health and Activity Limitation Survey (HALS)

The lightest colour shows areas where the educational level is highest, for example, the two Western provinces. As the areas become darker purple, they indicate that more people have not completed grade 9, an indicator of low basic literacy.

Canada -- 28.1%

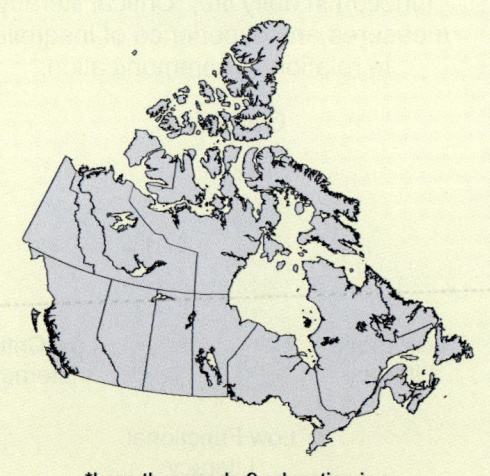

Percent of the population with disabilities with less than grade 9 education
- 1.3 - 22.6%
- 22.7 - 30.8%
- 30.9 - 37.8%
- 37.9 - 46.0%
- 46.1 - 74.6%
- Data suppressed^

*Less than grade 9 education is a crude measure of illiteracy.
^Data was suppressed when the CSD has a population less than 40 and for Indian Reserves, if the response rate was less than 25%.

Map 5.2

V. LITERACY AND DISABILITY AT THE CROSSROADS | 91

Percent of the Population Ages 16 and Older with Less than Grade 9 Education*, with and without Disabilities, Provinces

1996 National Population Health Survey (NPHS)

Adults with disabilities are less likely to have gone to school past grade 8 compared to adults without disabilities. Almost one quarter (23.8%) of people with disabilities have less than grade 9 education, compared to 11.3% of the population without disabilities. These data have not been adjusted to account for the different age structures of the two populations.

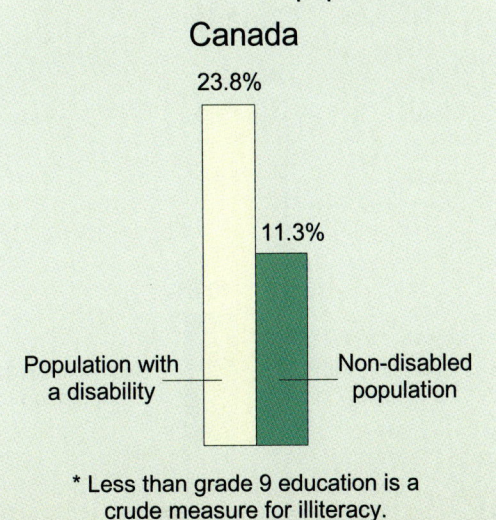

Canada

23.8% — Population with a disability
11.3% — Non-disabled population

* Less than grade 9 education is a crude measure for illiteracy.

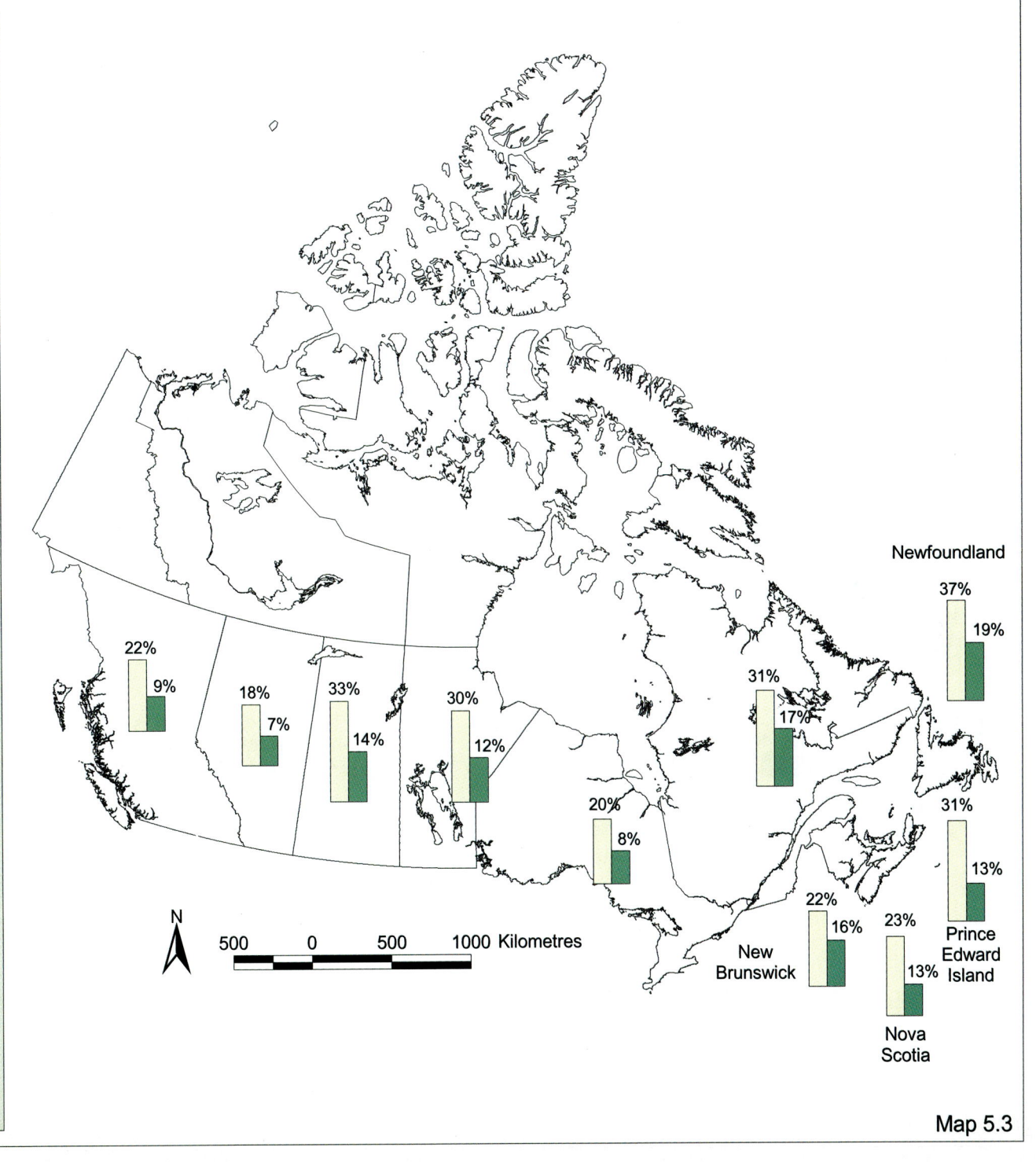

Provincial data (with disability / non-disabled):
- British Columbia: 22% / 9%
- Alberta: 18% / 7%
- Saskatchewan: 33% / 14%
- Manitoba: 30% / 12%
- Ontario: 20% / 8%
- Quebec: 31% / 17%
- Newfoundland: 37% / 19%
- New Brunswick: 22% / 16%
- Nova Scotia: 23% / 13%
- Prince Edward Island: 31% / 13%

Map 5.3

ATLAS OF LITERACY AND DISABILITY

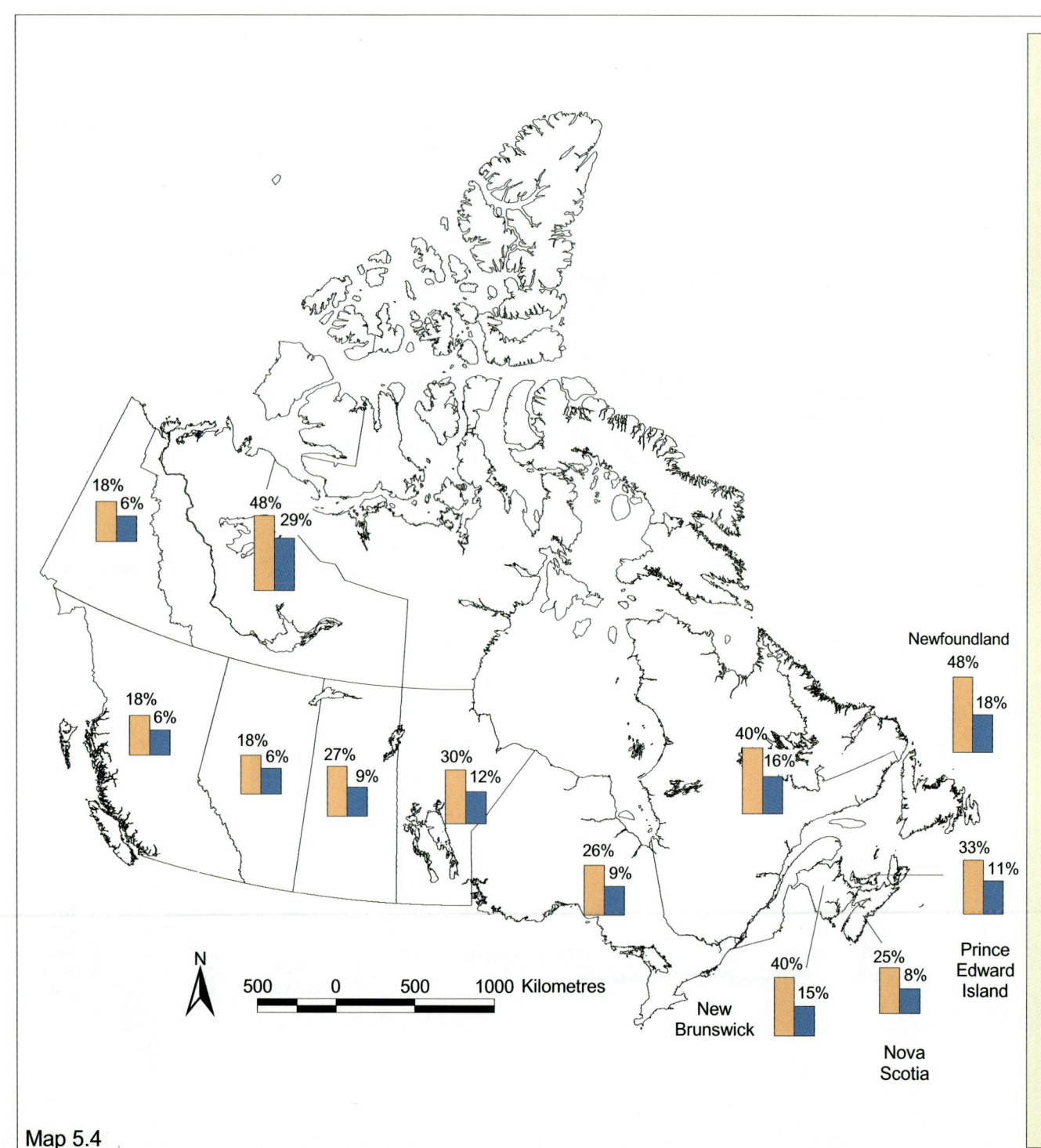

Percent of the Population Ages 15 and Older with Less than Grade 9 Education*, with and without Disabilities, Provinces and Territories

1991 Health and Activity Limitation Survey (HALS)

HALS data on basic literacy show a similar pattern to NPHS, although the numbers are somewhat different (Map 5.3). Regardless of what part of the country they live in, adults with disabilities were less likely to go to high school than adults without disabilities. They are nearly three times a likely to have less than a grade 9 education (28.1%) than other Canadian (10.8%).

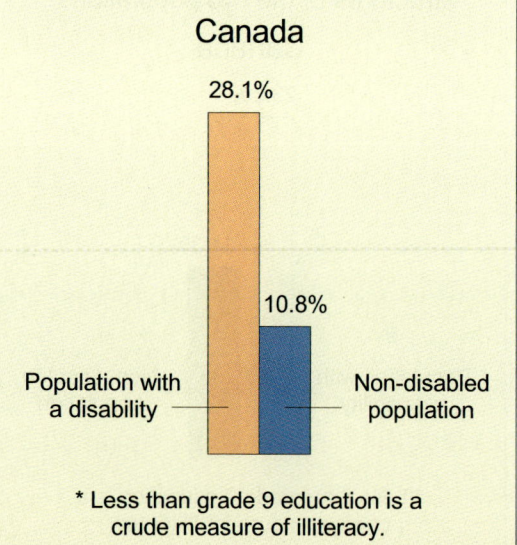

Canada: 28.1% (Population with a disability), 10.8% (Non-disabled population)

Yukon: 18% / 6%
Northwest Territories: 48% / 29%
British Columbia: 18% / 6%
Alberta: 18% / 6%
Saskatchewan: 27% / 9%
Manitoba: 30% / 12%
Ontario: 26% / 9%
Quebec: 40% / 16%
Newfoundland: 48% / 18%
New Brunswick: 40% / 15%
Nova Scotia: 25% / 8%
Prince Edward Island: 33% / 11%

* Less than grade 9 education is a crude measure of illiteracy.

Map 5.4

V. LITERACY AND DISABILITY AT THE CROSSROADS | 93

Functional Literacy* Levels for Ages 16 and Older with Disabilities, Provinces

1994 International Adult Literacy Survey (IALS)

Functional literacy is classified in 3 levels. Level 1 includes those who scored at the lowest end of the index that was created and level 3 were those who had the highest scores, suggesting more functional literacy. Most people (39.1%) fall into the middle range but there is wide variation across the country.

Canada

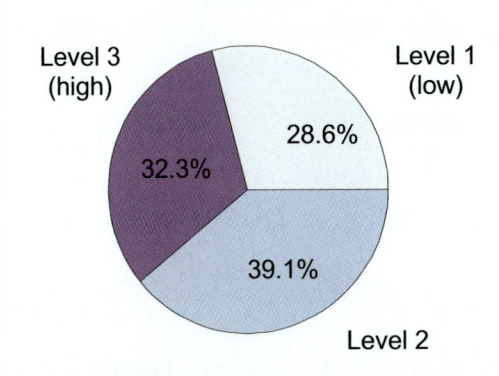

Level 3 (high): 32.3%
Level 1 (low): 28.6%
Level 2: 39.1%

*Based on an alternative proxy for functional literacy derived from IALS.

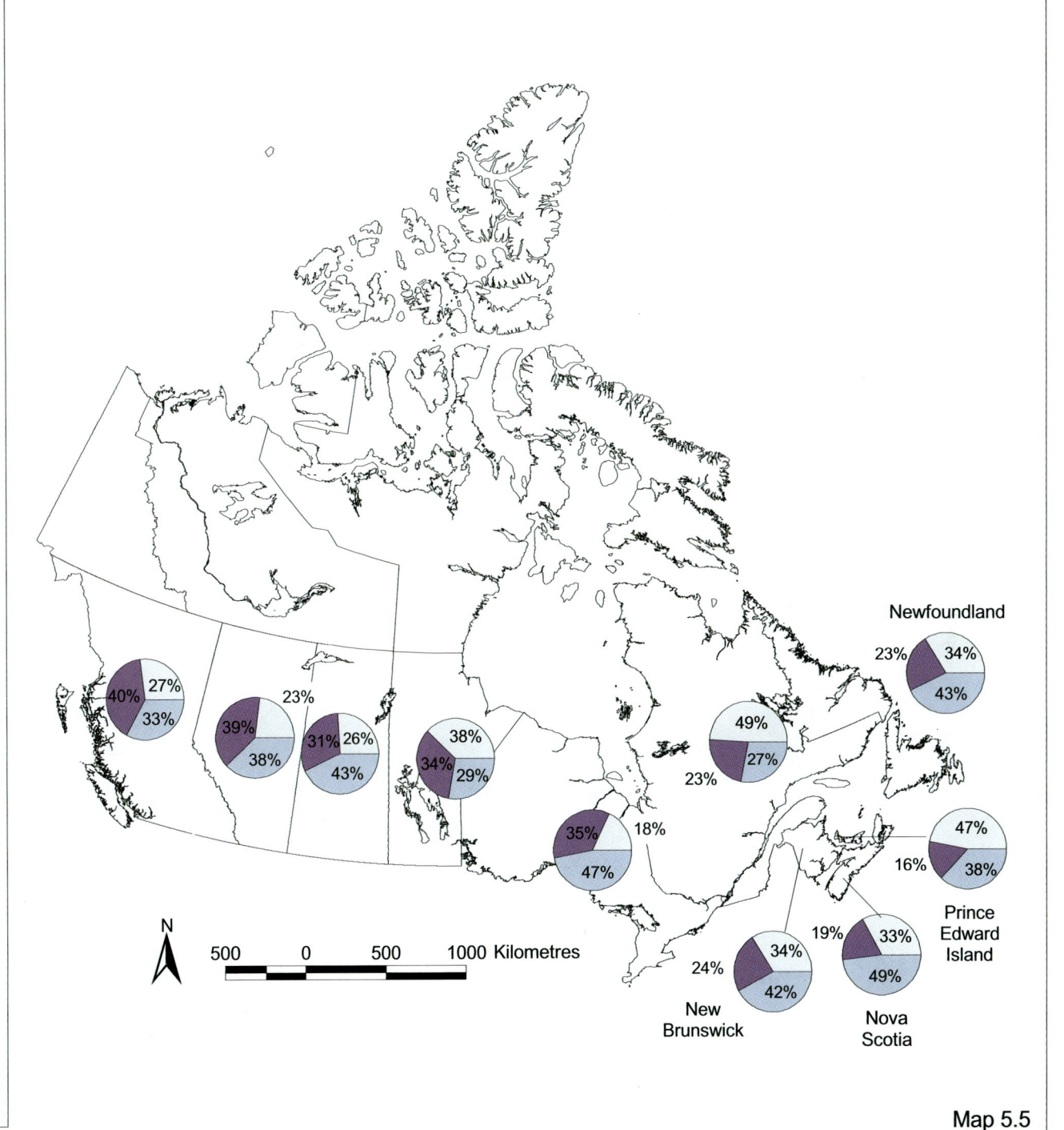

Provincial pie charts (Level 1 / Level 3 / Level 2):
- British Columbia: 27% / 40% / 33%
- Alberta: 23% / 39% / 38%
- Saskatchewan: 26% / 31% / 43%
- Manitoba: 38% / 34% / 29% (23% label)
- Ontario: 49% / 27% (23%)
- Quebec: 35% / 47% (18%)
- Newfoundland: 34% / 43% (23%)
- New Brunswick: 34% / 42% (24%)
- Nova Scotia: 33% / 49% (19%)
- Prince Edward Island: 47% / 38% (16%)

Map 5.5

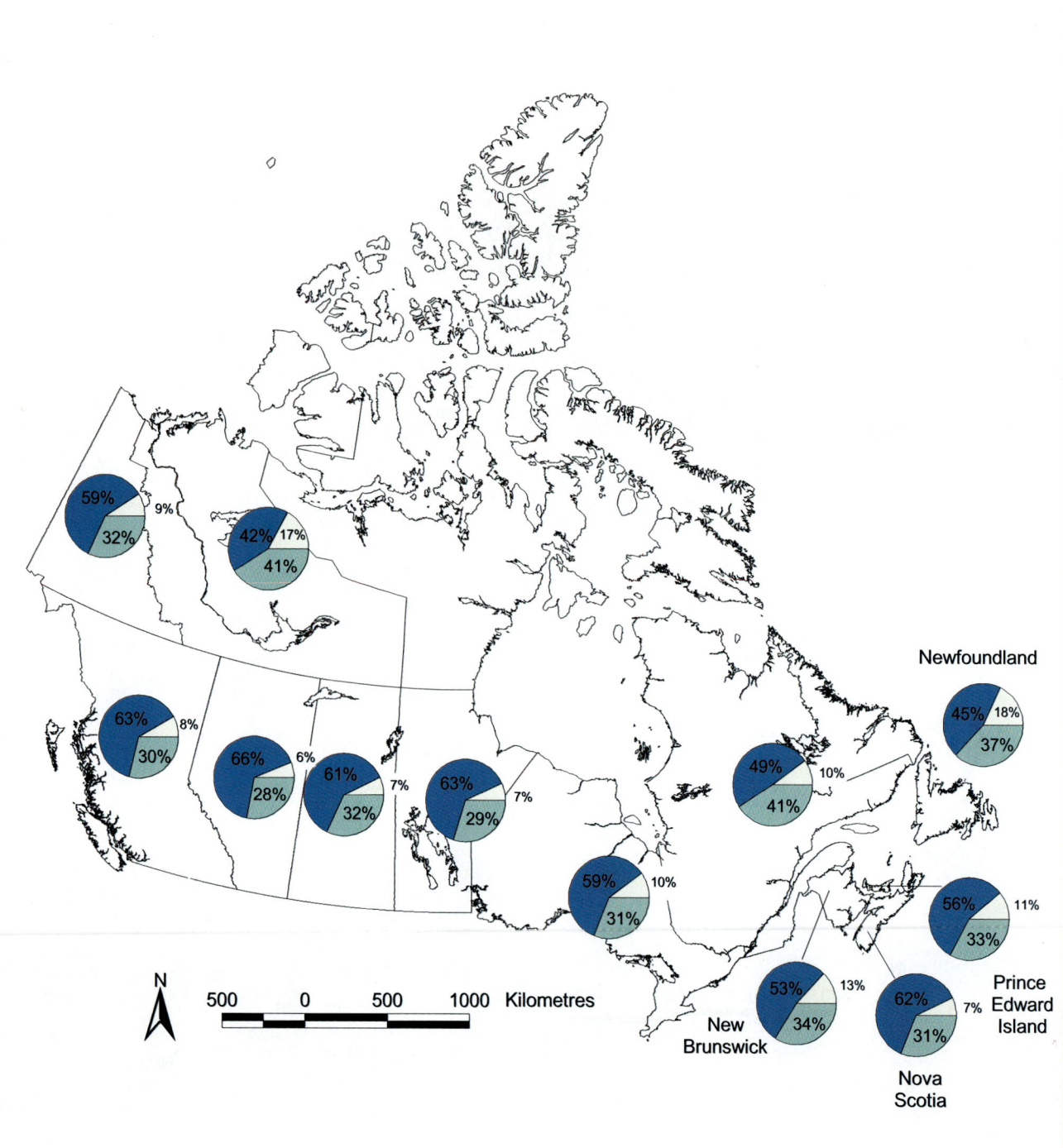

ATLAS OF LITERACY AND DISABILITY

Functional Literacy* Levels for Ages 15 and Older with Disabilities Residing in Households, Provinces and Territories

1991 Health and Activity Limitation Survey (HALS)

In most parts of the country, more than half of adults with disabilities score at the highest level of functional literacy. Nationally, 58.2% score at this level. The Northwest Territories, Quebec and Newfoundland are exceptions. Around a third of the disabled population (average 32.7%) are at the middle level and less than one in ten (9.1%) are at the lowest level.

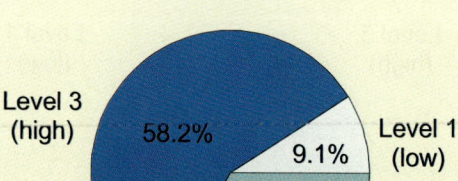

Canada

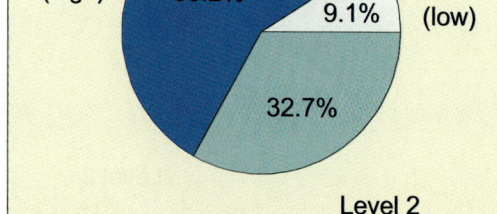

- Level 3 (high): 58.2%
- Level 2: 32.7%
- Level 1 (low): 9.1%

Provincial/Territorial values (Level 3 / Level 2 / Level 1):
- Yukon: 59% / 32% / 9%
- Northwest Territories: 42% / 41% / 17%
- British Columbia: 63% / 30% / 8%
- Alberta: 66% / 28% / 6%
- Saskatchewan: 61% / 32% / 7%
- Manitoba: 63% / 29% / 7%
- Ontario: 59% / 31% / 10%
- Quebec: 49% / 41% / 10%
- Newfoundland: 45% / 37% / 18%
- New Brunswick: 53% / 34% / 13%
- Nova Scotia: 62% / 31% / 7%
- Prince Edward Island: 56% / 33% / 11%

*Based on an alternative proxy for functional literacy derived from HALS.

Map 5.6

V. LITERACY AND DISABILITY AT THE CROSSROADS | 95

Earliest Age of Onset of Disability for Persons with Low Functional Literacy Skills*, Provinces and Territories

1991 Health and Activity Limitation Survey (HALS)

One quarter of adults with disabilities classified as having low functional literacy skills became disabled either at birth or before they reached age 5. Another 14% reported their limitation activity began between the ages of 5 and 19. This is much the same across the country.

Canada

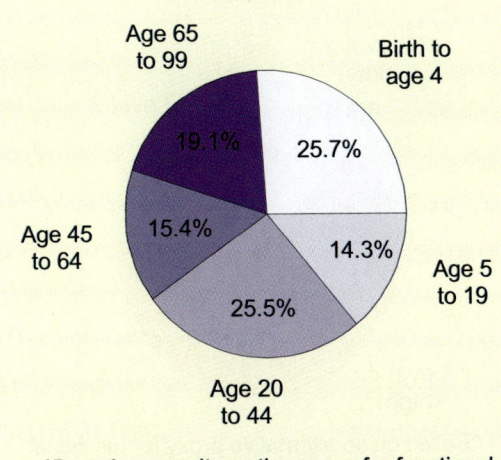

- Age 65 to 99: 19.1%
- Birth to age 4: 25.7%
- Age 5 to 19: 14.3%
- Age 20 to 44: 25.5%
- Age 45 to 64: 15.4%

*Based on an alternative proxy for functional literacy derived from HALS. Low functional literacy skills are level 1.

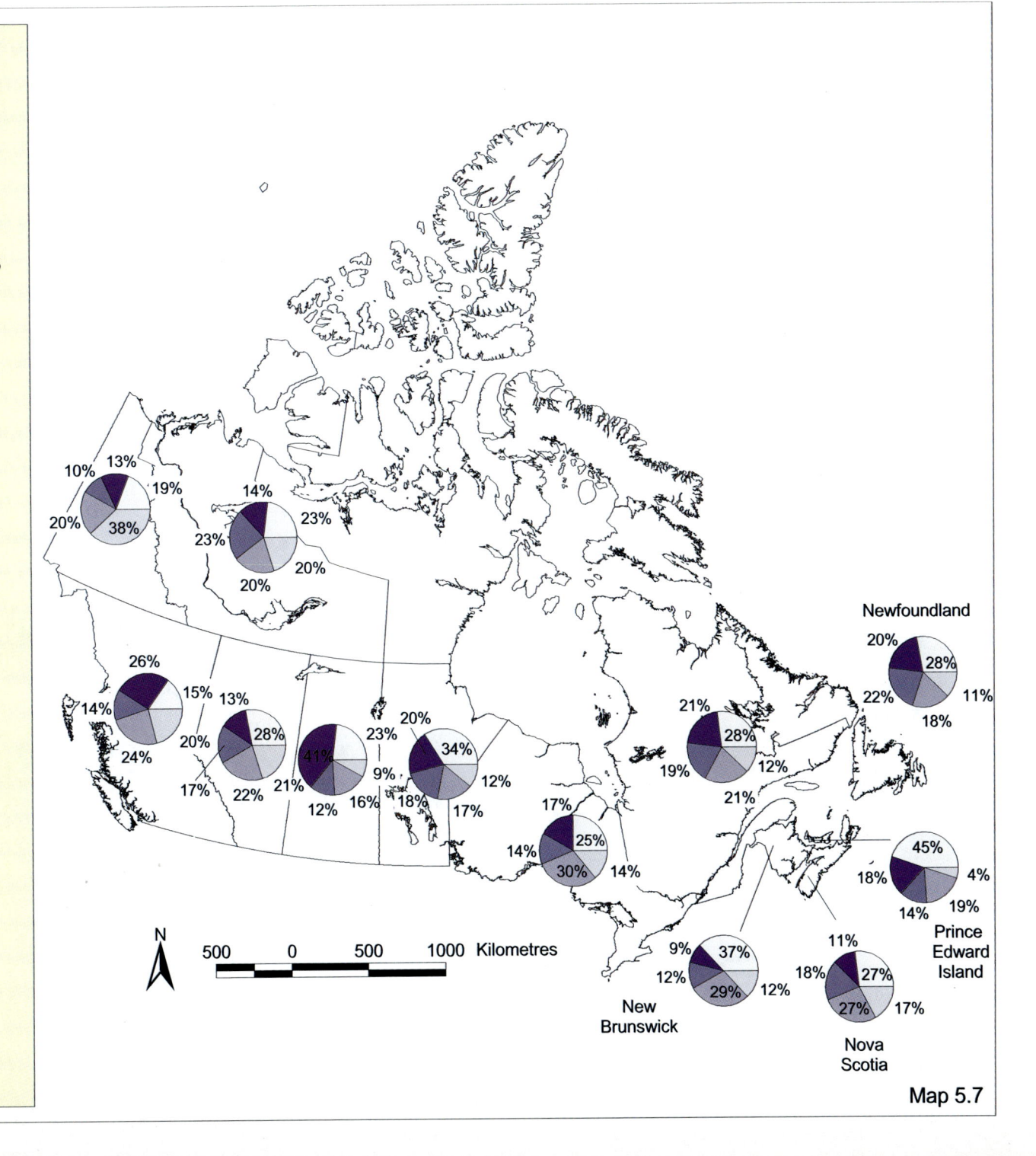

Map 5.7

ATLAS OF LITERACY AND DISABILITY

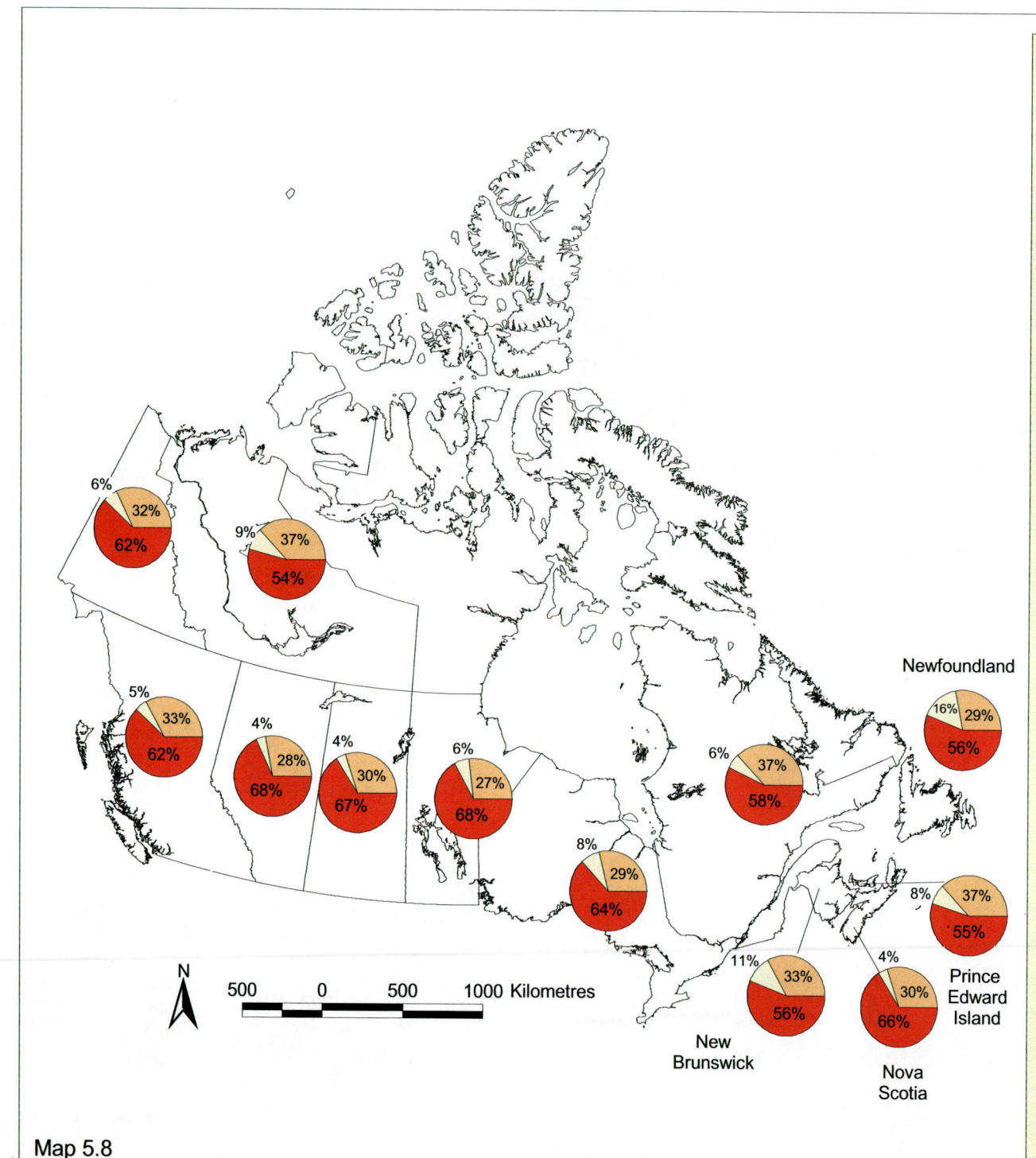

Functional Literacy* Levels for Adults with Disabilities Who are Active in the Labour Force, Provinces and Territories

1991 Health and Activity Limitation Survey (HALS)

Throughout the country, well over half of working age adults with disabilities who are in the labour force have functional literacy skills at the highest level (63.1%). More score at the highest level in Ontario, the western provinces and the Yukon, compared to the Northwest Territory, Quebec, and the eastern provinces.

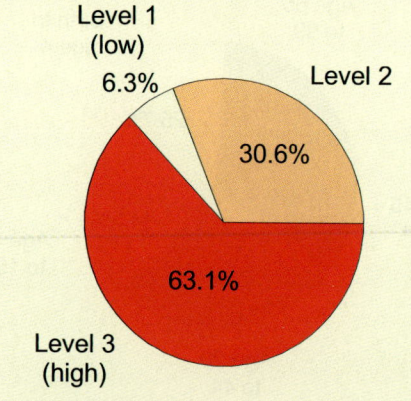

Canada

- Level 1 (low): 6.3%
- Level 2: 30.6%
- Level 3 (high): 63.1%

*Based on an alternative proxy for functional literacy derived from HALS.
Includes people ages 15 to 64 who are employed and those who are looking for work.

Map 5.8

Yukon: 6% / 32% / 62%
Northwest Territories: 9% / 37% / 54%
British Columbia: 5% / 33% / 62%
Alberta: 4% / 28% / 68%
Saskatchewan: 4% / 30% / 67%
Manitoba: 6% / 27% / 68%
Ontario: 6% / 37% / 58%
Quebec: 8% / 29% / 64%
Newfoundland: 16% / 29% / 56%
Prince Edward Island: 8% / 37% / 55%
New Brunswick: 11% / 33% / 56%
Nova Scotia: 4% / 30% / 66%

V. LITERACY AND DISABILITY AT THE CROSSROADS | 97

Functional Literacy Skills* for Ages 15 and Older with Disabilities Residing in Households Having Low Income, Provinces

1991 Health and Activity Limitation Survey (HALS)

About half of Canadians age 15 and older with disabilities who are poor have high functional literacy skills (50.3%), according to this proxy variable. 37% have a medium level of skill and 13% have low functional literacy skills.

Canada

Level 3 (high) — 50.3%
Level 1 (low) — 12.7%
Level 2 — 37.0%

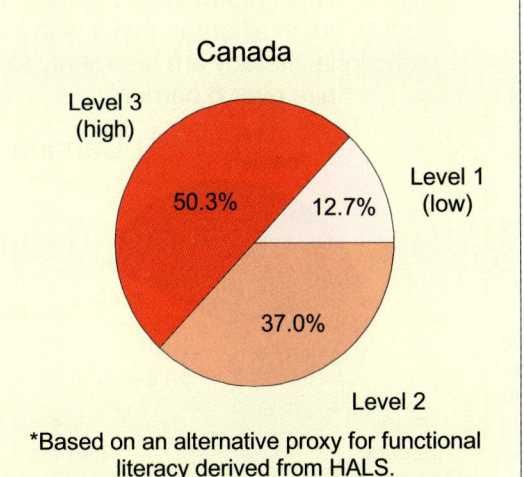

*Based on an alternative proxy for functional literacy derived from HALS.
Low Income is based on Statistics Canada's Low Income Cut-Off. LICOs are not available for the Yukon or Northwest Territories.

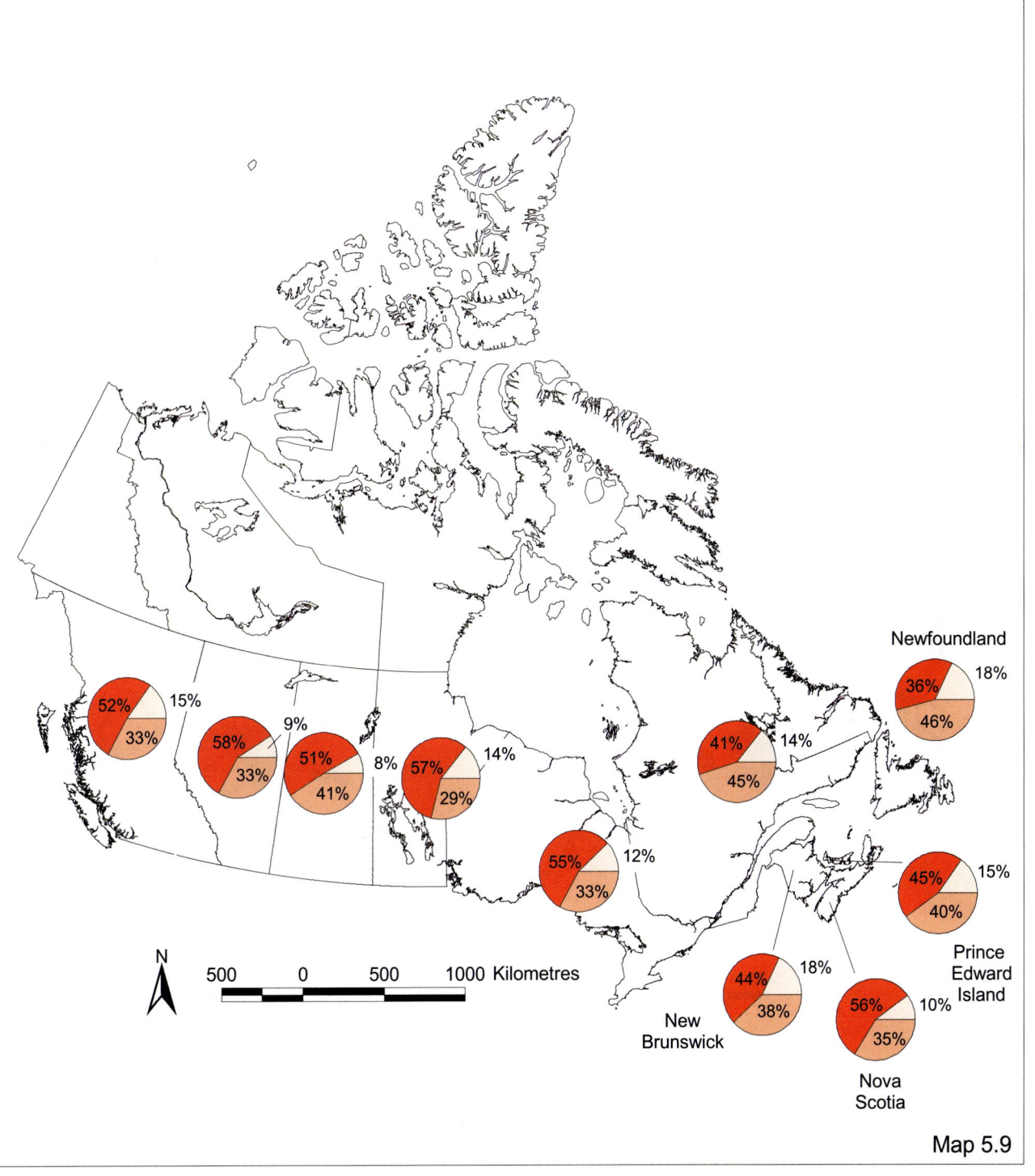

British Columbia: 52% / 33% / 15%
Alberta: 58% / 33% / 9%
Saskatchewan: 51% / 41% / 8%
Manitoba: 57% / 29% / 14%
Ontario: 41% / 45% / 14%
Quebec: 55% / 33% / 12%
New Brunswick: 44% / 38% / 18%
Nova Scotia: 56% / 35% / 10%
Prince Edward Island: 45% / 40% / 15%
Newfoundland: 36% / 46% / 18%

Map 5.9

ATLAS OF LITERACY AND DISABILITY

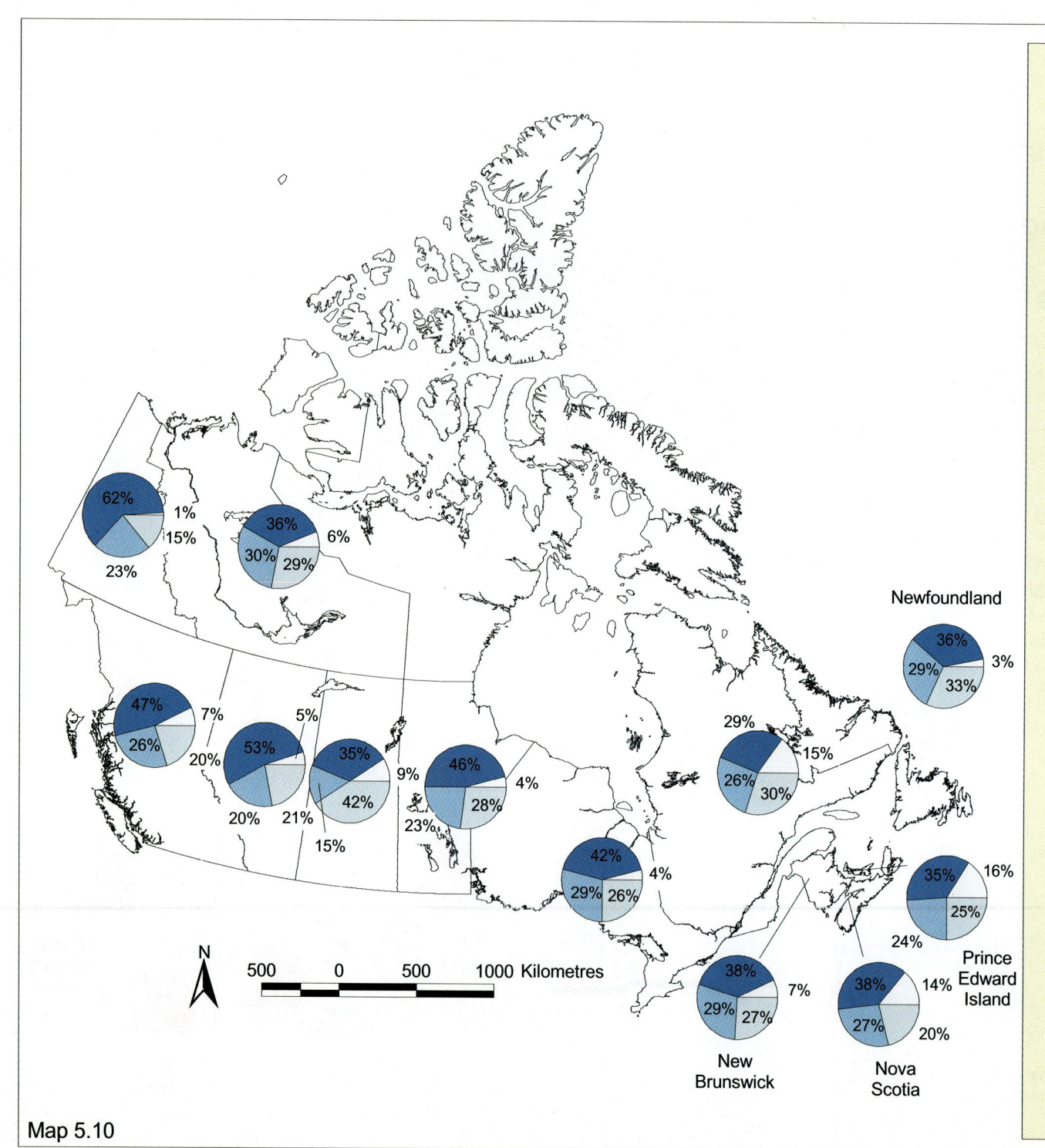

Number of Barriers Encountered for Ages 15 and Older with Disabilities who have Low Functional Literacy Skills*, Provinces and Territories

1991 Health and Activity Limitation (HALS) Survey

People with disabilities who have low functional literacy skills - the ability to use literacy skills to participate in the social and economic life of the community - are faced with many barriers to inclusion in their communities. Two-thirds of this population reported 6 or more barriers and only 7% reported no barriers. This pattern varies across the country, but in all areas those with low functional literacy are also likely to have over 6 barriers.

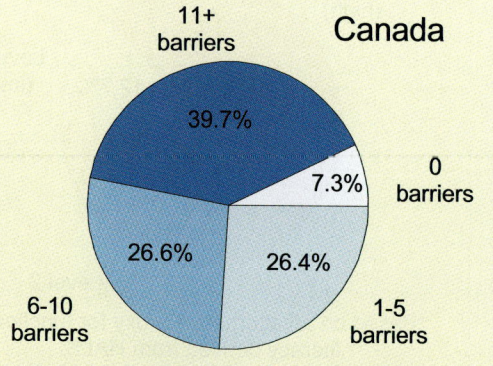

Canada
- 11+ barriers: 39.7%
- 6-10 barriers: 26.6%
- 1-5 barriers: 26.4%
- 0 barriers: 7.3%

*Based on an alternative proxy for functional literacy derived from HALS. Low functional literacy skills are level 1.

Provincial/Territorial Data

Yukon: 62%, 1%, 15%, 23%
Northwest Territories: 36%, 6%, 29%, 30%
British Columbia: 47%, 7%, 20%, 26%
Alberta: 53%, 5%, 21%, 20%
Saskatchewan: 35%, 9%, 42%, 15%
Manitoba: 46%, 4%, 28%, 23%
Ontario: 42%, 4%, 26%, 29%
Quebec: 29%, 15%, 30%, 26%
Newfoundland: 36%, 3%, 33%, 29%
Prince Edward Island: 35%, 16%, 25%, 24%
New Brunswick: 38%, 7%, 27%, 29%
Nova Scotia: 38%, 14%, 20%, 27%

Map 5.10

V. LITERACY AND DISABILITY AT THE CROSSROADS | 99

Number of Accommodations Received by Ages 15 and Older with Disabilities who have Low Functional Literacy Skills*, Provinces and Territories

1991 Health and Activity Limitation Survey (HALS)

Just over half (52.6%) of all adults with disabilities who had low functional literacy reported that they had received one to five accommodations to remove barriers that they encountered in their everyday activities. An additional 21.6% reported even more accommodations to remove barriers.

Canada

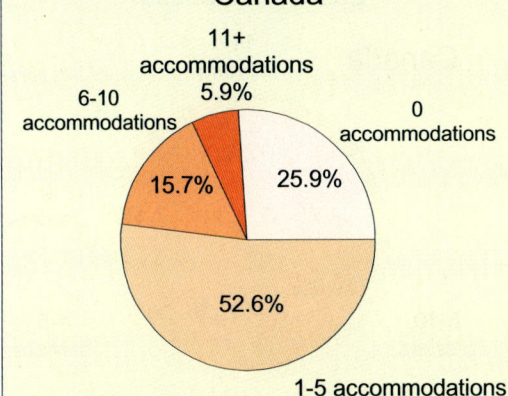

- 11+ accommodations: 5.9%
- 6-10 accommodations: 15.7%
- 0 accommodations: 25.9%
- 1-5 accommodations: 52.6%

*Based on an alternative proxy for functional literacy derived from HALS. Low functional literacy skills are level 1.

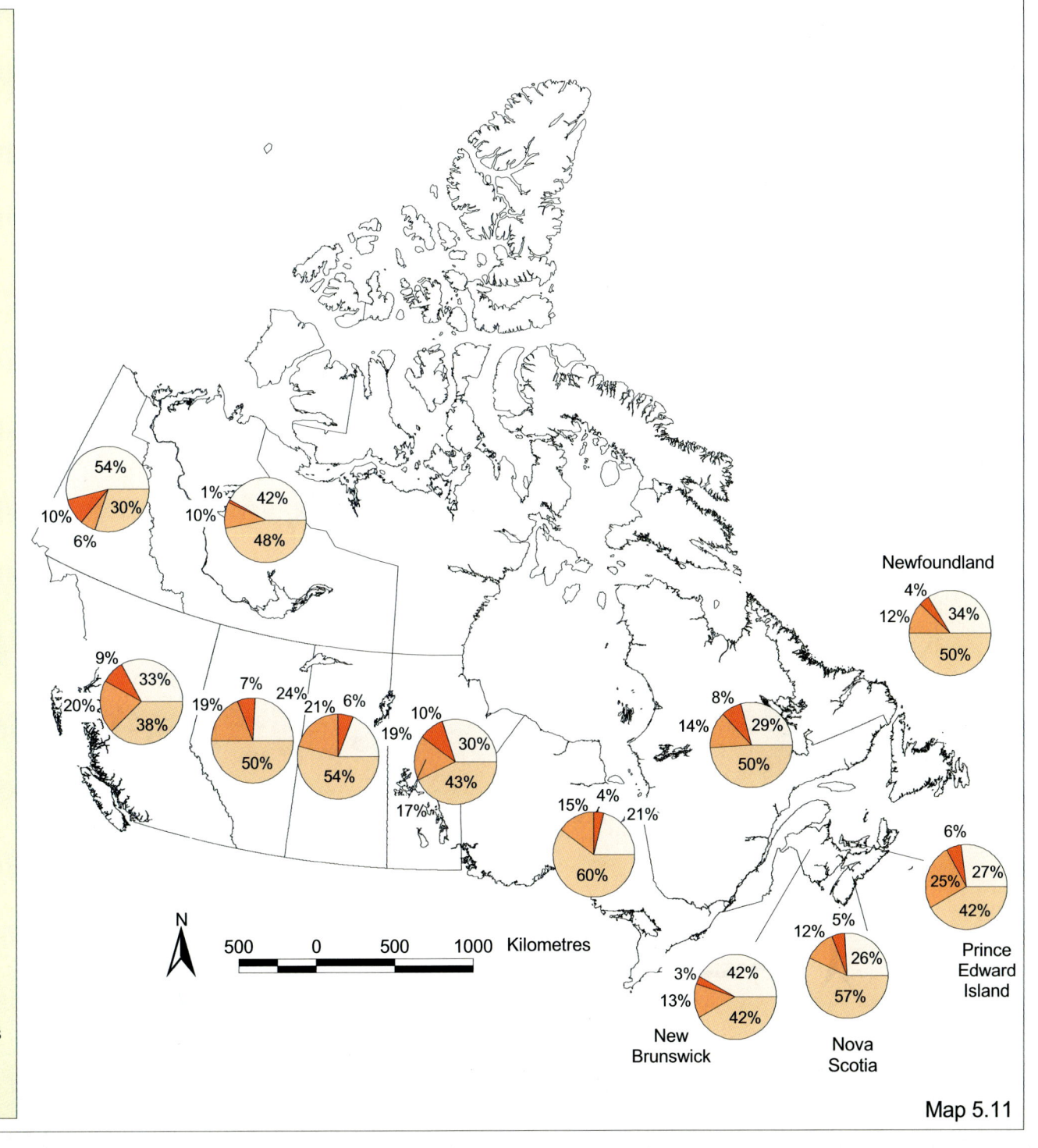

Map 5.11

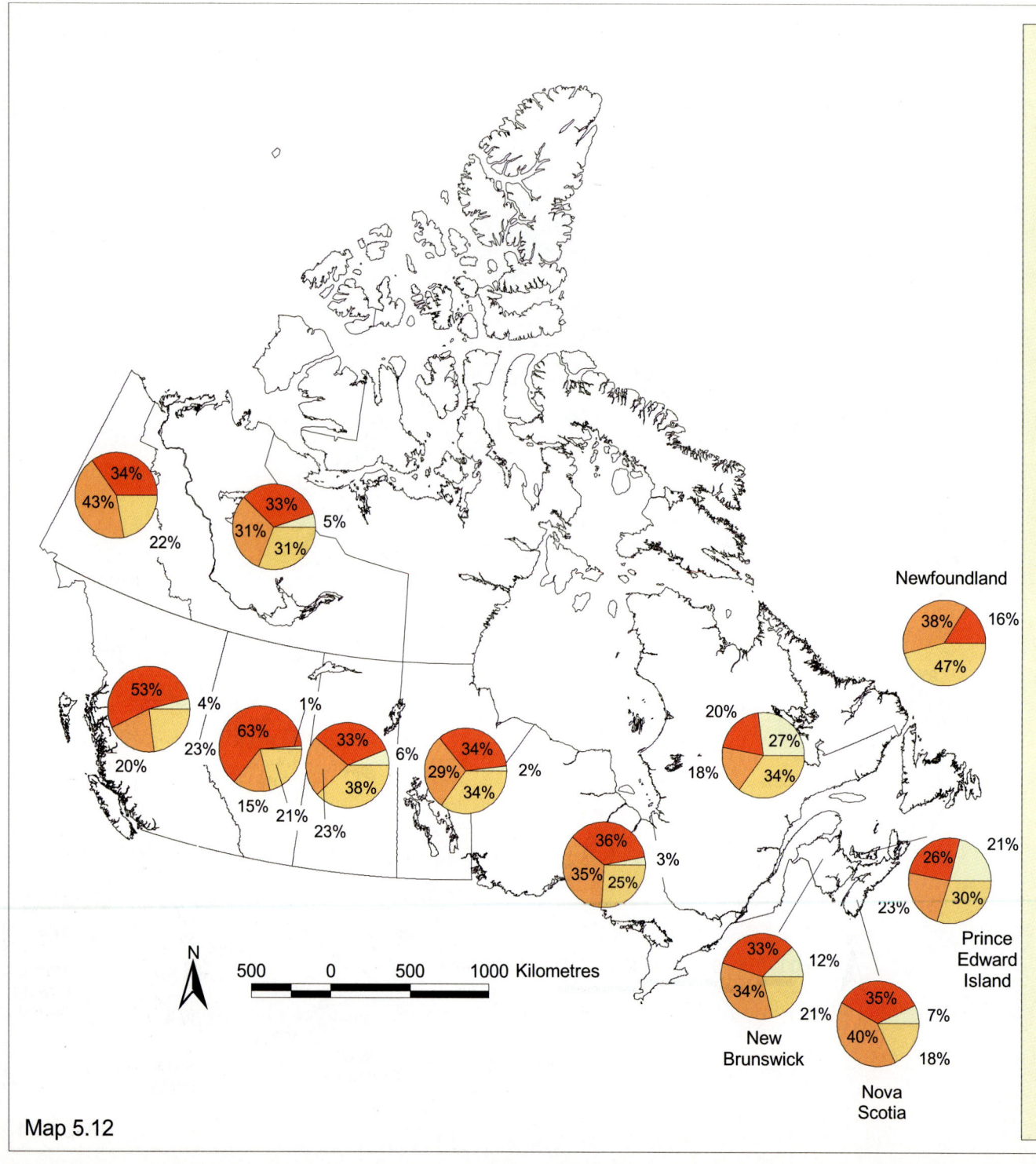

ATLAS OF LITERACY AND DISABILITY

Number of Barriers Encountered for Adults with Disabilities Who are Active in the Labour Force and Have Low Functional Literacy Skills*, Provinces and Territories

1991 Health and Activity Limitation Survey (HALS)

More than 90% of people with disabilities who have low functional literacy skills in Canada face at least one barrier in their everyday activities. A surprising 37% count 11 or more barriers in their daily living, with 29% reporting 6 to 10 barriers. The Western Provinces show a trend where fewer people have barrier-free lives compared to the Eastern Provinces.

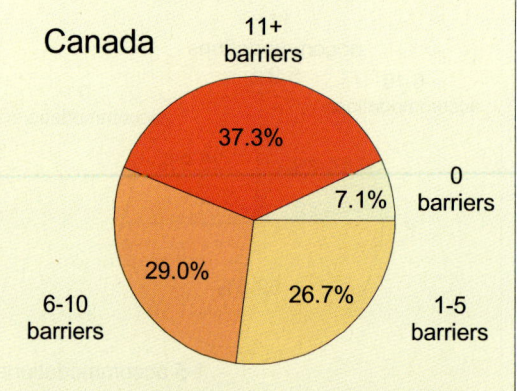

Canada
- 11+ barriers: 37.3%
- 0 barriers: 7.1%
- 1-5 barriers: 26.7%
- 6-10 barriers: 29.0%

*Based on an alternative proxy for functional literacy derived from HALS. Low functional literacy skills are level 1.

Yukon: 34% / 43% / 22% / (blank)
Northwest Territories: 33% / 31% / 31% / 5%
British Columbia: 53% / 23% / 20% / 4%
Alberta: 63% / 15% / 21% / 1%
Saskatchewan: 33% / 38% / 23% / 6%
Manitoba: 34% / 29% / 34% / 2%
Ontario: 36% / 35% / 25% / 3%
Quebec: 27% / 34% / 18% / 20%
Newfoundland: 38% / 47% / 16%
Prince Edward Island: 26% / 30% / 23% / 21%
New Brunswick: 33% / 34% / 21% / 12%
Nova Scotia: 35% / 40% / 18% / 7%

Map 5.12

V. LITERACY AND DISABILITY AT THE CROSSROADS | 101

Number of Accommodations Received by Adults with Disabilities Who are Active in the Labour Force and have Low Functional Literacy Skills*, Provinces and Territories

1991 Health and Activity Limitation Survey (HALS)

The majority of people in Canada with low functional literacy report 1 to 5 accommodations to deal with the barriers they face in everyday living (54.8%). About 38% receive no accommodation, although it is not possible to know how many of those need accommodations. This pattern is uneven across the provinces.

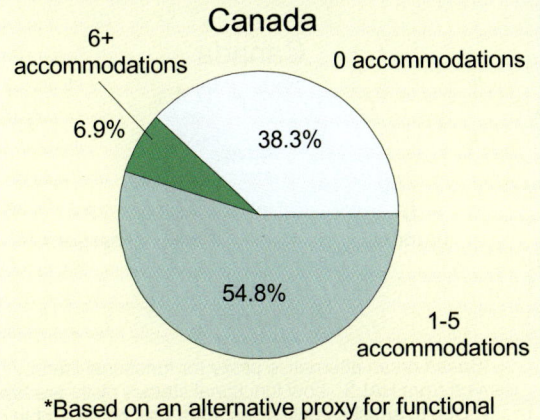

Canada
- 6+ accommodations: 6.9%
- 0 accommodations: 38.3%
- 1-5 accommodations: 54.8%

*Based on an alternative proxy for functional literacy derived from HALS. Low functional literacy skills are level 1.

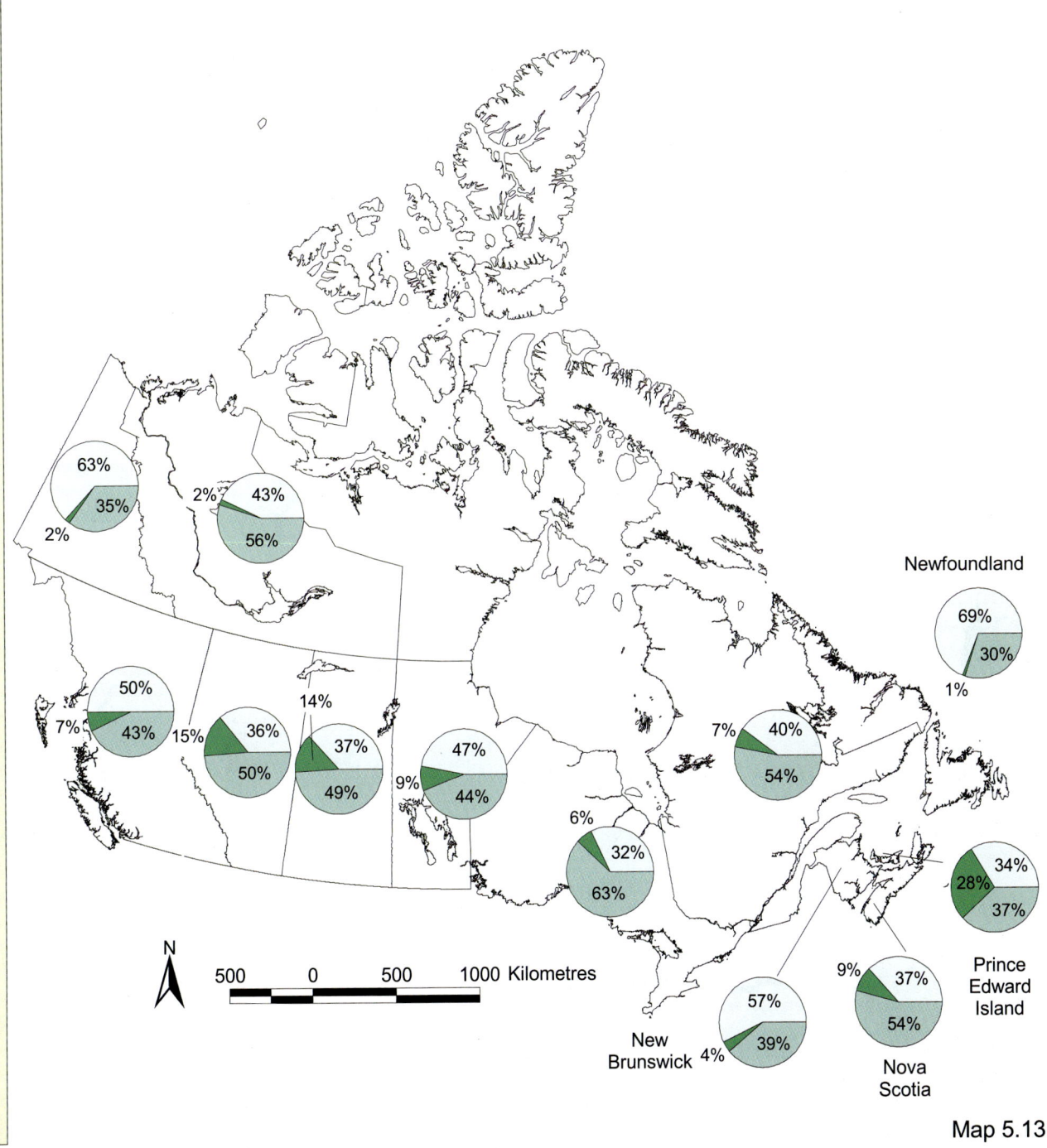

Yukon: 63% / 35% / 2%
Northwest Territories: 43% / 56% / 2%
British Columbia: 50% / 43% / 7%
Alberta: 15% / 50% / 36%
Saskatchewan: 14% / 49% / 37%
Manitoba: 9% / 44% / 47%
Ontario: 6% / 63% / 32%
Quebec: 7% / 54% / 40%
Newfoundland: 69% / 30% / 1%
Prince Edward Island: 34% / 37% / 28%
Nova Scotia: 9% / 54% / 37%
New Brunswick: 57% / 39% / 4%

Map 5.13

ATLAS OF LITERACY AND DISABILITY

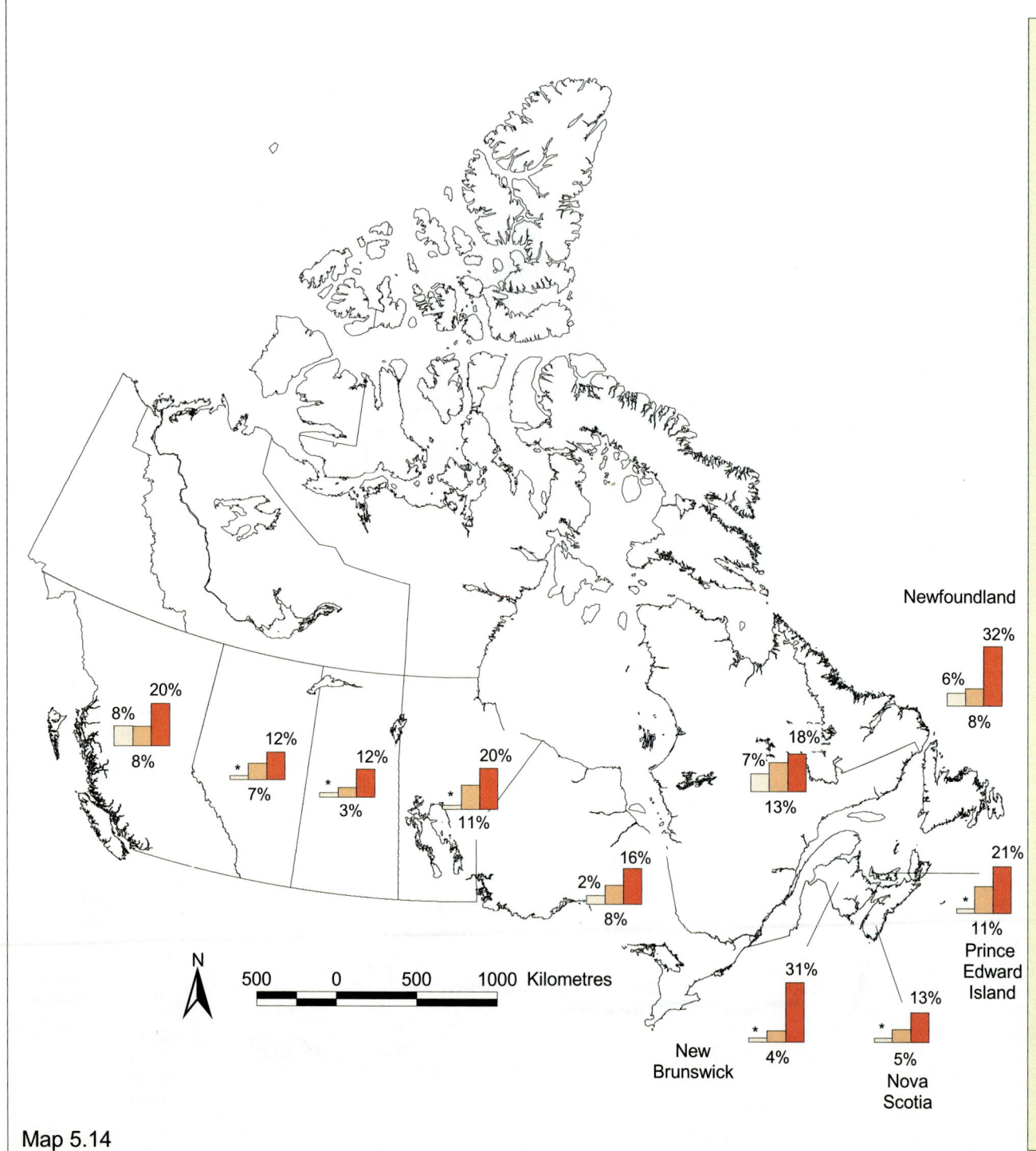

Number of Barriers Encountered for Ages 15 and Older with Disabilities Residing in Households with Low Income and Low Functional Literacy Skills*, Provinces

1991 Health and Activity Limitation Survey (HALS)

For adults with disabilities facing 6+ barriers 17.4% of them have both low income and low functional literacy. A smaller percentage, 9%, face 1-5 barriers. The pattern of decreasing numbers of people facing smaller numbers of barriers is consistent across the nation.

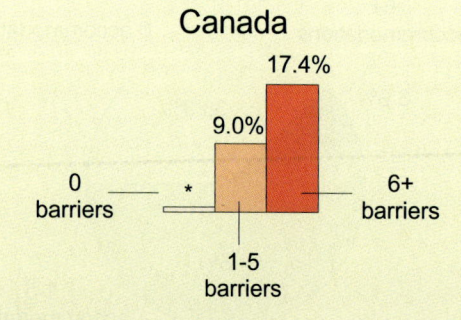

Canada

- 0 barriers: *
- 1-5 barriers: 9.0%
- 6+ barriers: 17.4%

*Based on an alternative proxy for functional literacy derived from HALS. Low functional literacy skills are level 1. Due to small sample sizes, data was not available for the Northwest and Yukon Territories. Data was suppressed for 0 barriers in several provinces.

Provincial data (0 / 1-5 / 6+ barriers):

- Newfoundland: 6% / 8% / 32%
- Prince Edward Island: * / 11% / 21%
- Nova Scotia: * / 5% / 13%
- New Brunswick: * / 4% / 31%
- Quebec: 7% / 13% / 18%
- Ontario: 2% / 8% / 16%
- Manitoba: * / 11% / 20%
- Saskatchewan: * / 3% / 12%
- Alberta: * / 7% / 12%
- British Columbia: 8% / 8% / 20%

Map 5.14

V. LITERACY AND DISABILITY AT THE CROSSROADS | 103

Number of Accommodations Received by Ages 15 and Older with Disabilities Residing in Households Having Low Income and Low Functional Literacy Skills*, Provinces

1991 Health and Activity Limitation Survey (HALS)

Of the people with disabilities who receive 6 or more accommodations one out of five adults have both low income and low functional literacy skills. Less than 15% had 1 to 5 accommodations. The pattern of decreasing percentages of adults corresponding to smaller numbers of accommodations is seen in the Eastern and Western provinces but not the central provinces.

Canada

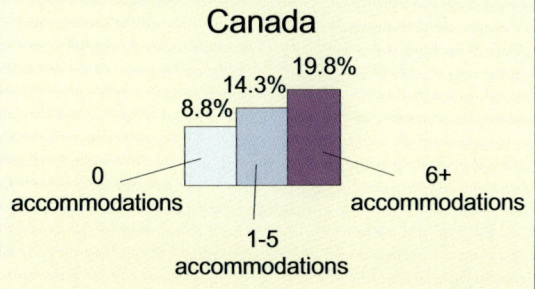

- 0 accommodations: 8.8%
- 1-5 accommodations: 14.3%
- 6+ accommodations: 19.8%

*Based on an alternative proxy for functional literacy derived from HALS. Low functional literacy skills are level 1. Due to small sample sizes, data was not available for the Northwest Territories and the Yukon Territory.

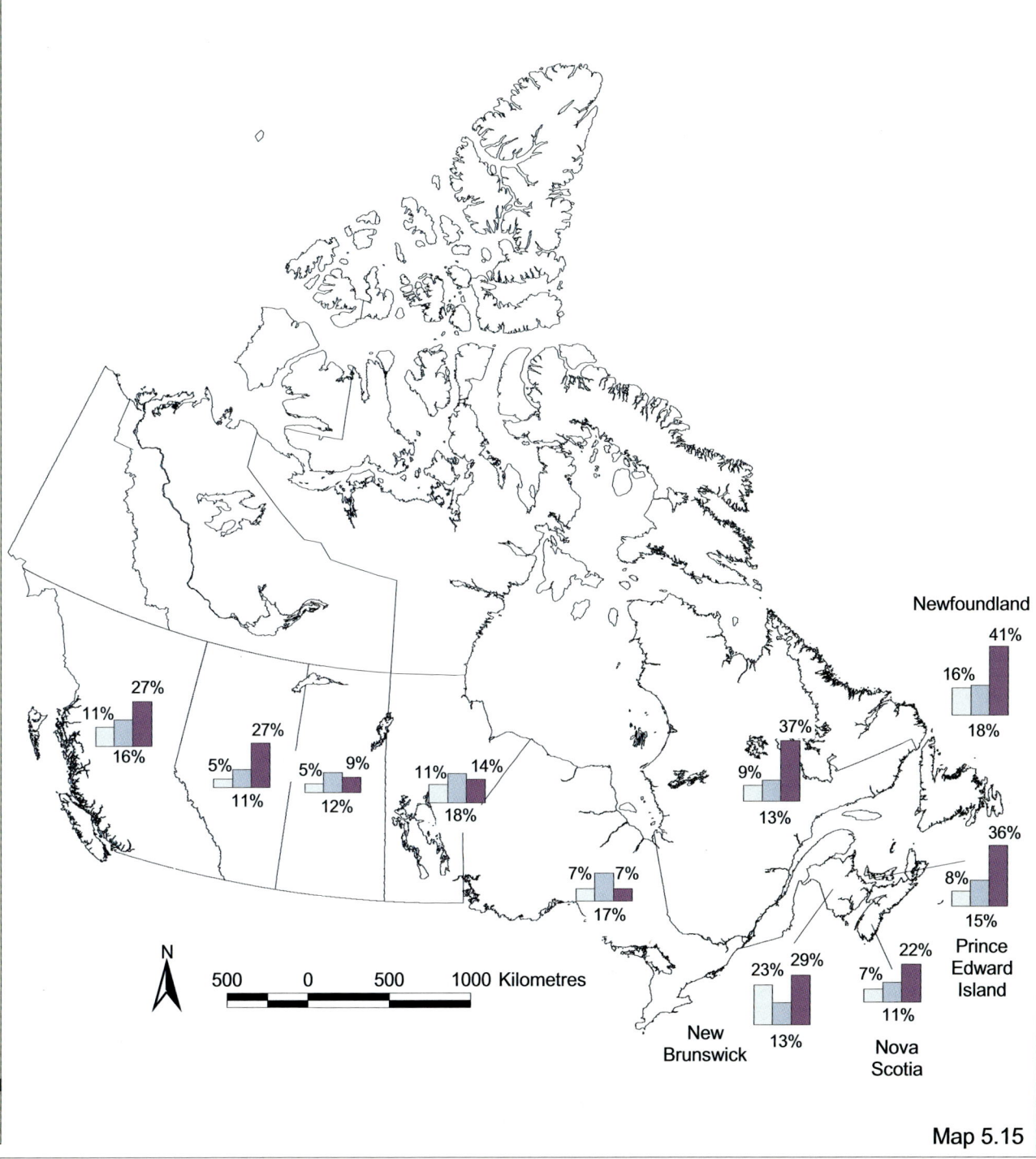

Provincial values (0% / 1-5 / 6+):
- British Columbia: 11%, 16%, 27%
- Alberta: 5%, 11%, 27%
- Saskatchewan: 5%, 12%, 9%
- Manitoba: 11%, 18%, 14%
- Ontario: 7%, 17%, 7%
- Quebec: 9%, 13%, 37%
- New Brunswick: 23%, 13%, 29%
- Nova Scotia: 7%, 11%, 22%
- Prince Edward Island: 8%, 15%, 36%
- Newfoundland: 16%, 18%, 41%

Map 5.15

V. LITERACY AND DISABILITY AT THE CROSSROADS | 105

Critical Literacy* Levels for Ages 16 and Older with Disabilities, Provinces

1994 International Adult Literacy Survey (IALS)

Dividing critical literacy into three levels shows that, according to IALS, most people with disabilities in Canada have the mid-level ranking. They are followed by about equal proportions in the low and high levels. There is an east-west pattern with the Eastern Provinces having lower levels of critical literacy.

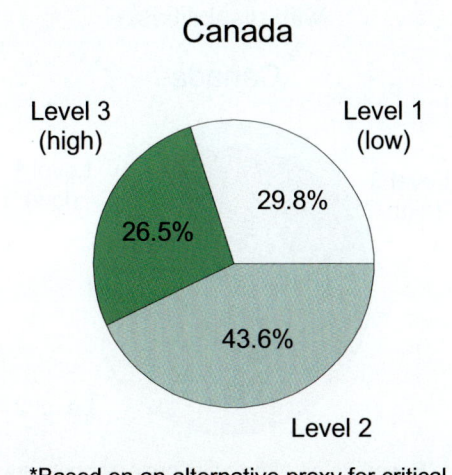

Canada

- Level 3 (high): 26.5%
- Level 1 (low): 29.8%
- Level 2: 43.6%

*Based on an alternative proxy for critical literacy derived from IALS.

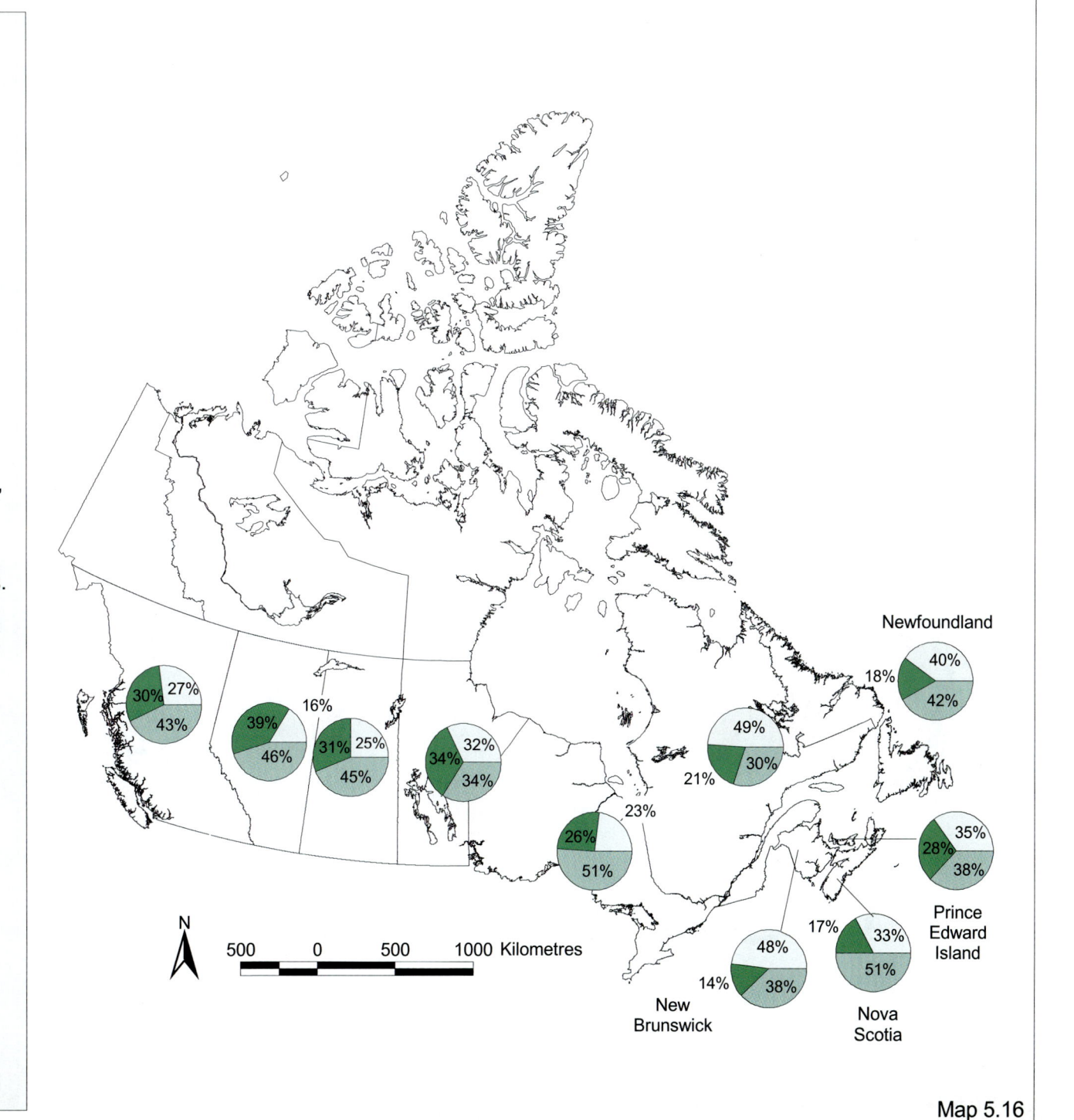

Provincial pie charts (Level 1 low / Level 2 / Level 3 high):

- British Columbia: 27% / 43% / 30%
- Alberta: 16% / 46% / 39%
- Saskatchewan: 25% / 45% / 31%
- Manitoba: 32% / 34% / 34%
- Ontario: 23% / 51% / 26%
- Quebec: 21% / 30% / 49%
- New Brunswick: 14% / 48% / 38%
- Nova Scotia: 17% / 51% / 33%
- Prince Edward Island: 35% / 38% / 28%
- Newfoundland: 18% / 42% / 40%

Map 5.16

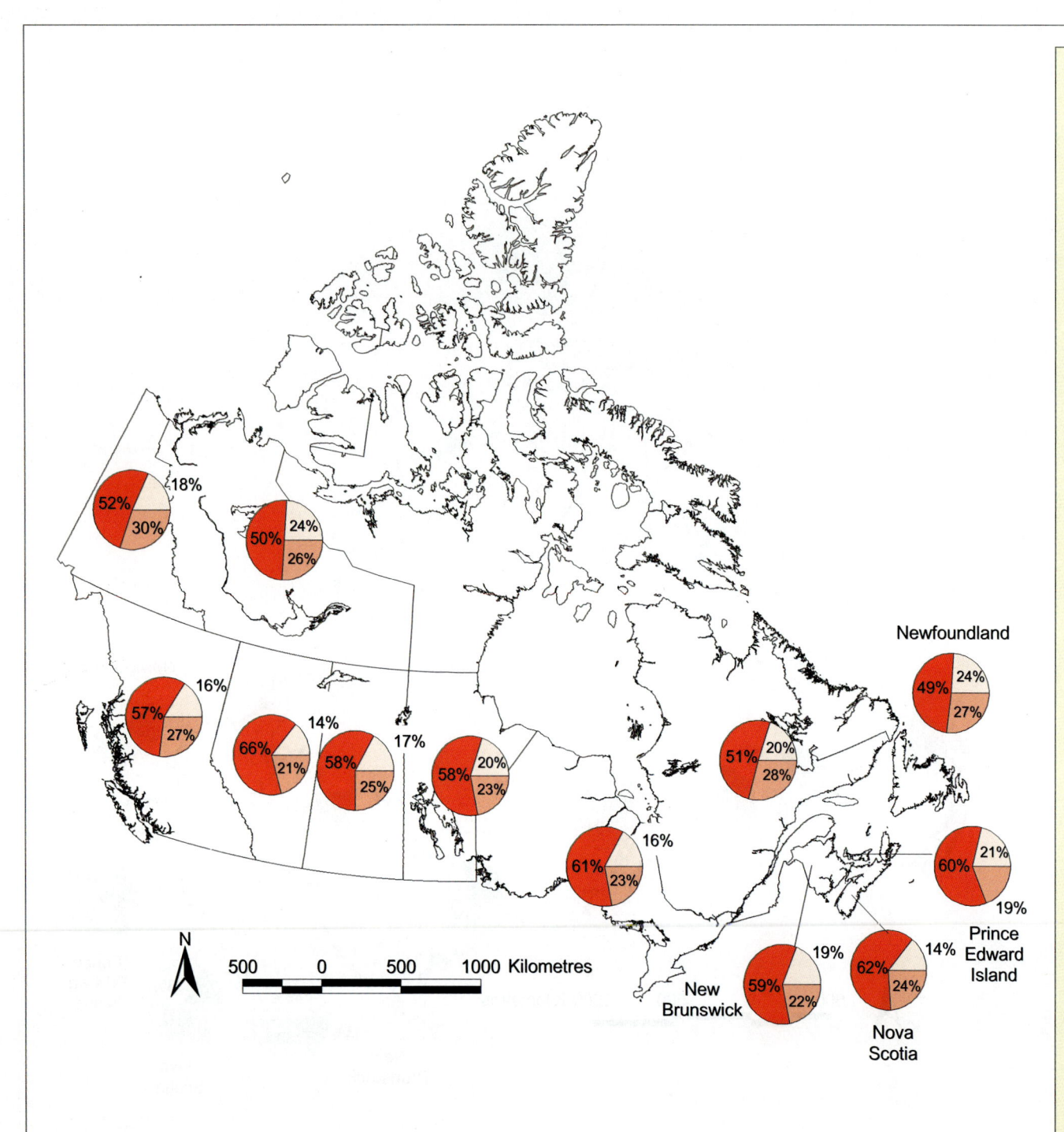

106　ATLAS OF LITERACY AND DISABILITY

Critical Literacy* Levels for Ages 15 and Older with Disabilities Residing in Households, Provinces and Territories

1991 Health and Activity Limitation Survey (HALS)

Almost 60% of Canadian adults with disabilities report experiencing high critical literacy - those skills and conditions that are necessary for socially marginalized individuals and groups to communicate their interests in public discourse. While there is some variation across Canada, the proportion of individuals reporting the highest level of critical literary never falls below half of the population with disabilities.

Canada

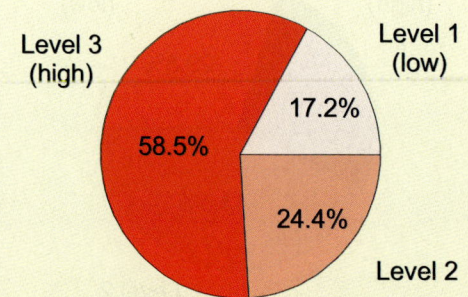

- Level 3 (high): 58.5%
- Level 2: 24.4%
- Level 1 (low): 17.2%

*Based on an alternative proxy for critical literacy derived from HALS.

Map values by province/territory:

- Yukon: 52% / 30% / 18%
- Northwest Territories: 50% / 26% / 24%
- British Columbia: 57% / 27% / 16%
- Alberta: 66% / 21% / 14%
- Saskatchewan: 58% / 25% / 17%
- Manitoba: 58% / 23% / 20%
- Ontario: 61% / 23% / 16%
- Quebec: 51% / 28% / 20%
- Newfoundland: 49% / 27% / 24%
- New Brunswick: 59% / 22% / 19%
- Nova Scotia: 62% / 24% / 14%
- Prince Edward Island: 60% / 21% / 19%

Map 5.17

V. LITERACY AND DISABILITY AT THE CROSSROADS | 107

Earliest Age of Onset of Disability for Persons with Low Critical Literacy Skills*, Provinces and Territories

1991 Health and Activity Limitation Survey (HALS)

The age of onset of disability does not appear to make a large difference in terms of the experience of low critical literacy skills. The differences were only slight between age of onset categories.

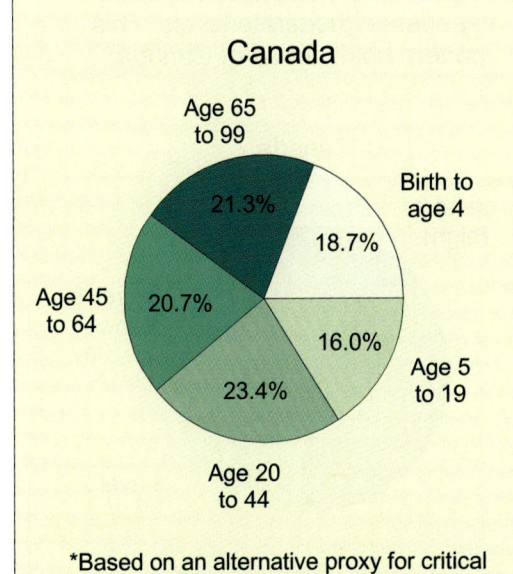

Canada

- Age 65 to 99: 21.3%
- Birth to age 4: 18.7%
- Age 5 to 19: 16.0%
- Age 20 to 44: 23.4%
- Age 45 to 64: 20.7%

*Based on an alternative proxy for critical literacy derived from HALS. Low critical literacy skills are level 1. Due to small sample sizes, the Yukon Territory and the Northwest Territory were combined.

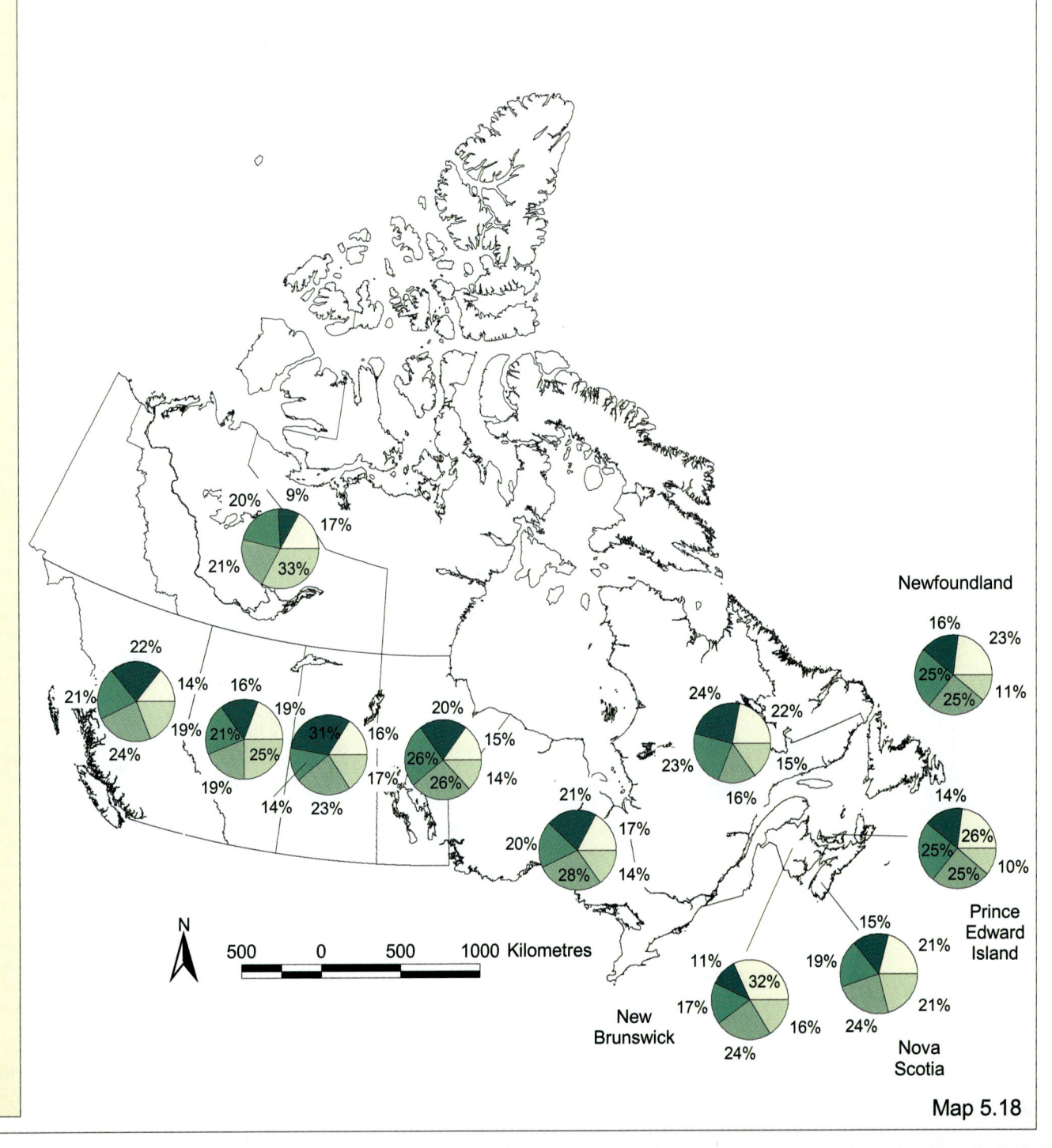

Map 5.18

ATLAS OF LITERACY AND DISABILITY

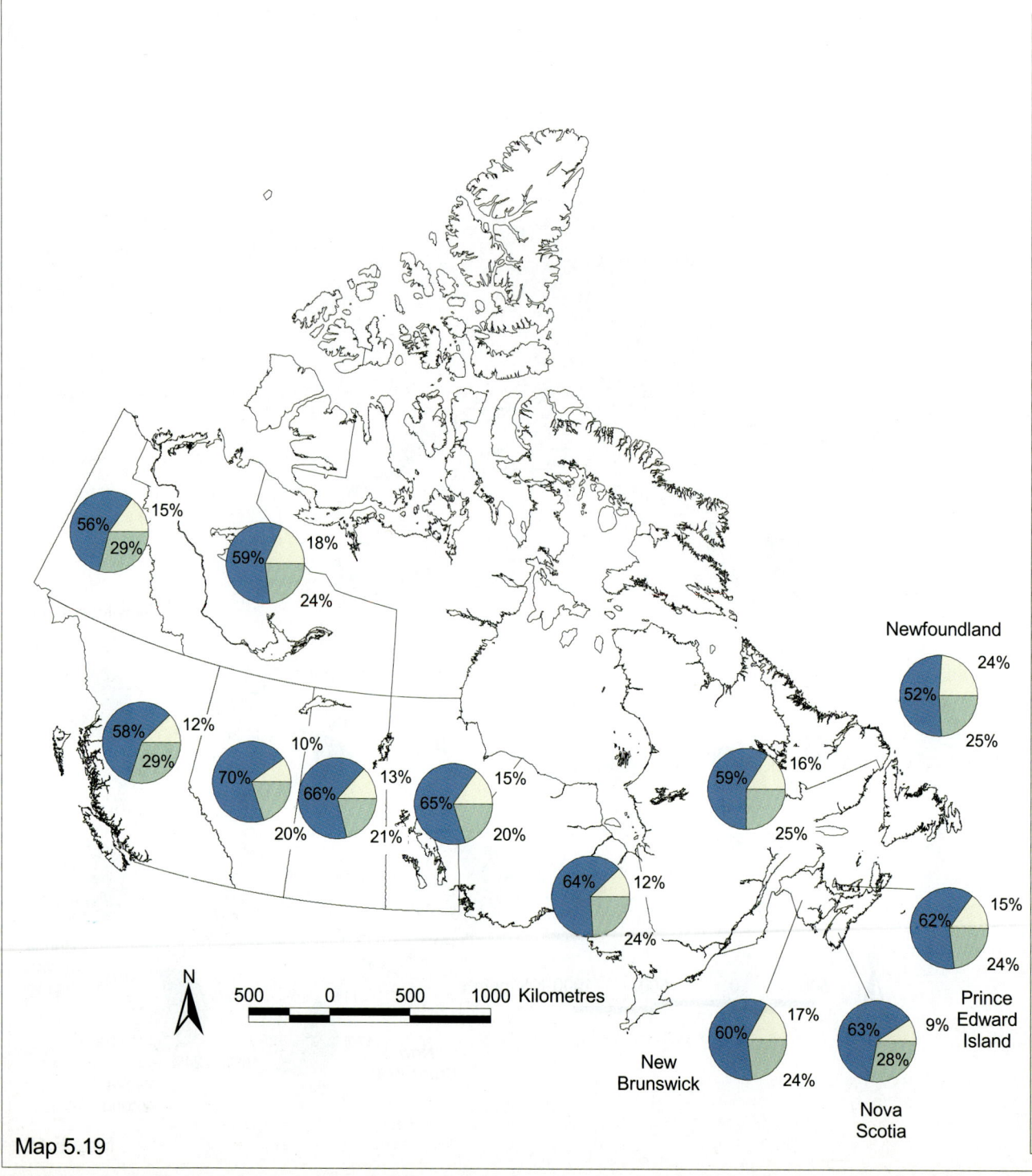

Map 5.19

Critical Literacy* Levels for Adults with Disabilities Who are Active in the Labour Force, Provinces and Territories

1991 Health and Activity Limitation Survey (HALS)

63% of adults with disabilties active in the labour force experience high critical literacy. One quarter experience moderate levels. This pattern holds for all of Canada.

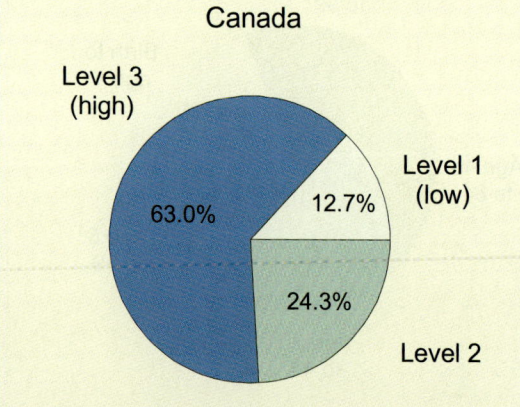

Canada
- Level 3 (high): 63.0%
- Level 1 (low): 12.7%
- Level 2: 24.3%

*Based on an alternative proxy for critical literacy derived from HALS. Includes people ages 15 to 64 who are employed and those who are looking for work.

Yukon: 56% / 29% / 15%
Northwest Territories: 59% / 24% / 18%
British Columbia: 58% / 29% / 12%
Alberta: 70% / 20% / 10%
Saskatchewan: 66% / 21% / 13%
Manitoba: 65% / 20% / 15%
Ontario: 64% / 24% / 12%
Quebec: 59% / 25% / 16%
Newfoundland: 52% / 25% / 24%
Prince Edward Island: 62% / 24% / 15%
New Brunswick: 60% / 24% / 17%
Nova Scotia: 63% / 28% / 9%

V. LITERACY AND DISABILITY AT THE CROSSROADS

Critical Literacy Skills* for Ages 15 and Older with Disabilities Residing in Households Having Low Income, Provinces

1991 Health and Activity Limitation Survey (HALS)

This exploratory literacy measure shows that the majority of Canadians age 15 and older with disabilities who are poor have high critical literacy skills (53.1%). This is consistent across the country with eight provinces above the 50% threshold.

Canada

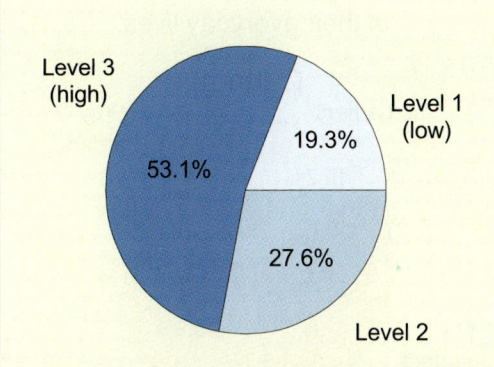

- Level 3 (high): 53.1%
- Level 2: 27.6%
- Level 1 (low): 19.3%

*Based on an alternative proxy for critical literacy derived from HALS. Low Income is based on Statistics Canada's Low Income Cut-Off. LICOs are not available for the Yukon or Northwest Territories.

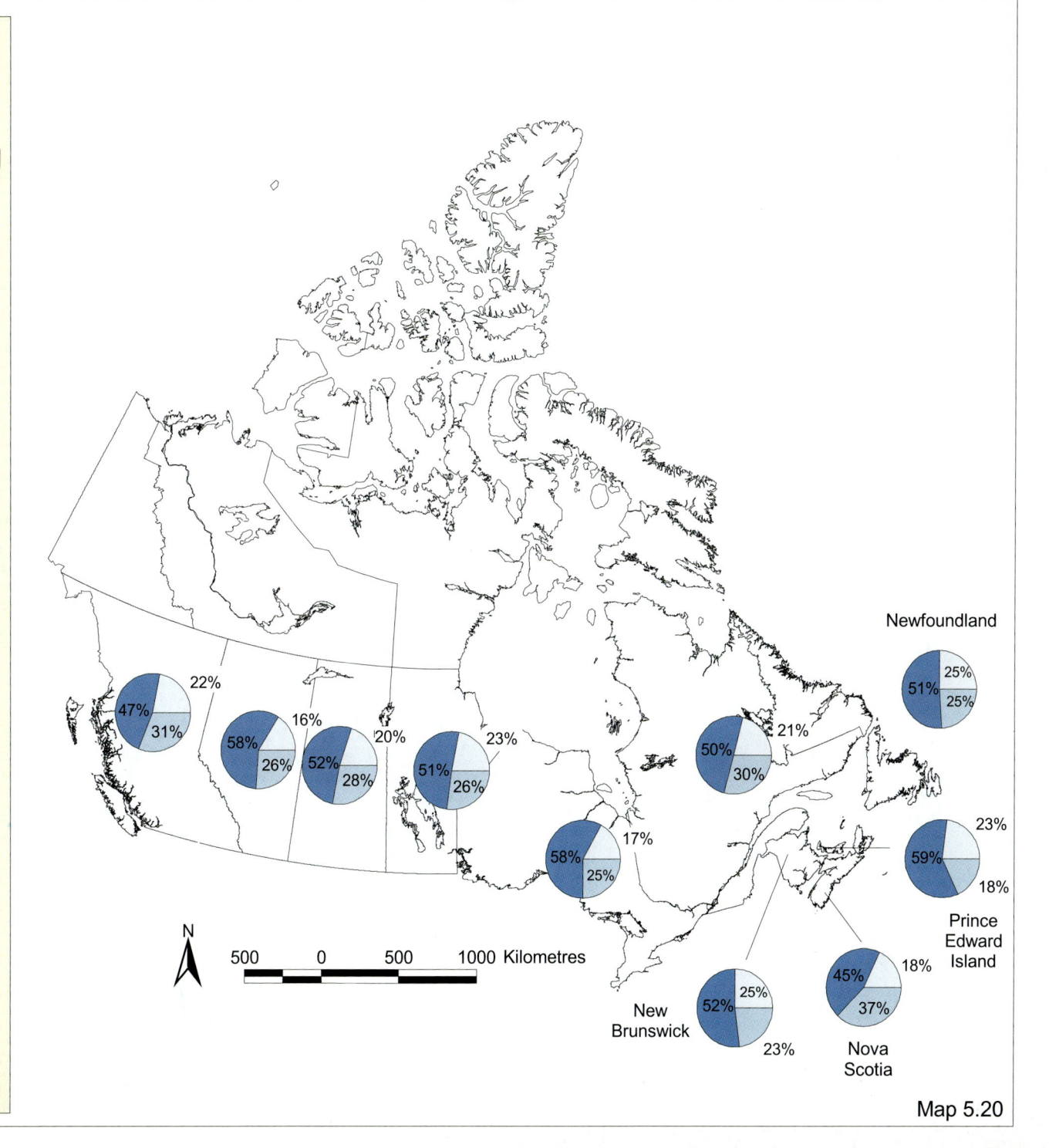

Provincial pie charts (Level 3 / Level 2 / Level 1):

- British Columbia: 47% / 31% / 22%
- Alberta: 58% / 26% / 16%
- Saskatchewan: 52% / 28% / 20%
- Manitoba: 51% / 26% / 23%
- Ontario: 58% / 25% / 17%
- Quebec: 50% / 30% / 21%
- New Brunswick: 52% / 23% / 25%
- Nova Scotia: 45% / 37% / 18%
- Prince Edward Island: 59% / 18% / 23%
- Newfoundland: 51% / 25% / 25%

Map 5.20

ATLAS OF LITERACY AND DISABILITY

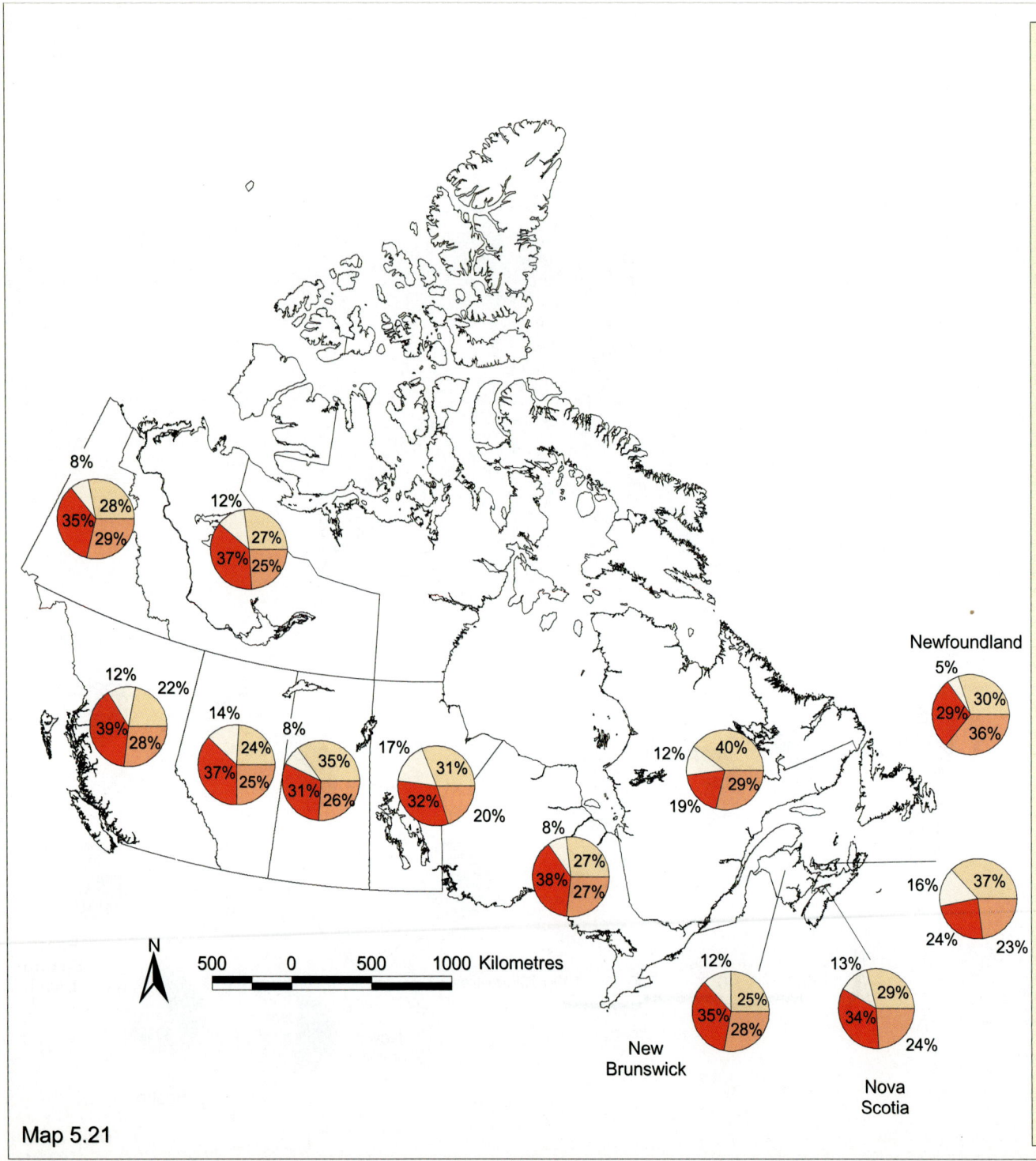

Map 5.21

Barriers Encountered for Ages 15 and Older with Disabilities who have Low Critical Literacy Skills*, Provinces and Territories

1991 Health and Activity Limitation Survey (HALS)

For those adults who were experiencing barriers at the time of the survey, almost equal numbers reported one to five barriers, six to 10 barriers and 11 or more barriers - 29.9%, 26.9% and 32.4% respectively. About 11% of adults with disabilities were experiencing no barriers at the time of the survey, either because they had received accommodations and were now barrier-free or because they had never experienced any barriers in their everyday lives.

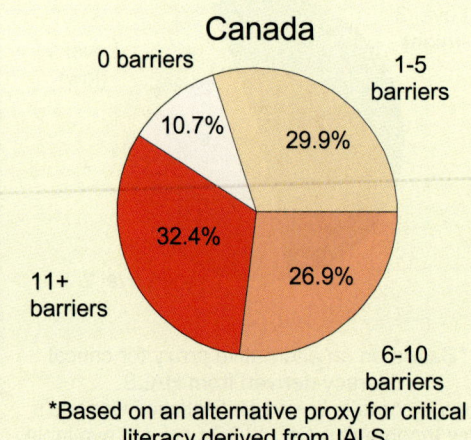

Canada

- 0 barriers: 10.7%
- 1-5 barriers: 29.9%
- 6-10 barriers: 26.9%
- 11+ barriers: 32.4%

*Based on an alternative proxy for critical literacy derived from IALS. Low critical literacy skills are level 1.

Provincial/Territorial pie charts

Yukon: 8%, 28%, 35%, 29%
Northwest Territories: 12%, 27%, 37%, 25%
British Columbia: 12%, 22%, 39%, 28%
Alberta: 14%, 24%, 37%, 25%
Saskatchewan: 8%, 35%, 31%, 26%
Manitoba: 17%, 31%, 32%, 20%
Ontario: 12%, 40%, 29%, 19%
Quebec: 8%, 27%, 38%, 27%
Newfoundland: 5%, 30%, 29%, 36%
Prince Edward Island: 16%, 37%, 23%, 24%
New Brunswick: 12%, 25%, 35%, 28%
Nova Scotia: 13%, 29%, 34%, 24%

V. LITERACY AND DISABILITY AT THE CROSSROADS | 111

Accommodations Received by Ages 15 and Older with Disabilities who have Low Critical Literacy Skills*, Provinces and Territories

1991 Health and Activity Limitation Survey (HALS)

Just over half (51.5%) of all adults with disabilities who had low critical literacy reported that they had received one to five accommodations to remove barriers that they encountered in their everyday activities. An additional 18.5% reported even more accommodations to remove barriers. 30.1% of those with low critical literacy have no accommodations.

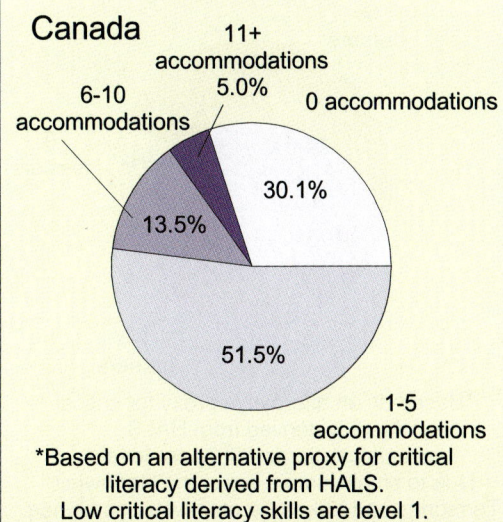

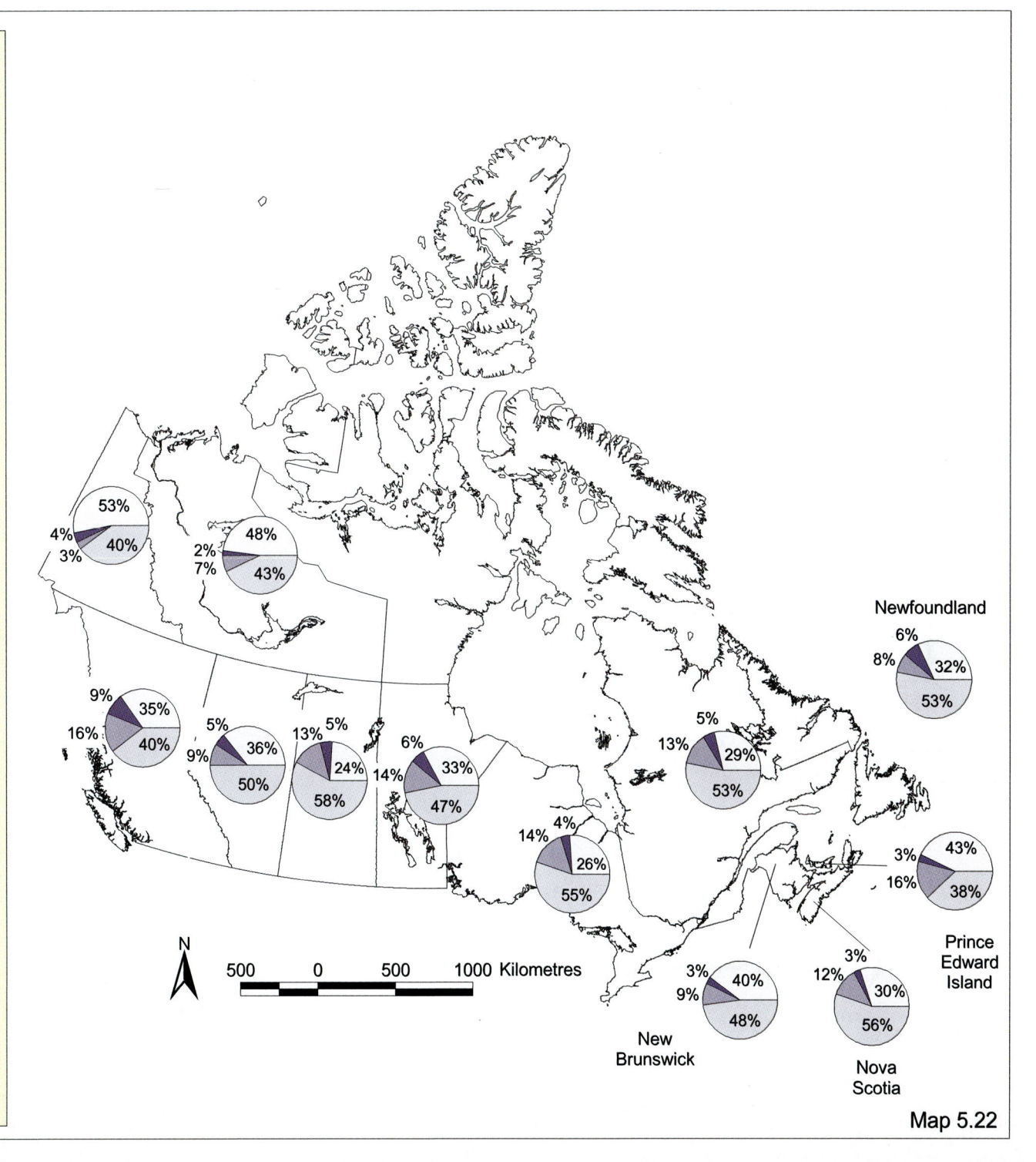

Canada

- 0 accommodations: 30.1%
- 1-5 accommodations: 51.5%
- 6-10 accommodations: 13.5%
- 11+ accommodations: 5.0%

*Based on an alternative proxy for critical literacy derived from HALS. Low critical literacy skills are level 1.

Map 5.22

ATLAS OF LITERACY AND DISABILITY

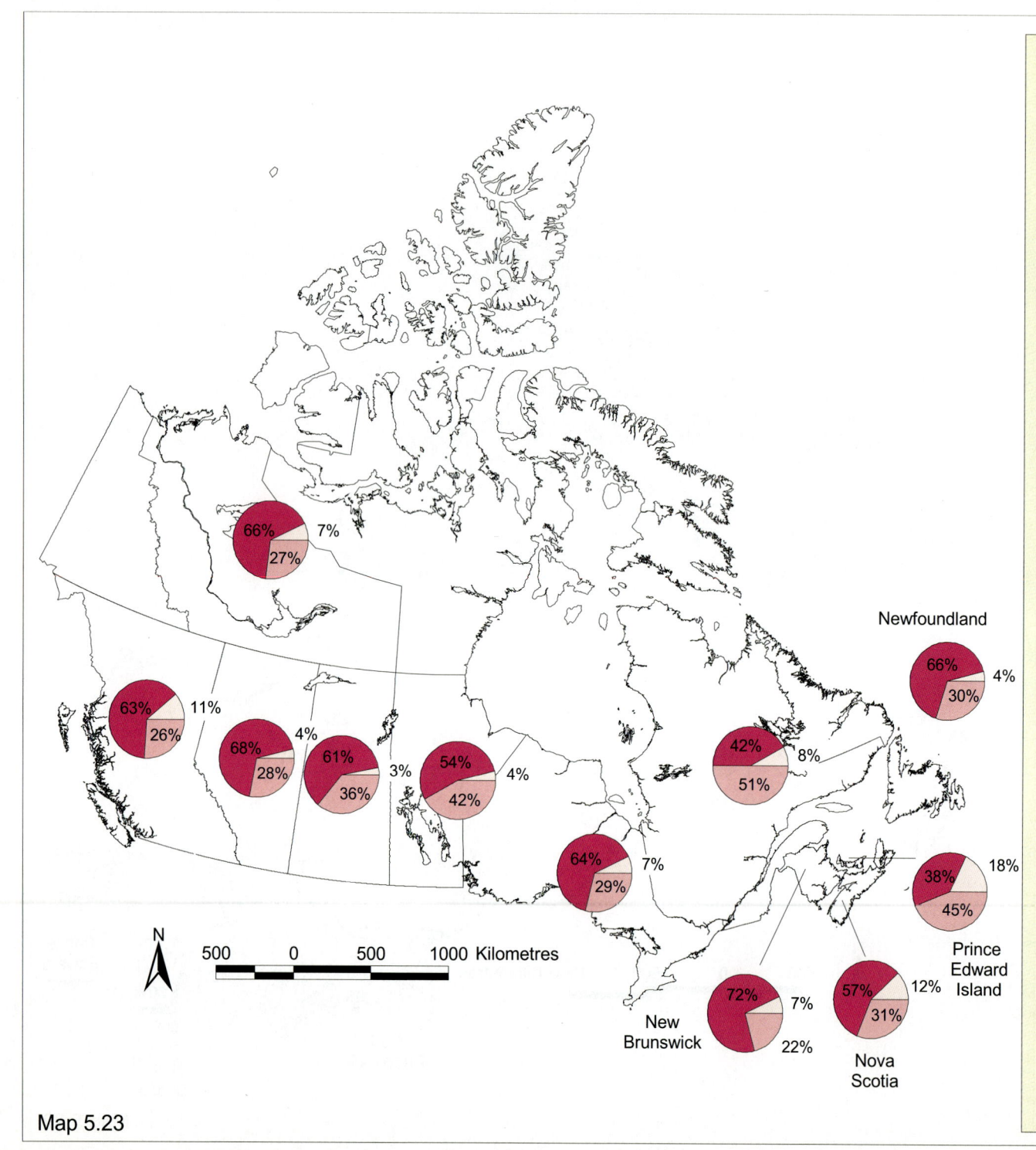

Number of Barriers Encountered by Adults with Disabilities Who are Active in the Labour Force and have Low Critical Literacy Skills*, Provinces and Territories

1991 Health and Activity Limitation Survey (HALS)

While nearly everyone experiencing low critical literacy who has a disability has at least one barrier (over 90%), the majority encounter 6 or more barriers in their daily lives (60%). A small percentage has no barriers. A province by province review shows differences across the country.

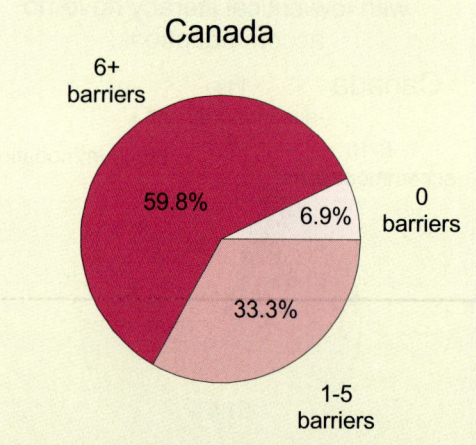

Canada

- 6+ barriers: 59.8%
- 1-5 barriers: 33.3%
- 0 barriers: 6.9%

*Based on an alternative proxy for critical literacy derived from HALS. Low critical literacy skills are level 1. Due to small sample sizes, the Northwest Territories and Yukon Territory were combined.

Northwest Territories/Yukon: 66% / 27% / 7%
British Columbia: 63% / 26% / 11%
Alberta: 68% / 28% / 4%
Saskatchewan: 61% / 36% / 3%
Manitoba: 54% / 42% / 4%
Ontario: 64% / 29% / 7%
Quebec: 42% / 51% / 8%
Newfoundland: 66% / 30% / 4%
Prince Edward Island: 38% / 45% / 18%
New Brunswick: 72% / 22% / 7%
Nova Scotia: 57% / 31% / 12%

Map 5.23

V. LITERACY AND DISABILITY AT THE CROSSROADS | 113

Number of Accommodations Received by Adults with Disabilities who are Active in the Labour Force and have Low Critical Literacy Skills*, Provinces and Territories

1991 Health and Activity Limitation Survey (HALS)

Fifty-eight percent of Canadians with disabilities experiencing low critical literacy indicate that they receive some accommodations. The vast majority (50%) has between 1 and 5 accommodations. There is a broad range in number of accommodations across Canada.

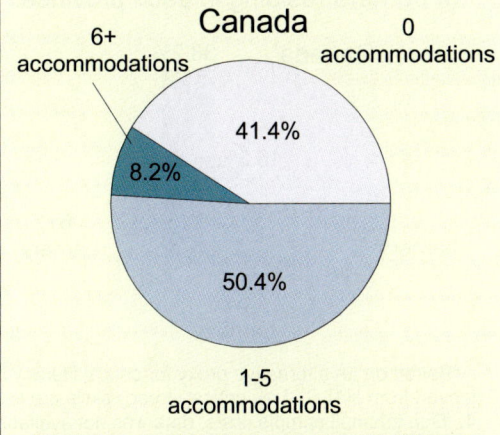

Canada
- 6+ accommodations: 8.2%
- 0 accommodations: 41.4%
- 1-5 accommodations: 50.4%

*Based on an alternative proxy for critical literacy derived from HALS. Low critical literacy skills are level 1. Due to small sample sizes, the Northwest Territories and Yukon Territory were combined.

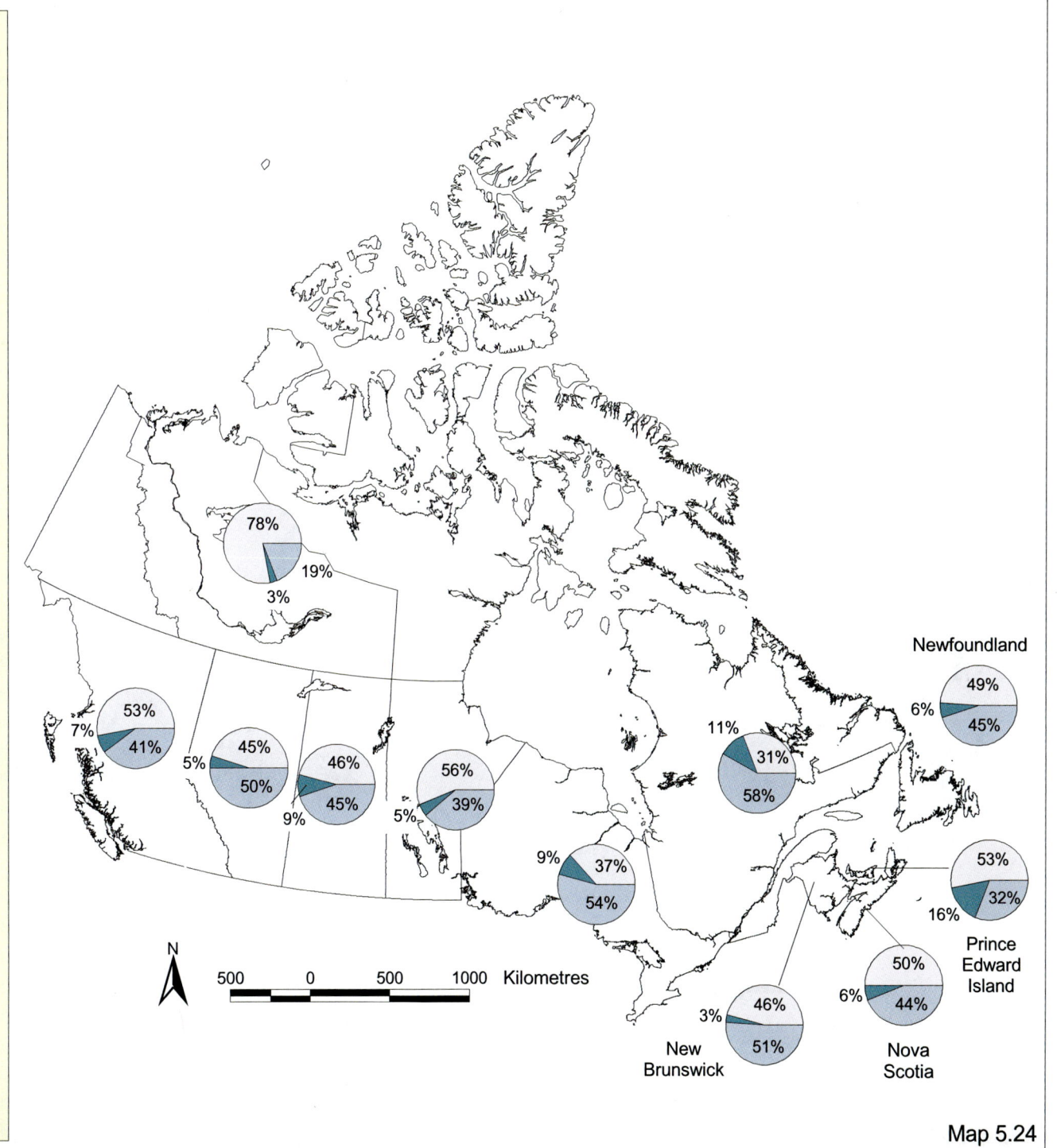

Territories (combined): 78% / 19% / 3%
British Columbia: 53% / 41% / 7% (approx)
Alberta: 45% / 50% / 5%
Saskatchewan: 46% / 45% / 9%
Manitoba: 56% / 39% / 5%
Ontario: 37% / 54% / 9%
Quebec: 31% / 58% / 11%
New Brunswick: 46% / 51% / 3%
Nova Scotia: 50% / 44% / 6%
Prince Edward Island: 53% / 32% / 16%
Newfoundland: 49% / 45% / 6%

Map 5.24

ATLAS OF LITERACY AND DISABILITY

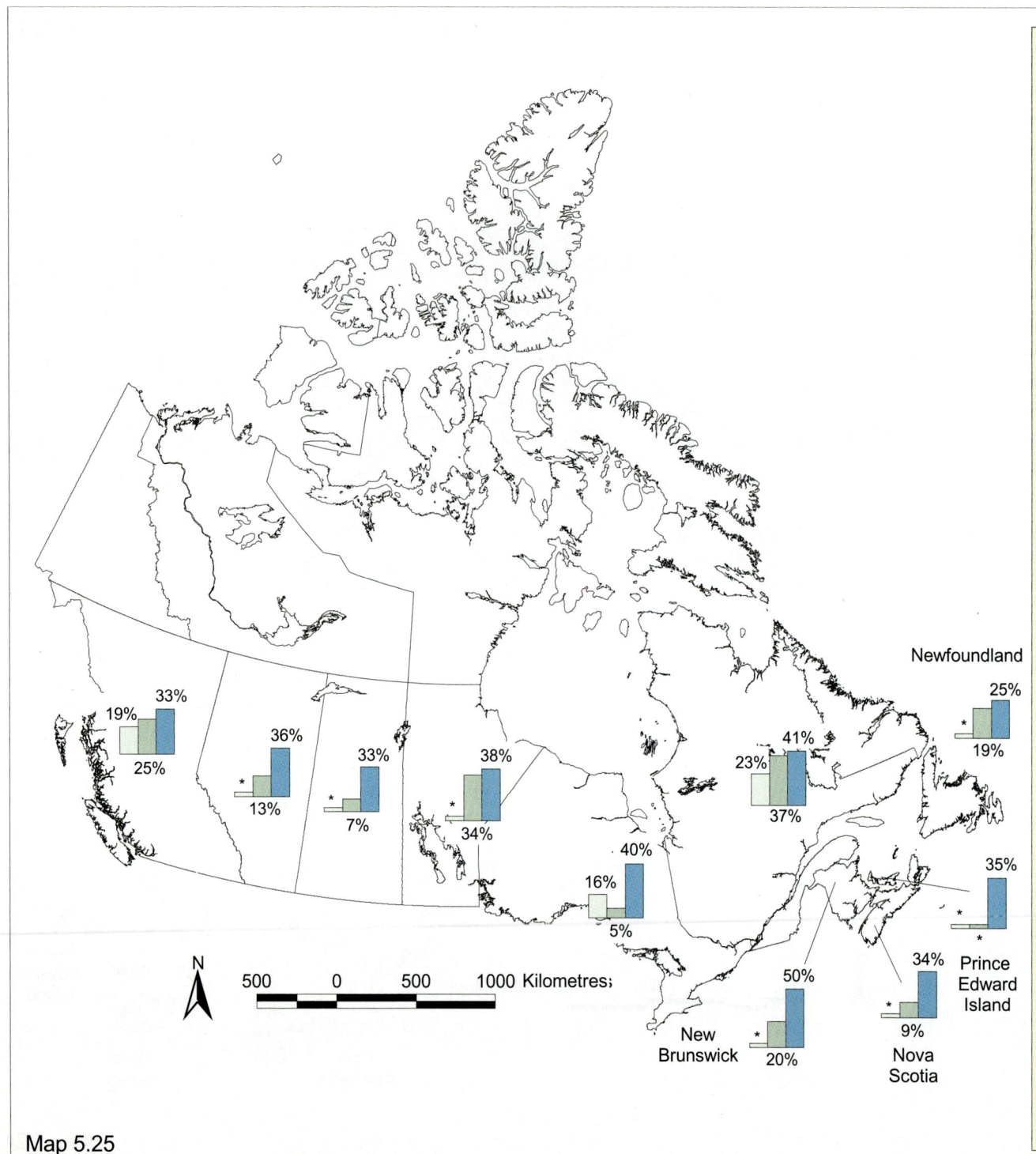

Number of Barriers Encountered for Ages 15 and Older with Disabilities Residing in Households with Low Income and Low Critical Literacy Skills*, Provinces

1991 Health and Activity Limitation Survey (HALS)

This map shows a relationship among income, critical literacy and barriers that people face. Of the adults with disabilities facing 6 or more barriers in their daily lives, 40% reside in households with low income and low critical literacy. Sixteen percent of the group face between 1 and 5 barriers. There are significant numbers of people facing large numbers of barriers residing in each province.

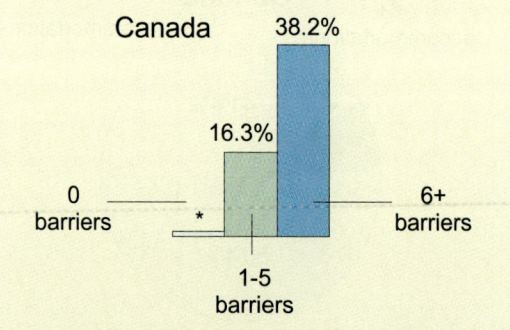

Canada: 0 barriers *, 1-5 barriers 16.3%, 6+ barriers 38.2%

*Based on an alternative proxy for critical literacy derived from HALS. Low critical literacy skills are level 1. Due to small sample sizes, data was not available for the Northwest and Yukon Territories. Data was suppressed for 0 barriers in several provinces. The Canada estimate for 1-5 barriers does not contain data for PEI.

Provincial values:
- British Columbia: 19%, 25%, 33%
- Alberta: *, 13%, 36%
- Saskatchewan: *, 7%, 33%
- Manitoba: *, 34%, 38%
- Ontario: 16%, 5%, 40%
- Quebec: 23%, 37%, 41%
- Newfoundland: *, 19%, 25%
- New Brunswick: *, 20%, 50%
- Nova Scotia: *, 9%, 34%
- Prince Edward Island: *, *, 35%

Map 5.25

V. LITERACY AND DISABILITY AT THE CROSSROADS | 115

Number of Accommodations Received by Ages 15 and Older with Disabilities Residing in Households Having Low Income and Low Critical Literacy Skills*, Provinces

1991 Health and Activity Limitation Survey (HALS)

This map shows a relationship among income, critical literacy and accommodations that people receive. Of the adults with disabilities receiving 1 to 5 accommodations in their daily lives 34.6% reside in households with low income and low critical literacy. 31.9% of the adults receiving no accommodations reside in households with low income and have low critical literacy. There are significant numbers of people receiving large number of accommodations residing in each province.

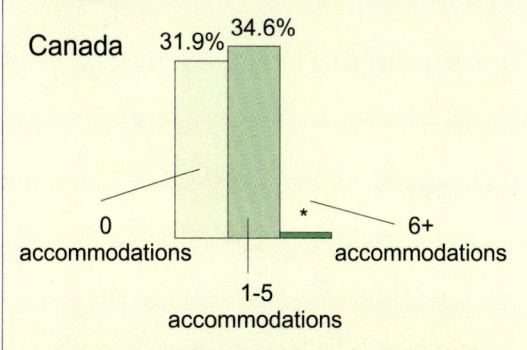

Canada: 0 accommodations 31.9%; 1-5 accommodations 34.6%; 6+ accommodations *

*Based on an alternative proxy for critical literacy derived from HALS. Low critical literacy skills are level 1. Due to small sample sizes, data was not available for the Northwest and Yukon Territories. Data was suppressed for 6+ accommodations in several provinces.

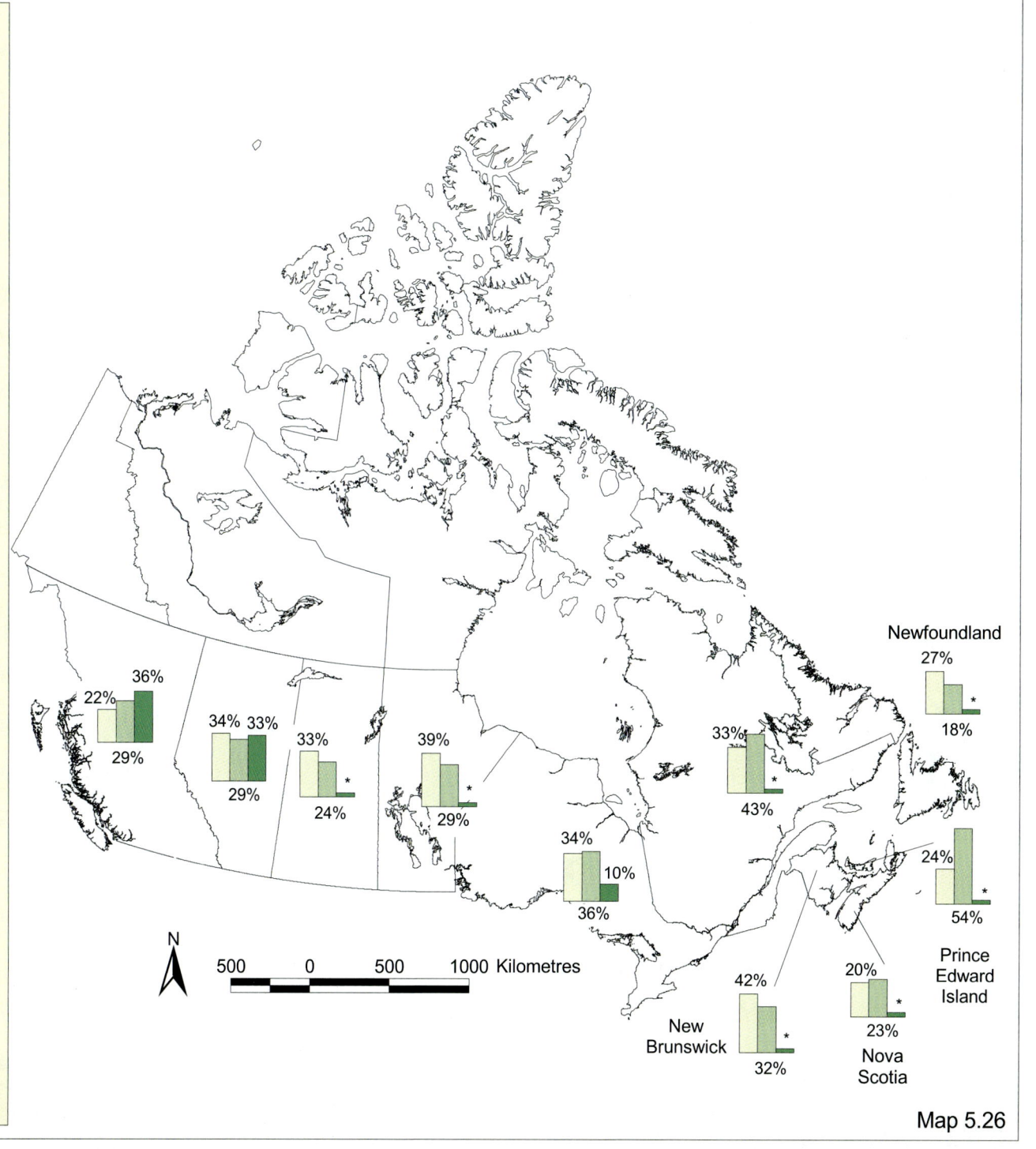

Provincial data (0 / 1-5 / 6+ accommodations):
- British Columbia: 22% / 36% / 29%
- Alberta: 34% / 33% / 29%
- Saskatchewan: 33% / 24% / *
- Manitoba: 39% / 29% / *
- Ontario: 34% / 36% / 10%
- Quebec: 33% / 43% / *
- Newfoundland: 27% / 18% / *
- New Brunswick: 42% / 32% / *
- Nova Scotia: 20% / 23% / *
- Prince Edward Island: 24% / 54% / *

Map 5.26

ATLAS OF LITERACY AND DISABILITY

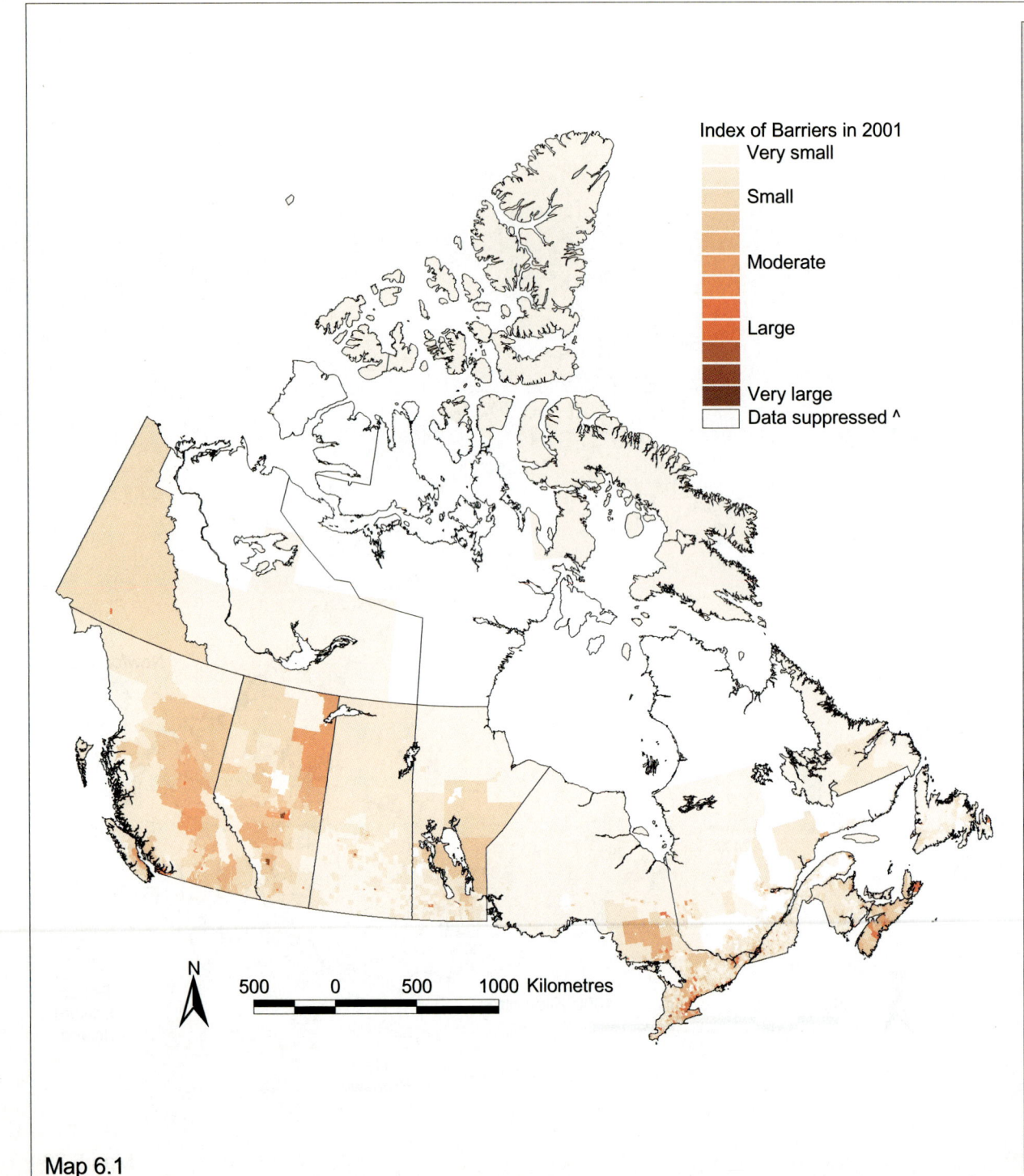

Index of Barriers in 2001
- Very small
- Small
- Moderate
- Large
- Very large
- Data suppressed ^

A Relative Index of 2001 Barriers Encountered by Ages 15 and Older with Disabilities, Census Subdivisions

Modeled Data based on 1991 HALS, 1994 IALS, 1996 NPHS, 1996 Census of Population and Verified Against 2001 PALS

The darker colours show areas where the population with disabilities should encounter larger number of barriers in their everyday activities. There is strong spatial variation with areas of greater lesser importance being contiguous to each other at all scales - local census subdivisions (inset), provincial, and national.

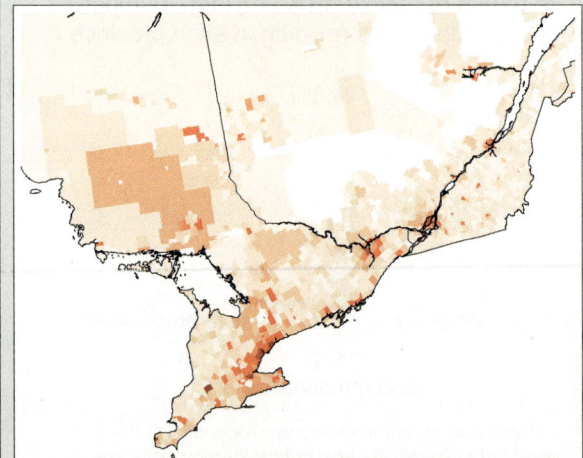

^Data was suppressed when the CSD had a population less than 40 and for Indian Reserves, if the response rate for the Indian Reserve was less than 25%.

Map 6.1

V. LITERACY AND DISABILITY AT THE CROSSROADS | 117

A Relative Index of 2001 Accommodations by Ages 15 and Older with Disabilities, Census Subdivisions

Modeled Data based on 1991 HALS, 1994 IALS, 1996 NPHS, 1996 Census of Population and Verified Against 2001 PALS

The lighter colours show areas where the population with disabilities receive a lesser number accommodations in their everyday activities. There is strong spatial variation with areas of greater lesser importance being contiguous to each other at all scales - local census subdivisions (inset), provincial, and national.

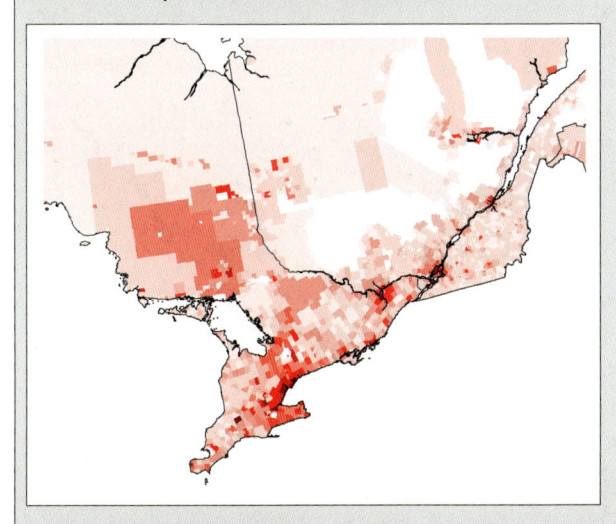

Index of Accommodations in 2001
- Very small
- Small
- Moderate
- Large
- Very large
- Data suppressed^

^Data was suppressed when the CSD had a population less than 40 and for Indian Reserves, if the response rate for the Indian Reserve was less than 25%.

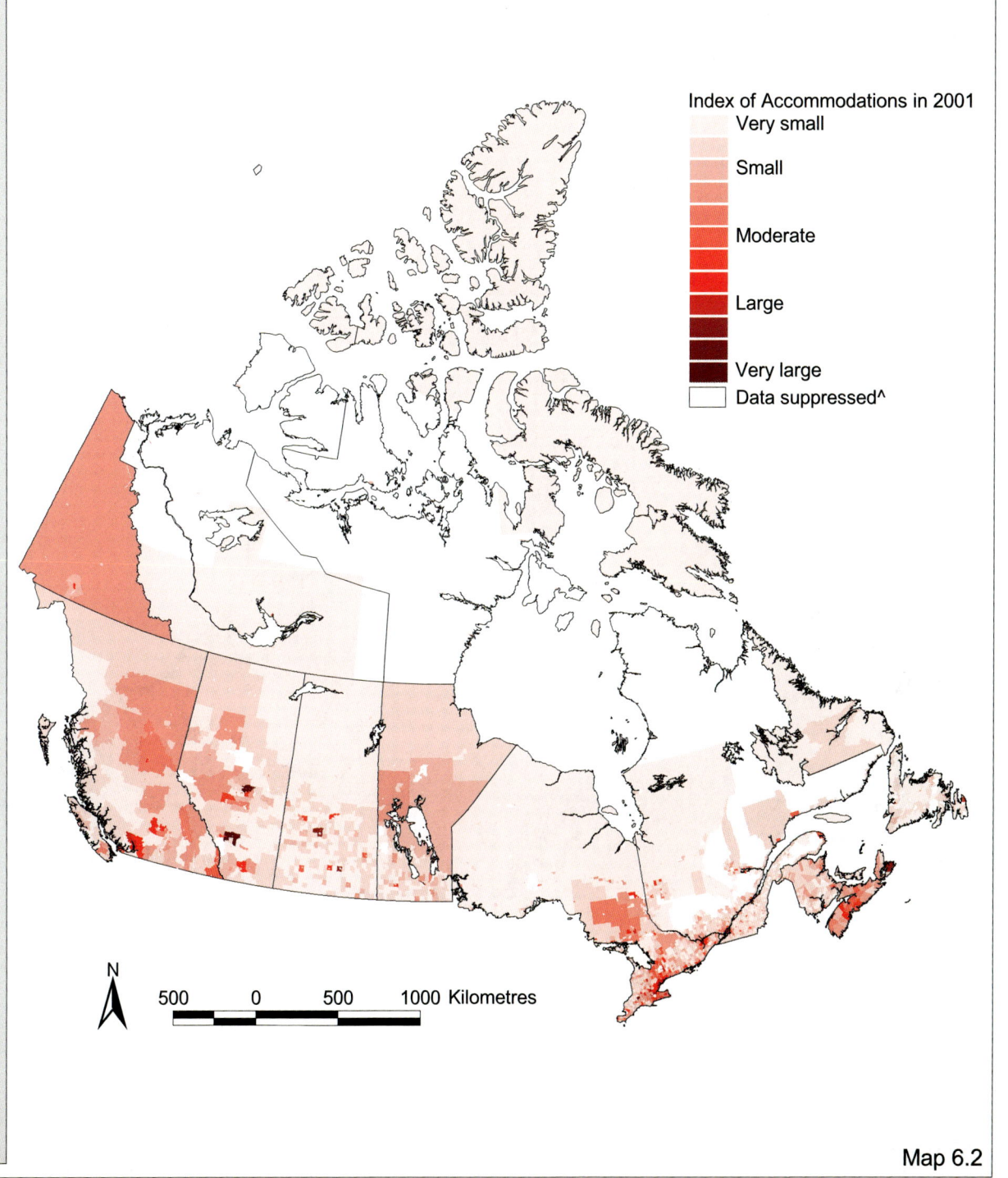

Map 6.2

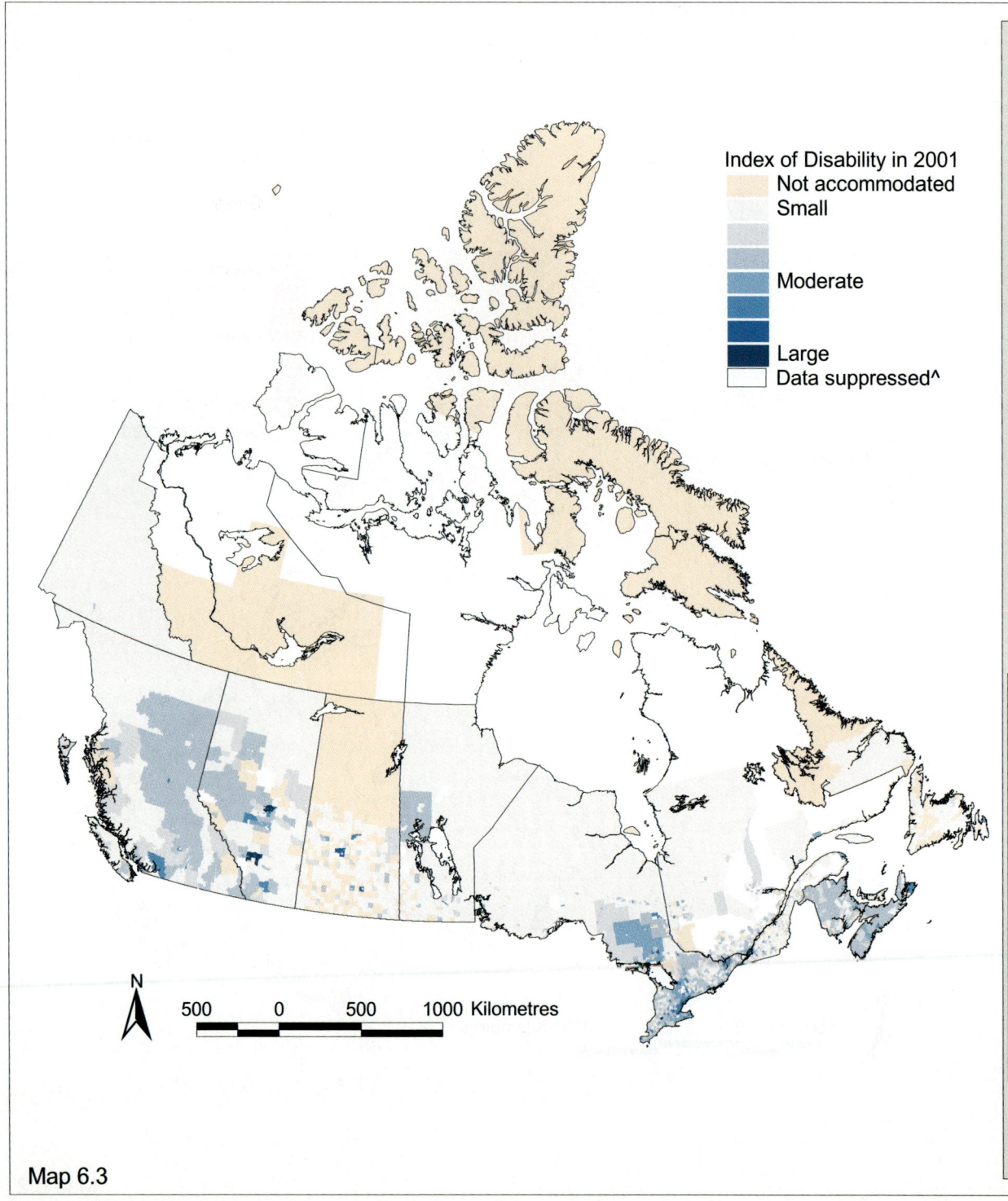

ATLAS OF LITERACY AND DISABILITY

A Relative Index of 2001 Accommodated Barriers by Ages 15 and Older with Disabilities, Census Subdivisions

Modeled Data based on 1991 HALS, 1994 IALS, 1996 NPHS, 1996 Census of Population and Verified Against 2001 PALS

The darker colours show areas where the population with disabilities barriers are the most accommodated in their everyday activities. There is strong spatial variation with areas of greater lesser importance being contiguous to each other at all scales -local (inset), provincial, and national.

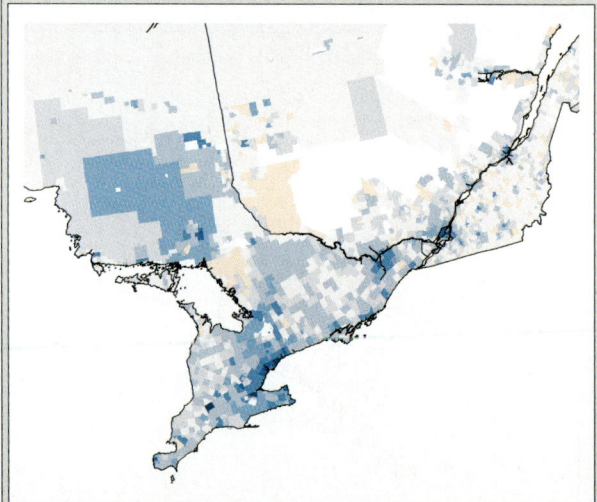

Index of Disability in 2001
- Not accommodated
- Small
- Moderate
- Large
- Data suppressed^

^Data was suppressed when the CSD had a population less than 40 and for Indian Reserves, if the response rate for the Indian Reserve was less than 25%

Map 6.3

VI. *Conclusion*

This project was driven by the hypothesis that there is a relationship between literacy and disability, and that this relationship is complex and multi-directional. Literacy skills are affected by experiences in education, at home and at work. We wondered, in connecting this work, if people who experience disability-related barriers to full participation also face barriers in developing literacy skills and in having their styles of communication recognized by others. A critical perspective of literacy and a rights-based perspective of disability informed our approach throughout this research project.

Critical literacy is not about the skills people have acquired. This is not to imply that literacy skills are not important, or that they fail to play a role in critical literacy. On the contrary, literacy skills such as reading, writing and math, and equal opportunities to gain them, have a clear impact on people's marginalization. However, it is the marginalization, not the skill acquisition, which is the primary focus of critical literacy.

Critical literacy includes strategies to ensure equitable access to literacy skill acquisition, but it also includes strategies to ensure that people are not marginalized as a result of their level of literacy skill. In a similar way, disability rights takes into consideration the systems of discrimination that disadvantage people with disabilities. IALS tells us that there is an association between disadvantage and low literacy skills. The findings clearly indicate that persons classified as having low literacy are less likely to be engaged in stable employment and more likely to be in low income groups. People with disabilities are similarly disadvantaged, as HALS data demonstrates.

With this understanding of critical literacy and disability, the study, drawing on different surveys, using GIS mapping, analyzing exploratory literacy and disability variables and using data modeling, uncovered some preliminary findings about this relationship that are grounded in a critical literacy and disability rights perspective.

Both HALS and IALS found that people with disability were disadvantaged in terms of their literacy skills. HALS found people with disabilities were less likely to have completed grade nine (basic literacy). IALS found people with disabilities were less likely to have adequate levels of prose document and quantitative literacy skills (functional literacy).

The proxy variables for functional and critical literacy both found that people with disabilities were disadvantaged. Using the derived proxy for functional literacy, approximately 1 in 10 adults with disabilities has functional literacy skills at the lowest level in most regions of Canada. This means that they do not have the literacy skills needed to function every day in the social and economic life of their community. Around one-third of those with disabilities (32.7%) are at the middle level, which means that they are functioning with some challenges. These findings suggest that nearly half of Canadians with disabilities face barriers related to functional literacy.

Similar proportions face barriers to meaningful participation in public discourse. Around 42% of Canadian adults with disabilities experience low to moderate critical literacy. This means they are either experiencing fairly severe exclusions related to communication or, minimally, they face barriers in this regard.

The findings showed that literacy and disability separately intersect with other demographic and socio-economic factors, making it difficult to identify precisely which factors are causal or the direction of causality. What is apparent is that people with disabilities are in double jeopardy with respect to basic, functional and critical literacy. The social determinants of disability and the social determinants of literacy operate together to create hurdles to equal participation in Canadian society for people with disabilities. This is reflected in correlations related to education attainment, age, regional differences, language and immigration, aboriginal status, labour force participation and income.

Survey Design and Information Gathering

Some of our findings relate to the availability of national, regional, provincial and subprovincial data about the relationship between literacy and disability. From the outset, we knew there was a gap in data in this area; however, the extent of this gap became evident as the research team faced a series of barriers in accessing statistical information about this relationship. Literacy and disability data exist in separate datasets in Canada. The primary source for literacy data at the time of this study was the International Adult Literacy Survey. The primary sources for disability data were the Health and Activity Limitation Survey and the Participation and Activity Limitation Survey. Each of these is based on a well thought out definition of its topic area (literacy or disability) and operationalized according to internationally acceptable standards of survey design. However, these studies, on their own and in combination, provided insufficient data for reliably exploring the intersection of literacy and disability from the perspective of critical literacy and disability rights. Further, the present sampling designs are inadequate at a fine level of spatial resolution. The following recommendations are based on the existing gaps in the data, and the kinds of data that need to be available, to better understand the relationship of literacy and disability.

- Standardized definitions of the concepts of literacy and disability that reflect contemporary theoretical perspectives on these issues are needed. These could be used in all national surveys, so that, for example, good disability data could be drawn from literacy surveys, and good literacy data could be drawn from disability surveys.

- New approaches in survey design that reflect recent paradigm shifts in literacy theory towards what has been termed critical, emancipatory or discursive literacy theory, and disability theory based on social determinants and rights, suggest new approaches are needed in survey design which reflect these perspectives.

- The Barriers and Accommodation Index, while still in its developmental stage, is adaptable to current disability surveys that include questions on barriers and accommodations. However, in the design on new disability surveys, indicators based on the BAI could be incorporated that better enable a survey to measure the impact of barrier accommodation on inclusion and socio-economic conditions. Further research is needed to determine the best types of survey questions to create such a tool. Such research should be informed by the input of members of the disability community, and be based on the disability-rights approach.

- Measures of critical literacy should be designed for use in future surveys. Such measures could include questions on the barriers people experience to acquiring literacy skills, to communicating with others, to accessing information, and to having their voices recognized in society.

A study of this nature is useful only to the extent that is understandable and helpful in revealing facts about social phenomena – facts that can be used and built upon by policy makers at all levels, and by other social animators in civil society. The use of maps to draw attention to the situation of literacy and disability in Canada, the theoretical underpinnings and the statistical knowledge in the areas both singly and in combination was a primary function of this study. Some findings were more interesting, more surprising and more useful than others. But in all cases, the maps provide a way of presenting data that we hope will make it easier to identify with, compared to the conventional tables and charts that are the trademark of statistical analysis.

Appendix A: Detailed Methodology

The general methodology of the project was a nine-step process (see figure A.1). The project was designed to be an integrated team approach with two areas of specialty. One team focused on data collection and interpretation while the other focused on data analysis and presentation. There was considerable overlap between the two teams.

The best available data on literacy and disability were collected from a variety of private, NGO, and governmental studies. This was supplemented by expert interviews which included recommendations of other studies and analyses. A total of 1000 studies were examined and 30 people interviewed. This provided a collective library that was fundamental to the research.

In order to access data at the finest spatial detail, the Research Data Centre (RDC) was approached. The RDC is a part of a new initiative by Statistics Canada to provide researchers with monitored access to previously unobtainable unsuppressed survey data. The RDC allowed us to sample, analyze, and model the data, with some restrictions. RDC regulations include a rule demanding suppression of data from any cell size of 5 or less, for reasons of privacy. Blank areas in maps shown in the atlas and report are where data has been suppressed.

Sampled and analyzed data files were obtained from the RDC data. These in turn were put on the "Applied Social Systems Laboratory" of the University at Buffalo server. In conjunction with the National Center from Geographic Information Analysis and Interdisciplinary Graduate Education Research Training programs the data files were prepared for other types of statistical analysis and comparison with other data files as well as for spatial and GIS analyses. These files were made into tables and graphs and were then sent for interpretation by the members of the research group most familiar with the survey, literacy, or disability aspects of the file. There was then an interactive process between the interpreters and the GIS developers in terms of exactly what variables should be used and how they should be mapped. The GIS maps were created and then sent back to the entire team for comment. As they were approved, the writing of articles, the creation of the atlas, and the drafting of the final report were undertaken.

THE DATABASES

The five databases that were the primary basis for the data for this study are described below.

1. 1994 *International Adult Literacy Survey (IALS) for Canada*

IALS was initiated with two goals:
   i. to develop an assessment instrument that would enable comparisons of literacy performance across languages and cultures, and
   ii. if such an assessment could be created, perform such comparisons, describing the literacy skills of people from different countries.

In 1994, nine countries including Canada (English and French-speaking populations) fielded the world's first large-scale, comparative assessment of adult literacy.

Literacy was defined as the individual's ability to use written information to function in society. The development of the survey instrument and the management of the survey was a joint effort of Statistics Canada and the Educational Testing Service of Princeton, New Jersey.

The focus of the survey was the direct assessment of the literacy skills of respondents using tasks of varying degree of difficulty drawn from a range of topic and knowledge areas. Each respondent completed a booklet of literacy tasks designed to measure their prose, document, and quantitative skills. Most of these tasks were open-ended requiring the respondent to provide a written answer. To achieve good content coverage of each of three literacy domains, the number of tasks in the assessment had to be quite large. Yet, the time burden for each respondent also had to be kept within an acceptable range. To accommodate these two conflicting requirements, each respondent was asked to complete only a selection of tasks — the selection of the tasks was made using a variant of matrix sampling.

Additional information was collected on a background questionnaire including demographic characteristics, education, labour market experience, self-assessment of literacy skills, training undertaken in the year previous to the survey, and perceived barriers to realizing enhanced literacy skill levels.

The main IALS sample was a sub-sample of the May 1994 Canadian Labour Force Survey (LFS) file using probability sampling at all stages. Residents of institutions, persons living on Indian reserves, members of the armed forces, residents of the Yukon and Northwest Territories are excluded from the sample.

The sub-sample of 6,427 LFS respondents aged 16 and older was stratified, with an over-sample of certain target groups of policy interest. The sample yielded 4,703 respondents.

A second sample was a three-stage probability sample of Francophones from the province of Ontario selected from the 1991 census. This sample resulted in 1,044 respondents.

The total number of respondents was 5,660. The overall response rate was 69%. To date, the geographic detail released from the 1994 IALS has been limited to four regions — Eastern region, Quebec, Ontario and the Western Region. Quality guidelines suggest that the sample size for any estimate should be 30 or greater. If the sample size less than 30, the estimate should be considered of unacceptable quality. However, all estimates can be released but those derived from a sample of less than 30 should be accompanied by a caution to users.

2. 1991 Health and Activity Limitation Survey (HALS)

The 1991 HALS was designed to collect data for a national database on disability that included all types of disabilities and all geographic areas in Canada. HALS was first conducted after the 1986 Census of Population, and it was repeated after the 1991 Census of Population.

HALS operationalized the definition of disability from the International Classification of Impairments, Disabilities and Handicaps (ICIDH), which was developed by the World Health Organization (WHO).

A modified version of the "Activities of Daily Living"[26] questions was used for Section A of the adult questionnaires. These questions _ developed by a working group of the Organization of Economic Cooperation and Development (OECD) _ represent a set of activities that measure the extent to which a health problem or condition limits the nature and extent of activities undertaken by an individual in his/her life. The questions asked respondents about the following:

  i. whether or not they are limited in specific activities such as walking up and down stairs, cutting food, and seeing newsprint; this method of evaluating a person's ability to perform specific tasks is called the "Functional Limitation

---

26 Special Study No. 5, Measuring Disability, O.E.C.D., 1982.

Approach" (corresponds to the Activities of Daily Living questions: A1-A19);

ii. whether or not they are limited in activities at home, school, work or leisure because of a physical or psychological condition;

iii. whether a health professional has ever told them that they had a learning disability or a mental handicap, or that they were developmentally delayed or mentally retarded; and

iv. whether or not they have any difficulty with learning or remembering.

The target population of HALS consisted of all persons with a physical or psychological disability who were living in Canada at the time of the 1991 Census, including residents of the Yukon and the Northwest Territories as well as permanent residents of most collective dwellings and health care institutions. Indian reserves were covered by the Aboriginal Peoples Survey, which was also conducted by Statistics Canada. Persons excluded for operational reasons were residents of penal institutions, correctional facilities, military camps, campgrounds and parks, soup kitchens, merchant and coastguard ships, and children's group homes.

HALS consisted of two separate components: the Household Survey, which was conducted immediately following the 1991 Census, and the Institutions Survey, which was conducted in early 1992.

The data used in this research included persons aged 15 and older who, at the time of the 1991 Census, were residents of private homes or small collective dwellings such as group homes.

Results of field tests conducted prior to the 1986 Census indicated that many persons with a disability did not respond "Yes" to the above questions on activity limitation. Typically, these persons were more active and had less serious disabilities than those individuals who responded "Yes" to the Census disability questions. These individuals represented a particular segment of the population of persons with disabilities and, therefore, needed to be sampled to avoid significant biases in the survey estimates. Consequently, it was decided to select and include in the 1991 HALS, a sample of individuals who responded "No" to both disability questions on the 1991 Census. This group of persons became the "No" sample. A sample of persons who responded "Yes" to at least one of the two Census disability questions constituted the "Yes" sample.

Approximately 35,000 individuals were selected for the "Yes" sample and 113,000 for the "No" sample, yielding a total of 148,000 adults (aged 15 years and older) and children (aged 0 to 14 years) for the household survey. The sample was selected such that estimates could be produced for the ten provinces, both territories and for persons aged 15 to 64 years residing in selected large urban centres.

Data collection for the Household Survey took place in the fall of 1991, immediately after the 1991 Census. Interviewers were trained on both survey content and procedures. The majority of the interviews were conducted by telephone. Personal interviews were conducted with all persons in the "Yes" sample who were aged 65 and older as well as with those individuals who requested one. Eighty-three percent of the interviews were conducted with the selected adult (persons aged 15 and older). However, some respondents were unable, because of a physical or psychological condition or because they were absent during the survey, to respond for him/herself. In these cases, a proxy respondent – another member of the household – was asked to answer the questions on behalf of the selected individual. The response rate for the household survey was 87%.

One of the advantages of a post-censal survey is that, for each respondent, information collected during the Census is linked to the data from the survey. For the household component of HALS, each person's record is a combination of the information collected in the survey as well as the information collected for the same individual in the Census.

i. Person-level variables provide a wide range of information (e.g., marital status, education, place of birth, citizenship, ethnic origin, mother tongue, language spoken at home).

ii. Household-level variables include size and type of household as well as data pertaining to the dwelling in which the person resides (e.g., dwelling owned/rented by household member, type of dwelling, date of construction, number of rooms, rent or mortgage costs).

iii. Since the Census divides the household into both "economic" and "Census" families, information is available for both of these entities (e.g., structure of the family, selected person's status within the family).

For persons who answered "No" to all of the HALS screening questions, the records on the database include the information from the Census only. This means that the database contains socio- and demographic data for persons without disabilities.

For persons who answered "Yes" to at least one of the HALS screening questions (the population with disabilities), the records include the responses to the HALS questionnaire as well as the information from the Census for those selected persons.

3. 2001 Participation and Activity Limitation Survey (PALS)

The Participation and Activity Limitation Survey (PALS) is a national survey designed to collect information on adults and children who have a disability. PALS provides information on the prevalence of various disabilities, the supports for persons with disabilities, their employment profile, their income and their participation in society.

PALS, like its predecessor HALS, is a post-censal survey that uses the 2001 Census as its sampling frame. The 2001 Census questionnaire included two general questions on activity limitations — different from those used in the 1986, 1991 and 1996 Censuses. The PALS sample was selected using the census information on age, geography and the responses to these two general questions. Only persons who answered "Yes" to one or both of the Census disability questions were eligible for sample selection. Unlike HALS, persons who answered "No" to both disability questions were not sampled.

The PALS sample was 43,000, consisting of approximately 35,000 adults and 8,000 children. The population covered by the survey was persons residing in private and some collective households in the ten provinces. Persons living in the Yukon, Northwest Territories and Nunavut, persons living in institutions and on First Nations reserves were excluded from the survey.

The interviews were conducted by telephone and the overall response rate was 82.5%.

The PALS screening questions include those used in the 1991 HALS with some modifications to better identify persons with learning disabilities, long-term memory difficulties, developmental disabilities and psychological disabilities. Questions were also added to identify persons who have limitation in their activities because of long-term pain.

During the period that data extraction and analysis were being completed for this research, the only data available from PALS were nature and severity of disability by age and gender. The remaining data will be released throughout the remainder of 2003 and early 2004.

4. 1996 National Population Health Survey (NPHS)

The NPHS collects information related to the health of the Canadian population and related socio-demographic information. The NPHS is composed of three components: the household survey, the Health Care Institution Survey and the Northern Territories survey. The household component includes household residents in all provinces, with the exclusion of populations on Indian Reserves, Canadian Forces Bases and some remote areas in Quebec and Ontario.

The National Population Health Survey (NPHS), a longitudinal survey, re-interviews a group of Canadians every two years. It is the first national health survey of its kind conducted in Canada. The initial wave of data collection Cycle 1 took place from June 1994 to June 1995. Data for Cycle 2 were collected from June 1996 to August 1997. Cycle 2 data were used in this research project.

From the longitudinal panel, a response rate of 93.6% was achieved in 1996/97. Of these 16,168 respondents, 15,670 provided full information, that is, general and in-depth health information for both cycles of the survey. The additional 498 respondents provided partial information (they gave at least general health information in both 1994/95 and 1996/97). As in cycle 1, additional respondents were surveyed in cycle 2 for cross-sectional purposes only—not as a part of the longitudinal panel. Their one-time participation produced a total of 210,377 respondents to the general health questions in cycle 2 (with 173,216 aged 12 or older and 37,161 under age 12) and 81,804 respondents to the in-depth health questions (with 73,402 aged 12 or older and 8,402 under age 12). Information from the 1996-97 NPHS used in this research included age, gender, activity limitation and educational attainment.

5. 1996 Census of Population

In mid-May 1996, Statistics Canada conducted the Census of Population to provide a statistical portrait of Canada and its people. The Census of Population provides the population and dwelling counts not only for Canada but also for each province and territory, and for smaller geographic units such as cities or districts within cities. The census also provides information about Canada's demographic, social and economic characteristics.

Not all respondents receive the same questionnaire. Four out of five households received the short form while the remaining one in five received a long form. The short form contains seven questions: the respondent's name, sex, age, marital and common-law status, family and household relationships and mother tongue. The long form includes the seven questions from the short questionnaire plus additional questions, including questions on education, employment and income.

The 1996 Census also collected information about people who have activity limitations at home, school, work or in other aspects of their lives, such as travel or recreation. In both the 1986 and 1991 Censuses, this information was used to identify the sample for the 1986 and 1991 HALS. Information from the 1996 Census of Population used in this research included age, activity limitation and educational attainment.

The study analyzes various variables from each of these databases as well as creating new variables which were derived from the extant variables. The ways that these derived variables were calculated are described below:

1. Barriers and Accommodations Index (BAI)

The Barriers and Accommodations Index developed is an alternative to the HALS' Severity of Disability Index. HALS operationalized the functional model of disability to identify the population with disabilities and augmented these questions with information on the barriers encountered by respondents and the accommodations they obtained. In this effort, HALS measured peoples' needs for, and access to aids, devices and other accommodations, building modifications and needs for specialized transportation in relation to their day-to-day experiences. The Barriers and Accommodations index provides an overall measure of peoples' experiences in terms of the accessibility of their environments at home, work, and in the community.

Creating the barriers and accommodations index
- Not all questions were asked of all respondents because of skip patterns that made the question not relevant to the respondent. In creating the barriers and accommodations index, these were treated as "No".

- Some respondents chose not to answer a question. When the HALS data was processed, these non-responses were left on the file and were identified with a "?" In creating the barriers and accommodations index, these were treated as "No".
- A "Yes" response to a question or category within a question was coded "1"; a "No" response was coded "0".
- The coded values were added to create the barriers index and the accommodations index and within each index by type.

1.1 The barriers component of the index

The following is the list of questions and response categories that were used in creating the barriers component of the index. The wording of the question has been truncated; the question is identified by the question number that appears on the HALS questionnaire; the response categories follow the question number – e.g. – aids and services needed by persons who are deaf or hard of hearing (A3d=01 to 11) where A3d is the question number on the Adult HALS questionnaire and the =01 to 11 are the response categories where the respondent could indicate the need for 11 different types of aids or personal services.

> Barriers to *aids and personal services* included any type of technical aids, specialized equipment, technical support, technical services and personal support that was needed but not obtained. Specifically, these included:
> - aids and services needed by persons who are deaf or hard of hearing (A3d=01 to 11)
> - aids and services needed by persons who are blind or visually impaired (A6d =01 to 11)
> - aids and services needed by persons who have difficulty speaking and being understood (A7g =1 to 6)
> - aids or specialized equipment needed to assist individuals with moving about (B4 =01 to 11)
> - aids or specialized equipment needed to support, replace or assist individuals in the use of hands or arms (B9 =3 to 6)
> - support need for preparation of meals (C5=3)
> - help needed with shopping (C10=3)
> - help needed with light housework (C15=3)
> - help needed with heavy housework (C20=3)
> - help needed with paying bills, banking, etc. (C25=3)
> - help needed with personal care (C29=3)
> - help needed to move around home (C33=3)
> - aids, devices or services needed to follow courses at school (D11=04 or =08 or =12 or =16 or =20 or =24 or =28 or =32 or =36 or =40)
> - aids, devices or services needed to work (E19 = 04 or =08 or = 12)
> - aids needed within home (G11 =3 or =8)
> - aids needed within home (G16 =01 or =04 or =05 or =06 or =08 or =09 or =10)
> - aids or personal support needed for leisure activities (H3 =07 or =13)
> - personal support needed for leisure activities (H7 =15).

Structural Barriers encountered within the *home and within the community* included:

- need for modifications to building features to attend school (D10 =04 or =08 or =12 or =16 or = 24)
- modifications needed to work environment (E20 = 04 or =08or = 12 or = 16 or =20 or =24)
- barriers that result in inability to undertake long distance travel (F21 =03 or=09 or=11 or=13)
- need for modifications to air terminals (F27 = 03 or =05 or=06 or=7)
- need for modifications to train terminals for train travel (F31 = 03 or =05 or=06 or=7)
- need for modifications to long-distance bus terminals (F35 = 03 or =05 or=06 or=7)
- need for modifications needed to ferry terminals for airplane travel (F35 = 03 or =05 or=06 or=7)
- need for specialized features to enter or leave personal residence (G11 =1 or =2 or =04)
- need for specialized features within personal residence (G16 =03 or =07)

Barriers encountered in using or attempting to use various forms of public *transportation* for local or long-distance travel included:

- suitable transportation to attend school (D10=20)
- inadequate transportation available to attend work-related training courses (currently employed) (E23 =05)
- inadequate transportation available to attend work-related training courses (currently unemployed) (E52 =05)
- lack of accessible transportation to go to work (currently not in the labour force) (E74 =17)
- inadequate transportation available to attend work-related training courses (currently not in the labour force) (E82 =05)
- needs specialized bus or van service (F10 =4)
- use of public transportation (short distance travel) (F17 =01 to 08)
- reasons why long distance travel is prevented (F21 = 01 or=17)
- obtaining information about specialized transportation services and facilities for long-distance travel (F24 =7)
- airplane travel (F27 = 01 or =05 or =09)
- train travel (F31 = 01 or =05 or =09)
- long-distance bus travel (F35 = 01 or =05 or =09)
- ferry travel (F39 = 01 or =05 or =09)
- long-distance travel in car, van or truck (F42 =5)
- inadequate transportation for leisure (H3 =09)
- inadequate transportation for leisure (H7 =13)

APPENDIX A: DETAILED METHODOLOGY

Barriers encountered in the *workplace* included:
- modified or different duties or modified hour, days, reduced work hours (E19 =16 or =20)
- work-related training courses not accessible (currently employed) (E23 =03)
- employer-related perception (currently employed) (E26 =02 or =07 or =12 or =17)
- current employer or perspective employer considers individual to be disadvantaged (currently employed) (E31 =1)
- work-related training courses not accessible (currently unemployed) (E52 =03)
- employer-related perception (currently unemployed) (E53 =02 or =07 or =12 or =17)
- current employer or perspective employer considers individual to be disadvantaged (currently unemployed) (E58 =1)
- work-related training courses not accessible (currently not in the labour force) (E82 =03)
- employer-related perception (currently not in the labour force) (E83 =02 or =07 or =12 or =17)

Financial barriers in various areas of daily life included:
- income and/or support impact (currently not in the labour force) (E74 = 01 or =03)
- specialized bus or van service too expensive (F13 =03)
- cost of airplane travel (F27 =23)
- cost of train travel (F31 =23)
- cost of long-distance bus travel (F35 =23)
- cost of ferry travel (F39 =23)
- financial assistance to move (G7 =1)
- financial assistance to make modifications (G20 =1)
- leisure activities (H3 =03)
- leisure activities (H7 =17)
- training to improve reading/writing skills (H13 =6)

Barriers encountered when interacting with *family members, friends and the community* at large included:
- labeling by others (A29a =01 or =03 or =06 or =09)
- education (D17 =01 or =07 or =09)
- attitudes of others (currently not in the labour force) (E74 =05 or =11)
- availability or rules concerning use of specialized bus or van (F13 = 05 or =07 or =09)
- attitude of public transportation staff (F17 =09)
- unsupportive staff or carrier rules and regulations re – airplane travel (F27 =15 or 19)
- unsupportive staff or carrier rules and regulations re – train travel (F31 =15 or 19)
- unsupportive staff or carrier rules and regulations re – long-distance bus travel (F35 =15 or 19)
- unsupportive staff or carrier rules and regulations re – ferry travel (F39 =15 or 19)
- difficulty obtaining support services to live independently (G6 =5)
- attitude of family and friends for increased leisure activity (H3 =15)
- attitude of family and friends for increased leisure activity (H7 =07)

1.2 The accommodations component of the index

The following is the list of questions and response categories that were used in creating the accommodations component of the index.

Aids and personal services included any type of *technical aids*, specialized equipment, technical support, technical services and personal support that were required and obtained. Specifically, these included:

- aids and services used for persons who are deaf or hard of hearing (A3b =01 or =03 or =05 or =07 or =09 or =11 or =13 or =15 or =17 or =19 or =21)
- aids and services used for persons who are blind or visually impaired (A6b =01 or =03 or =05 or =07 or =09 or =11 or =13 or =15 or =17 or =19 or =21)
- aids and services used for persons who have difficulty speaking and being understood (A7e =01 or =03 or =05 or =07 or =09 or =11)
- aids or specialized equipment used to assist individuals with moving about (B2 =01 or =03 or =05 or =07 or =09 or =11 or =13 or =15 or =17 or =19 or =21)
- aids or specialized equipment used to support, replace or assist individuals in the use of hands or arms (B7 =1 or =3 or =5 or =7)
- support obtained for preparation of meals (C5=4)
- support obtained with shopping (C10=4)
- support obtained with light housework (C15=4)
- support obtained with heavy housework (C20=4)
- support obtained with paying bills, banking, etc. (C25=4)
- support obtained with personal care (C29=4)
- support obtained to move around home (C33=4)
- physical or communication therapy (D7 =3)
- aids, devices or services used to follow courses at school (D11=02 or =06 or =10 or =14 or =18 or =22 or =26 or =30 or =34 or =38)
- aids, devices or services used to work (E19 = 02 or =06 or = 10 or = 26)
- aids or special devices used to drive (F6 = 01 or =03 or =05 or =07 or =09)
- aids or special devices used as a passenger in vehicles (F9 =1 or =3 or =5)
- aids used within home (G9 =05 or =07 or =13 or =15)
- aids used within home (G14 =01 or =03 or =07 or =09 or =11 or =15 or −17 or =19)
- aids used within home (G19 =01 or =07 or =15 or =17)

Structural Modifications required and obtained to move about within the home and within the community included:
- modifications made to work environment (E20 = 02 or =06 or = 10 or = 14 or =18 or =22)
- living in housing designed for people with disabilities (G3 =2)
- use of specialized features to enter or leave personal residence (G9 =01 or =03 or =09 or =11 or =17)
- use of specialized features within the home (G14 =05 or =13)
- use of modified appliances and fixtures within the home (G19 =03 or =o5 or =09 or =11 or =13)

Accommodations required and received when using various forms of public *transportation* for local travel included:
- use of specialized bus or van service (D12 =5)
- use of specialized van or service to get to work (E32 =4)
- use of specialized bus or van service (F11 =6)

Accommodations received in the *workplace* included:
- modified or different duties or modified hour, days, reduced work hours (E19 = 14 or =18)

2. Earliest Age of Onset

The earliest age of onset of disability is a derived variable based on responses to the following questions:

- At what age did you first have difficulty doing this (A1a, A2a, A4a, A5a, A7a, A8a, A9a, A10a, A11a, A12a, A13a, A14a, A15a, A16a, A17a, A18a, A19a)
- At what age did you first have activity limitation(s) (A20b)
- At what age did you first have difficulty with these activities (A21a)
- At what age did you first start having this activity limitation (A26a)

The derived variable "earliest age of onset" was the earliest age recorded by the interviewer to any of the above questions.

3. Disability (IALS)

An overall disability measure was created from IALS. A respondent was considered disabled if he or she answered yes (1) to any of the following questions:

G16a. Did you ever have eye/visual trouble of the kind that is not corrected by glasses?

G16b. Did you ever have hearing problems?

G16c. Did you ever have a speech disability?

G16d. Did you ever have a learning disability?

G16e. Did you ever have any other disability or health problem of six months or more.

A new variable was created with a value of 1 if the individual was disabled and a value of 0 if the individual was not disabled.

4. Functional Literacy (HALS)

A functional literacy variable was created from HALS using the following questions:

H1ii	How often do you read? Never – coded 1 All others including no response – coded 0
H1iii	How often do you talk on the telephone? Never – coded 1 All others including no response – coded 0
H1vi	How often do you shop? Never – coded 1 All others including no response – coded 0
A23i	Do you have difficulty telling your right from your left? Yes – coded 1 No and no response – coded 0
A23ii	Do people often say that you are not doing the right thing at the right time? Yes – coded 1 No and no response – coded 0
A23iv	Do you have any difficulty doing an activity that has many steps such as following a recipe? Yes – coded 1 No and no response – coded 0
A23v	Do you often have difficulty solving day to day problems? Yes – coded 1 No and no response – coded 0
H11	Do you feel that your reading and writing skills in English (French on French questionnaire) are adequate for you in your daily life? Yes – coded 0 No, don't know and no response – coded 1

Code values were then summed up across all identified variables to get an overall score for functional literacy. This overall score was then broken into three groups using the Natural Breaks statistical method. The highest values were recoded into Level 1 or low functional literacy.

5. Functional Literacy (IALS)

A functional literacy proxy was created from IALS using the following questions:

> G12. How would you rate your reading skills in English needed in daily life
> G13. How would you rate your writing skills in English needed in daily life
> G14. How would you rate your math skills needed in daily life
> ■ Possible answers to these questions are:
> 1. excellent
> 2. good
> 3. moderate
> 4. poor
> 5. no opinion

The codes for the responses were kept the same except for response 'no opinion' which was re-coded to a value of 0.

> E4. Rate reading in English at work
> E6. Rate writing skills in English at work
> E8. Rate math skills at work
> ■ Possible answers to these questions are:
> 1. excellent
> 2. good
> 3. moderate
> 4. poor
> 5. no opinion/not applicable

The codes for the responses were kept the same except for response 'no opinion/not applicable' which was re-coded to a value of 0.

> E5. Extent reading skills in English limit job opportunities
> E7. Extent writing skills in English limit job opportunities
> E9. Extent math skills limit job opportunities
> ■ Possible answers to these questions are:
> 1. Greatly limiting
> 2. Somewhat limiting
> 3. Not at all limiting

These variables were recoded so 'greatly limiting" = 3, 'somewhat limiting' = 2, not at all limiting' = 3. Missing or not stated values were recoded to 0.

G1. How often do you do the following activities:
   d. Write letters or anything else that is more than one page in length?
   g. Read books
   ■ Possible answers to these questions are:
      - daily
      - weekly
      - monthly
      - several times a year
      - never

These values were recoded into 'does these activities' (code of 0; daily, weekly, monthly, several times a year) and 'never' (code of 1).

G7. How often do you read or use information as part of your daily life
   a. Letters or memos
   b. Reports, articles, magazines, or journals
   d. Diagrams or schematics
   f. Material written in a language other than English
   ■ Possible answers to these questions are:
      - every day
      - a few times a week
      - once a week
      - less than once a week
      - rarely or never

These values were recoded into 'does these activities' (code of 0; every day, a few times a week, once a week, less than once a week) and 'never' (code of 1; rarely or never).

G11. How often do you need help from others with:
   a. Reading newspaper articles
   b. Reading information from government agencies, business, or other institutions
   c. Filling out forms such as applications or bank deposit slips
   d. Reading instructions such as on a medicine bottle
   e. Reading instructions on "packaged" goods in stores or supermarkets
   f. Doing basic arithmetic, that is, adding, subtracting, multiplying, and dividing?
   g. Writing notes and letters
   ■ Possible answers to these questions are:
      - often
      - sometimes
      - never

These values were recoded into 'needs help' (code of 1; often, sometimes) and 'does not need help' (code of 0; never).

APPENDIX A: DETAILED METHODOLOGY

> G8. I am now going to read you a list of different parts of a newspaper. Please tell me which parts you generally read when looking at a newspaper (mark all that apply).
> a. classified ads
> b. other advertisements
> c. national/international news
> d. regional or local news
> e. sports
> f. home, fashion, or health
> g. editorial page
> h. financial news or stock listings
> i. comics
> j. tv listings
> k. movie or concert listings
> l. book, movie or art reviews
> m. horoscope
> n. advice column
> o. other – specify

The choices for the above questions were yes or no. In addition there was a choice of 'Do not read the newspaper', which was coded as 98. These were recoded into 'reads the newspaper' (code of 0) and 'does not read the newspaper' (code of 1)

> G15. All things considered, how satisfied are you with your reading and writing skills in English? Are you…
> 1. very satisfied
> 2. somewhat satisfied
> 3. somewhat dissatisfied
> 4. very dissatisfied
> 5. no opinion
>
> The values were kept the same except for 'no opinion', which was re-coded to a value of 0.

The codes were then adjusted using a common denominator of 12 to give all questions equal weights based on number of possible responses.

Code values multiplied by 3: G12, G13, G14, E4, E6, E8, G15
Code values multiplied by 4: E5, E7, E9
Code values multiplied by 12: G1d, G1g, all G7, all G11, G8

Code values were then summed up across all identified variables to get an overall score for functional literacy. This overall score was then broken into three groups using the "Natural Breaks" statistical method. The highest values were recded into Level 1 or low functional literacy.

6. Critical Literacy (HALS)

A critical literacy variable was created from IALS using the following questions:

> B17   Does someone else organize the drugs or medication that you take?
> Yes – coded 1
> No or no response – coded 0
>
> A23iii   Do you have any difficulty explaining your ideas when speaking?
> Yes – coded 1
> No and no response – coded 0
>
> A23vii   Do you often need help to talk to people you don't know very well?
> Yes – coded 1
> No and no response – coded 0
>
> A23vi   Do you often need help to understand people you don't know very well?
> Yes – coded 1
> No and no response – coded 0
>
> H1iii   How often do you talk on the telephone?
> Never=0.5
> All other responses=0
>
> H1vi   How often do you shop?
> Never=0.5
> All other responses=0

Code values were then summed up across all identified variables to get an overall score for critical literacy. This overall score was then broken into three groups using the "Natural Breaks" statistical method. The highest values were recoded into Level 1 or low critical literacy.

7. Critical Literacy (IALS)

A critical literacy variable was created from IALS using the following questions:

> G1. How often do you do the following activities:
> a.Use a public libraryb ttend movie/play/concertc. Attend or take part in a sporting eventd. Participate in volunteer or community organizationse. Listen to radio, records, tapes, cassettes, or compact disksf.
> ■ Possible answers to these questions are:
> • Daily
> • Weekly
> • Monthly
> • Several times a year
> • Never

APPENDIX A: DETAILED METHODOLOGY   139

These values were recoded into 'does this activity' (value of 0; daily, weekly, monthly, several times a year) and 'does not do this activity' (value of 1; never)

G6. Which of the following materials do you currently have in your home
  a. Daily newspapers
  b. Weekly newspapers/magazines
  c. More than 25 books
  d. A (multi-volume) encyclopedia)
  e. A dictionary
  ■ Possible answers to these questions are:
    • Yes
    • No

Responses of yes were recoded as 0 and values of no were re-coded as 0. Any non-response was re-coded to 0.

G7. How often do you read or use information as part of your daily life
  c. Manuals or reference books, including catalogues
  e. Bills, invoices, spreadsheets, or budget tables
  g. Directions or instructions for medicines, recipes, or other products
  ■ Possible answers to these questions are:
    • Every day
    • A few times a week
    • Once a week
    • Less than once a week
    • Rarely or never

These values were recoded to 'uses this information' (code of 0; every day, a few times a week, once a week, less than once a week) and 'does not use this information' (code of 1; rarely or never). Any non-response was re-coded to 0.

G10. How much information about current events, public affairs, and the government do you get from:
  f. Newspapers
  g. Magazines
  h. Radio
  i. Television
  j. Family members, friends or co-workers
  ■ Possible answers to these questions are:
    • A lot
    • Some
    • Very little
    • None

These values were recoded to 'gets information from' (code of 0; a lot, some, very little) and 'does not get information from' (code of 1, none). Any non-response was re-coded to 0.

Code values were then summed up across all identified variables to get an overall score for critical literacy. This overall score was then broken into three groups using the "Natural Breaks" statistical method. The highest values were recoded into Level 1 or low critical literacy.

MODELLED DATA

In addition to the derived variables there was also modeled data.

1. Correction Factor Modeling

The Atlas includes two maps that were developed using correction factor modeling. This method of modeling develops data from the HALS sample and applies that developed data to the disabled/non-disabled 1996 Census data that was purchased from Statistics Canada.

	YES to at least one of the HALS screening questions	No to all of the HALS screening questions
YES to at least one of the 1991 Census disability questions	TRUE POSITIVES	FALSE POSITIVES
NO to all of the 1991 Census disability questions	FALSE NEGATIVES	TRUE NEGATIVES

This method assumes that:
- the relationship identified in 1991 between age and response to the Census disability questions and HALS screening questions will be the same relationship between age and the 1996 Census disability questions; and
- the relationship noted at the province/territory level will be the same for each census sub-division (CSD) within the province/territory.

- The 1991 HALS sample design includes a selection of individuals from those who answered "Yes" to at least one of the 1991 Census disability questions as well as a sample of individuals who answered "No" to all of the 1991 Census disability questions.
- Each selected individual was asked the HALS screening questions and the table summarizes the four possible outcomes.

1.1 Correction Factor Modeling – Disability Rates

For each province and both territories and for three age groups (15 to 34, 35 to 64 and 65 and older), we calculated the proportion — within an age group and province/territory — of persons who are true positives and the number who are false positives. We did the same for true negatives and false negatives.

The research team purchased 1996 Census data from Statistics Canada that provided the following information for every census sub-division (CSD) in Canada with a population of 40 or more:
- age groups — 15 to 34, 35 to 64 and 65 and older
- response to disability questions — yes to at least one disability question, no to all disability questions.

We "adjusted" the 1996 Census age/disability data for each CSD using the factors derived from HALS and produced "modeled" disability rates for the 1996 Census.

1.2 Correction Factor Modeling – Basic Literacy

For each province and both territories and for three age groups (15 to 34, 35 to 64 and 65 and older) and for two levels of educational attainment (Less than Grade 9, Grade 9 or more), we calculated the proportion — within an age group and province/territory — of persons who are true positives and the number who are false positives. We did the same for true negatives and false negatives.

The research team purchased 1996 Census data from Statistics Canada that provided the following information for every census sub-division (CSD) in Canada with a population of 40 or more:

- age groups — 15 to 34, 35 to 64 and 65 and older
- response to disability questions — yes to at least one disability question, no to all disability questions.

We "adjusted" the 1996 Census age/disability data for each CSD using the factors derived from HALS and produced "modeled" basic literacy rates for the 1996 Census.

INDEX CREATION

1.1 Index Calculations for 2001 Accomodations, Barriers, and Accommodated Barriers

Three maps showing 2001 Accomodations, Barriers, and Accommodated Barriers for populations with disabilities were created using the standard statistical and projection practices described below.

The first step was to verify that the temporal and spatial sampling of the data would not distort the data too much. In order to verify the temporal sampling, the HALS disability data, the IALS disability data, and the NPHS data were used to predict the PALS data. A polynomial quadratic regression equation was fitted to the HALS, IALS, and NPHS province by province with date being the independent variable. The general shape of the equations were an upside down "u". Once the regression equations were calculated the date of PALS was put into the equation. For every province the regression equations projected the PALS values within 5% and were significant. Most were between 1% and 2%. It was thus concluded that the temporal reqression equations were accurate.

Next, one had to determine to what extent the spatial variation in the hierarchical sampling designs of the surveys actually impacted the provincial values. In order to do so, common variables (although with slightly different definitions) were found for each survey. Their variations were compared in contrast to constructed variables for each variable from the census subdivisions. All were within one standard deviation of the constructed census variables and thus it was concluded that the sampling of the various surveys was acceptable at the provincial level. This is not surprising since that was one of the purposes of the sampling. Two more preliminary spatial tests were done. One was statistical and the other was manual and visual. First, spatial auto and cross-correlations were run on the census constructed variables to see to what extent the various sub-provincial areas were independent spatially. As expected, they werespatially independent except in the large cities and on the provincial borders. The provincial borders were caused by edge effects. When autocorrelation figures were recalculated, after including near border information on both sides of the border, independence was reasserted. Second, the maps and the variables of the sub-provincial data were examined for clusters of data. The clusters were then marked. Interpolations were calculated across the space using all values. These were projected as "contoured" values including all members of the cluster and then a second set of "contours were created" including randomly selected members of the cluster. The purpose was to see how much difference the inclusion of the spatially clustered data made in the locations of the contours. It varied from variable to variable and across the various provinces, but not enough to suggest that the clustering of sampled data invalidated conclusions.

Having completed these preliminary analyses, the indices were created. They were created by calculating a mean provincial barrier accommodation rate, using the barrier accommodation indices described above grouped individually into classifications of 0, 1-5, 6-10, 11+. These were calculated both by using the provincial figures and the disaggregated national figures to see whether there were significant differences. There were not. Using these mean figures as an adjustor they were then projected upon the 1996 activity limitation data for each individual census unit at a high degree of spatial resolution –the enumeration area. These were then projected forward through time using adjusted provincial individual temporal regression equations to get the 2001 values for each small district. Finally, the accommodations and barriers were combined in a single value for each small district. The new values were then aggregated at the census subdivision unit and mapped. These values are parametric. However, in order to be very conservative we used them in a non-parametric fashion. Thus, we mapped them as a non-parametric scale indicating only the relative strength of the barriers and accommodations, separately and together.

Sampling Issues

Each of the surveys IALS, HALS, PALS, NPHS, and the census itself is done with differing purposes and using differing sample designs. The issues of comparability are of course complex. There are two major issues to consider. First, to what degree does each survey actually succeed in doing what it purports. Second, to what degree is one able to compare and combine samples, Let us consider each of these issues in turn.

Each does successful sampling:

IALS is a nationally representative sampling design based upon adults aged 16-65. It used random stratifiers from 2 LFS rotations with 3 additional rotations in New Brunswick. However, in the case of Canada, the IALS sample was drawn from the 1994 Labour Force Survey frame and thus has similar sub-national characteristics. Although the LFS is valid at the provincial level, IALS chose to report at the regional level (ie. Atlantic provinces, Western provinces, etc.). It excludes residents of thse Northwest Territories and Yukon, inmates of institutions, persons living on Indian reserves and full-time members of the Canadian Forces. Oversampling took place for some key-groups (for example out-of-school youth) but this oversampling process was adjusted in the final data. Although the sample sizes are small in the neighborhood of 0.5-0.1% of the population, they are carefully chosen and since their significance is reported -choices were made accordingly and many people have used them to derive appro
priate meanings.[27]

HALS data are estimates based on a sample that consists of approximately 1 out of 75 persons in the " yes" sample and 1 out of 200 persons in the "no" sample. The data is weighted and then modified to offset non-responses and discrepancies. For HALS, when the sampling error is more than 33 1/3% of the estimate itself, it is considered to be too unreliable and all errors of less than 16 2/3% are acceptable. With respect to HALS, the response rate of 87% compares favorably with the rate generally observed for this type of survey.

For PALS the stratification and sample selection methods consisted of the cross-classification of the ten provinces, the age and the severity of disability, four age groups, and two levels of severity. The sampling design is a two-stage stratified design. It uses the 2001 Census long form sample using one in five households for the Enumeration Area. The overall response rate was 82.5% and data accuracy was checked using both the estimated standard error of the estimate, and the estimated coefficient of variation (CV). As one checks these tables, most of the estimates are well within the successful rates.

27 See The International Adult Literacy Survey (IALS): Understanding Whatwas Measured by Irwin Kirsch
28 In Quebec the NPHS sample is selected from dwellings participating in a health survey organized by Santé Québec: the 1992-93 Enquête sociale et de santé (ESS).

The National Population Health Survey (NPHS) household component includes household residents in all provinces, with the principal exclusion of populations on Indian Reserves, Canadian Forces Bases and some remote areas in Québec and Ontario. A minimum of 1,200 households in each province was needed to ensure reliable estimates by sex and age groups. Some provinces chose to increase the sample size to increase the utility of the survey. In all provinces except Quebec[28] the NPHS used the multi-purpose sampling methodology developed for the redesign of the Labour Force Survey (LFS). That methodology provides general household surveys with clustered samples of dwellings. Error indicators were the slippage rate, the discrepancy between NPHS population estimates and the most recent census-based population estimates as well as standard errors. In addition, as a means of assessing the quality of tabulated estimates, there are the Approximate Sampling Variability Tables that may be used, and were used by us to obtain approximate coefficients of variation for categorical-type estimates and proportions. Our estimates were within the range of acceptable variation.

The Canadian Census uses a wide variety of statistical and sampling techniques to obtain the best statistical estimates for comparison. The 1996 Census data were collected either from 100% of the population or on a sample basis (i.e. from a random sample of one in five households) with the data weighted up to provide estimates for the entire population. There are few problems with the actual sampling and the many studies that the cenus has produced have developed sufficient correction factors that it is seldom a problem. However, the bigger problem with the accuracy of the data is the privacy policy. There are three anti-corrections that are made by the census to make the data inaccurate and create problems with linking data trends to individuals. They are the random rounding policy, the areal and the cell suppression policy. Random rounding means that all figures, are randomly rounded either up or down to a multiple of "5", and in some cases "10". While simultaneously, areal suppression means all areas in which the cell values are less than a value between 200 and 40 (depending upon the particular sample) are suppressed while cell suppression has an arbritrary cut off value. In our case, it was 5 at the RDC. However, one needs to be aware that for small numbered areas the variation is assumed to be high. The suggested standard error is 20% for cells of 100, 4% for 2000, and 2% for 10,000.

The issue of comparison and combination is complex. It may be subdivided into two different issues and an question of style. The first issue emerges in the question about whether it is appropriate to present data from the different surveys in a single GIS analysis. The answer is clearly yes. One of the most important aspects of GIS is that it allows one to meaningfully compare concepts that are very different. These concepts have a commonality that allows comparison that is often overlooked. This is the common geography. The samples and purposes of the survey may be different, but the geography is the same. It is clearly appropriate to do a 10% stratified sample of x in Quebec and a different 15% sample of y in Quebec and show the results in the same space. In other words, a map of Canada showing the estimated amount of x for Quebec and the estimated amount of y for Quebec as two different values would be no problems since there are both x and y in Quebec and each sample is being shown differently. Quebec has remained with the same boundaries for the last 6 months during which the surveys were done.

The second issue is a bit more complicated. If one has a representative sample of one area and different representative sample of the same area, i.e. the same x and y surveys, can one create appropriate estimates of combined or crossed variables. The answer depends far more precisely on what and how one does it. For example it will be appropriate to estimate the total potential "x and y production" if x and y are parametric and have the characteristic of being addable. Similarly, it would be appropriate to estimate those areas of Quebec where "x and y production" is above or below a certain threshold or where no "x and y" production is taking place. On the other hand, one needs to be very careful when considering "xy". In this study, we have been very careful to maintain this differentiation except in the modeled and indexed variables where extensive testing was done prior to combination.

Finally, there is the question of style. We are unabashedly being aggressive regarding comparability. This is an experimental study that is trying to break new ground on what should be done. In the absence of surveys that more directly illuminate the information of interest to thi study, these methods are the best we could do toward reaching conclusions across these interdisciplinary and inter-subject barriers.

GIS METHODOLOGY

The GIS methodology was standard. The researchers used ArcView 3.2 with the standard spatial and statistical extensions to create templates. The extensions used were spatial analyst, 3D analyst, jpeg image support, database access, network analyst, project utility wizard, and others. There were problems obtaining appropriate digitized maps of Canada. Once obtained the projection had to be changed from Mercator to the more northern accurate Lambert Conformic projection. A variety of different analyses was tried including spatial buffering, filtering and contouring both the literacy and disability data. However, most of these were rejected in favor of using a variety of overlays.

GIS maps fit some general categories. Some are labeled "reference" in that they show different features and their spatial interrelationships so that the user may see where specific phenomena are located relative to others. Others are "thematic", showing a distribution where the user wants to see a pattern of data. There is actually a continuum between these two categories and most of the maps in this study are somewhere in between the extremes but tending to be more heavily weighted towards the thematic end of the continuum.

One of the most powerful capabilities of GIS, particularly for policy studies is that it allows one to derive new attributes from attributes already held in the GIS database. We have seen this in the various derived variables and crossed maps. The many basic types of function used for derivations of this kind are often provided as standard functions or operations in many GISs, under the name of 'map algebra'.

Map algebra includes the Boolean concepts of "Inclusive and Exclusive Union", "Inclusive and Exclusive Intersection", "and" and "or". They may be used simultaneously on the spatial characteristics of the data (spatial layer) and the attribute data (literacy, disability, socio-economic, or educational data). In this study, only the index maps took full advantage of all of these characteristics. However, most took advantage of the "spatial" and "attribute" layers and the concepts of "and" and "or".

On the other hand, no map stored in a GIS is truly error-free. There are of course errors in the sense of "mistakes and blunders" as well as statistical concepts of error meaning 'variation'. One needs to be careful that errors from maps stored in a GIS database do not propagate to the output of the new map when used as input to a GIS operation. In short, while this study has been aggressive with regard to variable definition and survey comparability it has been conservative with regard to GIS methodology.